SINGLE TO SINGLE

DOUGLAS L. FAGERSTROM, EDITOR

VICTOR BOOKS®

A DIVISION OF SCRIPTURE PRESS PUBLICATIONS INC.
USA CANADA ENGLAND

Unless otherwise indicated, all Scripture quotations are from the *Holy Bible, New International Version*, © 1973, 1978, 1984, International Bible Society. Used by permission of Zondervan Bible Publishers. Other quotations are from the *New American Standard Bible* (NASB), © the Lockman Foundation 1960, 1962, 1963, 1968, 1971, 1972, 1973, 1975, 1977. Used by permission; J.B. Phillips: *The New Testament in Modern English* (PH), Revised Edition, © J.B. Phillips, 1958, 1960, 1972, permission of Macmillan Publishing Co. and Collins Publishers; and the *King James Version* (KJV).

Library of Congress Cataloging-in-Publications
Single to single / [edited] by Doug Fagerstrom.
     p.   cm.
  ISBN 0-89693-258-3
    1. Single people — Prayer–books and devotions — English.
  2. Devotional calendars.   I. Fagerstrom, Douglas L.
BV4596.S5S565   1991   90-22090
242'.64 — dc20   CIP

1   2   3   4   5   6   7   8   9   10   Printing/Year   95   94   93   92   91

CONTENTS
■ ■ ■ ■

FOREWORD
■ ■ ■ ■

There is a significant difference between having devotions and having a devotional life. Single adults begin to grow spiritually when they make that discovery.

In an era of a frenzied single lifestyle, with a hundred and one time management techniques promising to make time in our lives for what we want to do, with many "good" things competing for our attention, how do we find time to quiet our hearts? How do we make time for God's Word as a daily ingredient in our lives?

We *decide* this is important to us.

The psalmist wrote, "I have hidden Your Word in my heart that I might not sin against You" (Ps. 119:11).

Single to Single is a way of "hiding" some truths for the spiritual "rainy days."

In times of temptation and stress, of disappointment in matters of the heart, the Word of God is a resource to the single adult. Not always providing solutions but always offering strength, encouragement, and hope.

It is a powerful proclamation that God loves us.

"How can a [single adult] keep his way pure?" is a paraphrase of a question asked centuries ago by the psalmist. The answer then, the answer now, is the same: "By living according to Your Word" (v. 9).

Henrietta Mears, a single adult, reached thousands of single adults as a talented Bible teacher in Southern California. Her book, *What the Bible Is All About* is still a bestseller.

She wrote the book after a single adult came to her and confessed, "What's wrong, Miss Mears? I've gone to Sunday School all my life, but if I had to take an exam on the Bible today, I'd flunk."

Miss Mears resolved to find ways to make Scripture come alive for single adults. *Single to Single* does the same thing.

Some single adults complain, "Why didn't God make it

plainer? Easier to understand?" One might as well ask why didn't God put coal closer to the surface? God rewards the miner.

In an era when singles are looking for heroes and advice givers, it is easy to ask, "What does so-and-so say?"

Rather, the wise single adult asks, "What does the Bible say?"

After a year with *Single to Single,* you will know what the Bible has to say on a lot of topics and issues.

Listen to some sage advice from Miss Mears:

Read it to be wise.

Believe it to be safe.

Practice it to be holy.

Harold Ivan Smith is the founder of Harold Ivan Smith and Associates and the author of more than 20 books. Harold is also a co-founder and a present board member of the National Association of Single Adult Leaders.

INTRODUCTION
■ ■ ■ ■

A FEW PERSONAL WORDS TO THE USER OF THIS BOOK:

"Devotions" is one of those words in the Christian life that leads to pangs of guilt and increases the blood pressure of spiritual awareness or unawareness. We know that it is a "discipline" for our lives that is necessary for growth and maturity in Christ. Yet for most, it brings on feelings of boredom, irrelevancy, and doubt about the return on the time invested.

The Psalmist David begins his book of poetry with the truth that the single adult who invests his life in God's good Word along with counsel from the godly will be blessed (happy), delighted, and productive (Ps. 1:1-3). And God says even more. He promises to guide our path, to grant understanding, to keep us from sin and provide for our every need—especially during the toughest times. What a return for a few brief moments of reading, praying, and considering the things that the God of this universe has for us.

This book is written to help each single adult reader know God better and to discover the wonderful life that He has outlined for every believer in His Son Jesus Christ. Here are a few ideas on how to use the book:

THE WRITERS. The book is a year-long treasury of Bible commentaries and personal responses to God's Word. Over fifty single adult leaders from the National Association of Single Adult Leaders have contributed the "DAY ONE COMMENTARY" for each week. The next six days are "applications" written by six single adults from the leader's ministry. Over 300 single adults from coast-to-coast have made a personal contribution to this devotional guide. Some have never been married. Others have experienced the pain of divorce. Widows and widowers have contributed. Many are single parents. They are here to lead us on our spiritual journey.

THE COMMENTARY. It is an in-depth look at the passage

of Scripture selected for the week. Each single adult leader selected his or her own Bible passage. Their study and scholarly exploration has led to a wonderful collection of thoughts, ideas, and a deeper understanding of God's Word.

THE APPLICATIONS. It was the assignment of each contributing single adult to give a personal response to their leader's Bible Commentary. They speak from their heart to yours. Many have become very transparent and vulnerable. Some share your story and will relate to your experience in your Christian journey. Others will make an indelible impression on your heart allowing God's Word, work, and person to encourage your life and daily walk with Jesus Christ.

ADDITIONAL VERSES. At the end of each day's devotional, two portions of Scripture are listed. The portions feature an Old Testament and a New Testament selection. The additional verses relate to the day's commentary or the application written by a single adult.

GETTING STARTED FOR THE JOURNEY. It will be a wonderful journey for you. Here are three suggestions for getting ready for your adventure in daily Christian living.

1. Set a time and place where you can quietly spend about 10 minutes alone with God.
2. Use a Bible to read some of the additional verses.
3. Find a small pad of paper and pen to write down some of your own personal thoughts and responses.

GROWING AHEAD. Now you are ready to go (grow). Let me offer you one way to enjoy your journey and adventure in living.

1. Pray before you read. Ask God to show you one special thing each day that will draw you closer to Him.
2. Read the entire Bible portion listed for the week.
3. Read the commentary or application.
4. If time permits, read the "additional" verses.
5. Write down one thing that God showed you today.
6. Thank God for the time that you had with Him.

THERE CAN BE MORE. When you get going in God's Word, it is sometimes hard to stop. Add a verse to your memory. Write it down on a business-size card and carry it everywhere you go. Add your own verses to each day's devotional reading. Write them down in this book. Consider a small group of fellow travelers to compare what you are discovering in your journey. Ask one friend to hold you accountable for the path that you find yourself traveling.

Most of all **ENJOY THE TRIP.** You will grow if you go. Don't miss one exciting day. And if you do, catch up the next day. And be sure to share with a friend what you see and experience along the way.

Single to Single is designed to be your personal growth guide. You will meet many new friends. Most of all you will get to know God better.

Doug Fagerstrom

WHY HAVE DEVOTIONS?

■ ■ ■ ■

There's this guy across the street. I don't know his name, but every day as the garage door slowly drones open to a new and equally unwelcome morning, he's there watering his perennials. He's an older man. I can tell because his hair is white and thinning on top, and he kind of slouches over the hose as it sags out of his hand. He stands in the same spot, splashing the flowers with a thick stream of water, and always gives his head a slow, automated turn in my direction as if a gear were attached to his neck from my garage door. Even in my haste, I do not ignore my responsibility to neighborly conduct, and always give him a quick wave as I'm getting into the car. I guess it doesn't matter if he sees me or not. I probably would never have bothered if the garage door wasn't so awfully slow. He seems like a nice enough man though, unobtrusive and all. But I don't know his name. It's a funny relationship we have.

But could I call it a relationship, I wondered to myself as I raced to work one day? I have never *related* to him. There hasn't been a word between us *really*. Oh, sure, we have a certain understanding. There's the motion of his looking at me and my ritualistic flourish of the arm, but I haven't really *talked* to him. Our only communication has been for show. I have made no effort to get to know this man. Well, I can't know everyone, I rationalize.

Every day I return home from work and sneak out to get the mail. He's usually in the backyard then. I always try to hurry so I won't be confronted by him. It's embarrassing after all these years! I wouldn't know what to say.

Just yesterday, I was having a particularly difficult time scooping all my mail order catalogues from out of my box, trying to stuff them under my arm for the mad dash back inside. They were so slippery in my sweaty palms I couldn't hold onto them. Suddenly, the sound of splashing water, slapping the pavement directly behind me froze my frantic movements. He was there.

The jig was up. I turned my head slowly, automatically. He stood in the road with his hose upheld and gushing. I smiled sheepishly in my hunched over position, one hand filled with catalogues, the other fluttering in a nervous, habitual wave. He smiled at me, a warm smile. My hand stopped moving and dropped slowly to my side.

"The name's Jesus," he said very quietly, finally looking straight into my eyes. The water continued to ricochet off the blacktop from the green hose as if nothing had changed, staining my good trousers with little dark dots.

I was once asked—why have devotions? Why meet with God? I, in turn asked, "Why eat, why sleep if you are a man? What else is there if you are a 'Christian'?" Christianity is nothing if you refuse to interact with God. Christianity is a relationship of both *listening* and *responding* to the Almighty Creator. It is a developing of love for Him, through the discovering of who He is, like getting to know a friend. As a Christian do you find yourself waving at God, or have you finally invited Him over for dinner?

Theo Bennett is a single adult student at Wheaton College in Wheaton, Illinois.

WHY DO I FAIL TO HAVE DEVOTIONS?

■ ■ ■ ■

There are a lot of reasons, OK excuses actually, for failing to be faithful in having a time of daily devotions.

- *"I'm too busy."* Probably true; most of us are too busy. But not a good excuse because even busy people seem to find time for some things less important than daily devotions, because they have developed a daily habit of, for example, eating at certain times, watching the 6 o'clock news, or reading the newspaper after dinner. Reading from God's Word and talking daily with Him should be one of our habits with which even busyness cannot interfere.

- *"I don't know how."* Daily devotions are intimidating to some people who feel that they must invest serious time pondering deep spiritual truths and using seminary-level Bible commentaries and study helps. Actually, our daily devotions are simple times apart with our best Friend, Jesus, who loves us and wants to share in our lives. Reading the Word, using a devotional guidebook, and praying are the basic components to developing a successful quiet time with the Lord.

- *"I don't feel like it."* It's easy to get so caught up in the cares of the day that we don't feel like coming to God and quieting our hearts. Maybe we are struggling with sin or temptation and don't want to listen to the urging of the Holy Spirit to make the right choices. Maybe we are nursing a grudge or are unwilling to forgive our brothers or sisters who have wronged us, and don't want to face God with our stubbornness.

- *"I'm lazy."* Sitting in front of the television, or sleeping in is sometimes easier than getting up and taking time to be with the Lord. We have good intentions, but we allow laziness to keep us away from meeting with Him.

There are lots of other excuses for not being successful in having daily devotions, just as there are a lot of excuses for not being successful in life. But the most significant reason for failing at living is failing to be faithful in sharing our lives on a daily basis with our Lord Jesus Christ.

Help us to be more faithful, Lord.

Bobbie Reed, Ph.D. is Associate Warden for the Donovan Correctional Facility in San Diego, California. While a single parent, Bobbie authored the book, *Prescription for a Broken Heart.* She is also a member of the board of the National Association of Single Adult Leaders (NSL). Bobbie has written 10 additional books in the field of single adult ministry.

WEEK ONE
■ ■ ■ ■

GOD'S BEST FOR US!

TEXT FOR THE WEEK: GENESIS 37–50

KEY VERSE: GENESIS 50:20   "You intended to harm
                                          me, but God intended it
                                          for good."

DAY ONE ■ Commentary on Genesis 50:20

You probably know the story: sold into slavery by his own brothers as a teenager; falsely accused of rape and imprisoned for it; promised by a released inmate that he would be helped out of prison, but then forgotten. After a strange twist of events, he was elevated to be prime minister of Egypt. And then the day came. His brothers came to him for help, not recognizing him and possibly assuming he was dead. What did he do? How did he respond? He applied the "50:20 Principle"! In Genesis 50:20, we read how this man, Joseph, responded to his brothers. With no malice or bitterness, he revealed his identity and then said, "You intended to harm me, but God intended it for good." Joseph was the victim of horrible cruelty from his brothers. But he was wise enough to look beyond their actions to God's intentions.

One year ago I resigned from a pastoral position. It was certainly one of the most painful events of my life. I was depressed, angry, and confused. People hurt me deeply, though it was unintentional. But out of that hurtful situation, I am now working in a different church where I am ministering to others, and being ministered to!

What about you? Has someone hurt you—either intentionally or unintentionally? Perhaps it was a parent, teacher, friend, or spouse. Can you, like Joseph, see God at work in that hurtful incident? Do you believe what Christians say so readily—often without much conviction—that "God is in control"?

16

The fact that God is in control does not mean that we can live irresponsibly and then blame God. Nor does it eliminate our part in prayer, spiritual warfare, forgiving our offenders, or seeking reconciliation. What it does mean is that when someone wrongs us, we can trust that God is at work. For reasons sometimes known only to Him, He has allowed the situation to work His wise, loving purposes in our lives.

In Joseph's case, God allowed him to be forcefully taken into Egypt, knowing that one day as prime minister, he would save the Hebrew race from starvation. In my case, God used my severed church relationship to place me in a church where I have found incredible joy and fulfillment.

The 50:20 Principle really works. Get hold of it. Let it get hold of you. It can change your life!

For Additional Reading: Jeremiah 31:3-10; Philippians 1:12-14
Mark Vanderput is the Singles Advisor at the Heights Cumberland Presbyterian Church in Albuquerque, New Mexico. Six single adults from Heights Cumberland church write the following.

DAY TWO ■ Genesis 50:20

One of the hardest situations I have had to face as a single person is keeping my spirits up during lonely, painful, or stressful times. Facing the pain of a broken relationship after 23 years, learning how to mourn the loss, being at home by myself, and handling the stress of job, finances, and family are just some of the daily problems that being alone entails.

As I begin each day I can now honestly pray, "May the words of my mouth and the meditation of my heart be pleasing in Your sight, O Lord, my Rock and my Redeemer" (Ps. 19:14).

When my husband, a graduate of a renowned Bible college, left for the third and final time, I thought my world had ended. I became hostile and defeated. But the Lord faithfully and patiently showed me He loved and cared for me and promised to continue to do just that for the rest of my days. I have discovered that my thoughts can be positive and an example to others.

For Additional Reading: Psalm 26:1-7; Philippians 4:4-9
Claudia, Age 48
Stockbroker and Investment Advisor

DAY THREE ■ Genesis 50:20

It can be extremely hard to look beyond today's pain or setback and believe there's a brighter future. My divorce experience was like a "bolt from the blue," but through Christ's healing love I was able to grow beyond bitterness and confusion and rejoice in becoming a person God could use for His purposes.

The key to this process is making positive choices. Joseph could have given up on God and lived in hatred and bitterness but he made the choice to have faith in God. In time, Joseph realized the great plan God had for him. The process may begin painfully but we need to be open for seeking His will in His time. Our hearts must be open to make the right choices to live within God's plan for our lives.

Like Joseph, we need to find God's victory in our human defeats. I have been amazed at the way God can use our past brokenness to touch others with His love.

For Additional Reading: Jeremiah 29:10-14; 1 Thessalonians 5:16-24
John, Age 32
Helicopter Pilot

DAY FOUR ■ Genesis 50:20

As I read Genesis 50:20, I realized that one problem we have as sinful human beings is judging good and evil. That, I believe, is one reason that God forbade Adam and Eve from eating from the tree of the knowledge of good and evil. Only He has the complete picture and only He truly knows what is in our best interest and what is not.

Probably the ultimate example of this was Jesus' death on the cross. From a purely human viewpoint, it was the greatest tragedy in the history of the human race; the Son of God, the only perfect Man, dying a sinner's death for doing nothing worthy of death. But in God's perfect plan, He turned this terrible event into the greatest gift that He could give, so that we would no longer be in bondage to sin, but have eternal life with Him through His Son Jesus Christ!

In my own life, I have also seen how God can use evil for good. I was born with a rare congenital birth defect which caused my bones to be very brittle. I have had over 40 broken bones and 20 operations to correct the problems with my condition. Many people would be broken and bitter with a life like that. But God has brought me closer to Him through all of the pain and fear that I have had to endure. He has been faithful to me through it all, bringing me through college and helping me to learn to walk after spending 18 years in a wheelchair! In my weakness, I have had to depend on Him for everything in my life. What a wonderful gift my handicap has been!

For Additional Reading: John 16:7-11; Lamentations 3:22-23
Mark, Age 37
Electrical Engineer

DAY FIVE ■ Genesis 50:20

Five years ago, I was working two projects at my job which were taking 10 to 16 hours a day to accomplish, as well as going to night school four nights a week. I had told my boss that I needed additional help, but he relied on me totally to perform above the norm. I had been told by my superiors that in order to get a promotion, I would have to get a college degree. Therefore, I started back to school.

After months of working two jobs and going to school in the evenings, I became very ill with pleurisy and pneumonia and ended up in the hospital. While lying in my hospital bed, I thought a lot about what I really wanted out of life. The one thing that continually came to my mind was getting involved in a Bible study group.

With the realization that I needed to change my priorities, I came to the conclusion that if I was going to change, it was necessary to put the things that meant the most to me at the top of my schedule. I had given up a lot of things that were very important to me in order to meet my work obligations and go to school. My boss, by this time, was forced to hire some additional help. As it turned out, I cut back on my schooling and now start the week out in a Bible study on Monday nights. The study of God's Word has given me new insight into how I want to change my life.

I thank God for my illness. It was what I needed to get my life back on track with the Lord.

For Additional Reading: 2 Chronicles 20:15-17; Matthew 6:28-33
Mary, Age 40
Data Manager

DAY SIX ■ Genesis 50:20

In March of 1985, when my wife of 19 years died of brain cancer, I knew, intellectually, God had a reason beyond and bigger than the needs of five kids and me. It has only been lately that I have grown to appreciate emotionally the good that has come and will come from what was a real tragedy to us.

We had discovered the tumor two and one half years before, and Gay lived a full, meaningful life in the meantime. She lived long enough to give each of us time to grow in understanding and to see our oldest graduate from high school. We all feel blessed for having had the extra two and one half years.

The emotional as well as intellectual understanding has been brought to the forefront as I have:

● Been put in a position to discuss critical issues with others having to deal with the loss of a spouse or having a terminally ill spouse.

• Seen a grown daughter be put in a position to be of comfort to a law school classmate who lost his dad.

• Seen a college-age son become acquainted with a classmate who had lost her mom at the same time in the same way without a supportive family environment to help deal with it.

• Seen another college-age daughter show concern for a classmate who is dealing with leukemia.

• Grown to more fully appreciate the love that is poured out by others who know and care for our family. What an opportunity they have had to share and be supportive.

• More fully appreciated the tremendous example my wife, Gay, was to those who knew her, and to handle a rotten deal joyfully with faith, inspiring all who knew her.

• Watched our five children accept responsibility and mature without forgetting how to have fun and enjoy life.

All of us are saddened and feel a void from the loss of a mom and spouse, and yet we understand there is a purpose in God's plan that supersedes us and that makes it all OK.

Perhaps Matthew 11:28 is an appropriate verse showing where our Saviour is during difficult times.

For Additional Reading: Psalm 69:1-21; 2 Corinthians 1:3-7
Bill, Age 45
Insurance Executive

DAY SEVEN ■ Genesis 50:20

Call me anytime. . . . Let me know if you need anything. . . . We're always here for you. . . . GONE! Friends and relatives surrounded me in the days after my husband's death with loving words of comfort and support; but in days, the numbers dwindled almost as dramatically as they had risen. Oh, a few stayed .and were true to their words, and offered their assistance, but for the most part I was alone—alone with loneliness, anger, and pain.

I searched for someone to take the pain away, but each new or old face let me down. Only God was faithfully there, day after day; putting people in my life who directed me again and again to the healing and growth available through God's faithfulness and Word. God turned my anger and despair into hope through His promises for today and eternity. He's the only One we can really depend on to never give up. Joseph knew, and I learned— CALL GOD ANYTIME!

For Additional Reading: Psalm 40:1-5; Matthew 14:13-21
Karen, Age 36
Nurse

WEEK TWO
■ ■ ■ ■

FORGET NOT GOD'S FAITHFULNESS

TEXT FOR THE WEEK: **DEUTERONOMY 8:1-20**

KEY VERSE: DEUTERONOMY 8:2   "Remember how the Lord your God led you all the way in the desert these forty years, to humble you and to test you in order to know what was in your heart, whether or not you would keep His commands."

DAY ONE ■ Commentary on Deuteronomy 8:1-3

I was anticipating great things as I drove into the city of Boston to begin my new job working with college students in a Christian student ministry. I was excited about my first assignment 800 miles from my home state of West Virginia. But that first year proved more difficult than I anticipated. People were less open and more formal than I was accustomed to. Adjusting to new roommates was hard, and most students did not appear at all interested in spiritual truths. By the end of my first year, I felt as if my time on the campus had been a total failure. I was ready to quit and return home.

The Children of Israel were ready to quit and return to Egypt many times on their journey to the Promised Land. In fact, the people took a 12-day journey and turned it into 40 years. God told them to go in and possess the land but they were not willing to trust Him and they rebelled. It was a time of great failure.

Now, 40 years later, this passage in Deuteronomy 8 finds Moses reminding Israel of God's faithfulness during those wilderness years. Verse 2 states, "Remember how the Lord your

God led you." Israel had not wandered around in the wilderness on her own all those years. The Lord had always been present with her. It had not been wasted time. He had taken her failure and used it to humble, to test, and to instruct as to the real source of life.

The word *humble* means "to be empty of pride and self-sufficiency." God wanted them, as He wants us, to be dependent on Him and not on our abilities. Yet we will never trust God until we have to. Often the only way we become convinced of our inability is for God to remove the resources and supports which we by nature depend on. Sometimes He does this by failure. According to verse 3, failure can reveal to us the true basic source of life which is God Himself. We must first experience hunger in order to know we need food.

I realize now that my year in Boston was not a waste of time or resources. God was using my failure to remove the self-sufficiency in my life and to teach me to depend on Him and His resources. I have learned not to be discouraged with failure. We are going to fail as Christians but God can use even our failures.

For Additional Reading: 2 Chronicles 7:11-14; 1 Peter 5:5-7
Pamela L. Harper is the Director of Young Adult Ministries at Ward Presbyterian Church in Livonia, Michigan. Six young adults from Ward Presbyterian write the following personal applications.

DAY TWO ■ Deuteronomy 8:1-3

Tests. The thing about college I always hated the most was tests. Like my college professors, God at times puts us through tests. One particularly difficult test came shortly after I became a Christian. Because of my job, I had to spend several months away from my Michigan home working in Arkansas. Loneliness quickly set in and I became angry at God for sending me away from my "place of security." Yet God was faithful to me (1 Cor. 10:13). Throughout my stay in Arkansas, God consistently provided me with loving Christian friends who cared for me and helped me grow as a new Christian. Indeed, I grew to love Arkansas deeply.

After I saw how lovingly God provided for me, I felt I had failed Him with my anger. However, I soon realized God had used my failure to teach me about Him and to shape my character. I now know God tests me because He cares.

For Additional Reading: Psalm 117:1-2; James 1:2-4
Randy, Age 28
Banker

DAY THREE ■ Deuteronomy 8:1-3

Have you ever been asked the question, "What has God been doing in and through you?" Occasionally a friend will ask me that question and it will send my mind wandering. Initially, I tend to recall all the wonderfully positive things God has been doing. After all, in a world that is glamour- and results-oriented, is it not appropriate to focus on the positive?

Yet, if I am specifically asked, "What is God teaching you?" It is not easy to think about. Why? Because it causes me to focus on "less than favorable" situations and circumstances.

Moses told Israel in Deuteronomy 8:2, "Remember how the Lord your God led you," in what I would call a less than favorable memory of wandering. Yet it was during this time that Israel became dependent on God.

One way which I deal with the less than favorable situations or circumstances God sends my way is to keep what I call an "Honest to God" journal. First, it allows me to express to God my honest thoughts and feelings (Ps. 62:8). Second, a month or year later, it is encouraging to read my journal to remember how God was working in my life, causing me to be dependent on Him so that His will would be done in and through me.

For Additional Reading: Psalm 105:1-5; 1 Peter 1:6-7
Joyce, Age 26
Staff Member, Campus Crusade for Christ

DAY FOUR ■ Deuteronomy 8:1-3

Do you ever catch yourself retranslating the Bible? One classic example is Romans 8:28 where I find myself saying, "All things work out good for those who love God," instead of the proper, "In all things God works for the good of those who love Him." It is funny how we do that.

Trials are as much a part of the Christian walk as the miracles with which we are graced every day. In a society where we take an aspirin at the slightest sign of pain, this sure is a hard concept to swallow. The pressures of being single in our society and all its "busyness" often make me feel just as the Israelites must have in Deuteronomy 8; as if I've been deserted by God. I find myself on my knees pleading, "Lord, why have You forsaken me?" But that's exactly where He wants us. And God didn't even spare His Son this test as we hear the echo of our own familiar words from Jesus' lips on the cross, "My God, My God, why have You forsaken Me?" (Matt. 27:46)

I think Amy Carmichael said it best:

No wound, no scar?

Yet, as the Master shall the servant be,

And, pierced are the feet that follow Me;

But thine are whole: can he have followed far

Who has no wound nor scar?

For Additional Reading: Psalm 22:1-11, 19-26; John 1:10-13
Elaine, Age 26
Mechanical Engineer

DAY FIVE ■ Deuteronomy 8:1-3

When I was asked to lead a mission trip for our singles group to the Dominican Republic, I was elated and cautious; elated because our director had so much confidence in me, and cautious because I had never led anything like this before.

During the 10 months of planning, many obstacles crossed my path: verbal commitments I had received from potential team members were withdrawn, outside pressures from graduate school courses sprang up, and a physical ailment struck me. The Lord said in Deuteronomy 8:2 that He would humble and test me, but He also promised He would lead me through the desert. He did.

The challenges continued on the trip; and again the Lord fed and sustained me. In Deuteronomy 8:3, the Israelites were faced with the challenge of a food shortage, but the Lord was faithful and provided for them. This was done so that both the Israelites (and myself) would realize that not just food was needed, but also the Lord.

The main thing that I learned from the missions trip was that completing it was like possessing only a small portion of the land that God ultimately is calling me to enter. I am now back out in the wilderness, being humbled, tested, and taught perseverance, so that when God calls me to enter the land again, I will be ready to use His strength and might to possess the *entire* land for His glory!

For Additional Reading: Isaiah 55:1-6; Matthew 25:31-35
Doug, Age 25
Financial Analyst

DAY SIX ■ Deuteronomy 8:1-3

It is funny how much we often want something. Then when we get it, it is not at all what we expected. The desire can be for a job, a new friend, or in my case, a relationship. I never dated much when I was younger, but I often wanted to. I would secretly and not-so-secretly long for a relationship, someone with whom to share my life, my hopes, disappointments, and expectations. Such a relationship was elusive. There were expanded flirtations from time to time, but I was like Israel lost in the desert—not for 40 years but for at least 12. The failure of Israel in not depending on God in Deuteronomy 8:3 was my failure in seeking a relationship.

When I finally turned the matter over to God, I was given the relationship for which I had longed. Why, I have wondered, is this one working where others before have failed? It is because God is at the center (Matt. 6:33). I needed to be stripped of my self-sufficiency in this area and let God run the show. He has, and regardless of what comes of this relationship, I have learned to depend on God in an area in which for years I thought I held all the answers.

For Additional Reading: Proverbs 3:1-8; 2 Corinthians 1:8-11
Alan, Age 31
Journalist

DAY SEVEN ■ Deuteronomy 8:1-3

I was fortunate to have been brought up in a Christian home and I made a commitment to Christ at an early age. My youth was filled with friends and activities involving the church. This environment was loving and secure, but it did not provide many opportunities to really trust God.

That opportunity to trust came during my college years. I had great difficulty in choosing a career path and changed my course of study a number of times. I felt as if God had let me wander in the wilderness. Eight years after entering a university, I left with a four-year degree. It was a time of testing. During those eight years I learned that my obedience to God and my relationship with Him were more important than how I earned a living.

In the years since, the Lord has shown His faithfulness to me. I better understand how a loving God can say to His children, "Remember how the Lord your God led you all the way in the desert these forty years, to humble you and to test you."

For Additional Reading: Deuteronomy 8:10-18;
Matthew 4:1-11
Clark, Age 33
Insurance Claims Representative

WEEK THREE

■ ■ ■ ■

SUCCESS FROM GOD'S WORD

TEXT FOR THE WEEK: **JOSHUA 1:1-18**

KEY VERSE: JOSHUA 1:8

> "Do not let this Book of the Law depart from your mouth; meditate on it day and night, so that you may be careful to do everything written in it. Then you will be prosperous and successful."

DAY ONE ■ Commentary on Joshua 1:8

The word "success" conjures up images of fancy cars, nice homes, ideal relationships, and money in the bank. What does the Bible say about success? How is success to be properly defined? The Hebrew term for "success" means to bring to successful completion what is intended. The term for "prosperity" means to put to its intended use.

Joshua was called on by God to lead His people into the Promised Land. The Lord gave him three commands, that if obeyed, would make him successful.

First, the Word of God was to characterize his conversation. This is what is meant by, "Do not let this Book of the Law depart from your mouth." God was telling Joshua to talk about His Word with others, that is, to relate all of life to the teachings of Scripture.

Second, Joshua was told to meditate on God's Word. The word "meditate" means to think deeply about, mull over in your mind, give time to. Meditation is to the soul what digestion is to the body. Without the slow and lengthened process of digestion, food would not nourish the body. Without meditation the soul will not be strengthened.

Third, Joshua was told to be careful to obey what was written.

He was not to be just a hearer of the Word, but a faithful doer as well.

Joshua never drove the latest model chariot, nor owned the biggest house in the land of Canaan, but Joshua was a success because He accomplished the intended purpose that God had for his life.

What does the Lord want of you as a single adult? If you are careful to follow the commandments of God as revealed in Scripture, you too will be a success.

For Additional Reading: Psalm 1:1-3; 2 Timothy 2:14-19
Bret Avlakeotes is the Single Adult Pastor at Fellowship Bible Church of Dallas, Texas. Six single adults from his church write the following.

DAY TWO ■ Joshua 1:8

I meditate on the Word of God day and night. I lean on it, depend on it, trust in it, and am comforted by it.

When I'm tired, I go to the Word. When I'm disappointed, I go to the Word. When I'm lonely, I go to the Word. When I feel like no one cares, I go to the Word.

Jesus is my security and my life. I wake up in the morning and He is there; I go to bed at night and He is there. Jesus cares when no one else does.

My life is nothing without Jesus. Jesus gave me the Word and I meditate on it. "The grass withers and the flowers fall, but the Word of our God stands forever" (Isa. 40:8).

For Additional Reading: Psalm 139:1-10; Romans 8:35-39
Chris, Age 25
Insurance Salesman

DAY THREE ■ Joshua 1:8

When I was a little girl, I loved playing with puzzles. In order to complete a puzzle, I had to learn to study each piece for colors, patterns, and individual shape. Then I would look at the picture on the box lid to see into which spot that small piece would fit.

In my life, meaningful meditation is much like putting a puzzle together. It is taking one piece of Scripture and reading it word by word, examining each word for its significance. I then gather that dissected piece of Scripture together again and look at how it fits in the whole scope of God's Word and my life. When I take the time to meditate on God's Law in this way, I complain less and obey more faithfully. Through God's Word I am more certain that the "piece" of my life is fitting into God's plan for me.

For Additional Reading: Psalm 119:33-40; 2 Peter 1:3-4
Kristie, Age 27
Teacher

DAY FOUR ■ Joshua 1:8

If there's one thing I'm learning in my single life, it is that God is not at all who I imagine Him to be. I've spent a lot of time thinking of Him as Someone who is available to give me what I think I need, when I think I need it.

But when God promises me success and prosperity, I have to look very carefully at that promise to understand what He means by those words. God's promise of success in taking possession of the Promised Land comes after 40 years of great difficulty and suffering in the desert. He also says that success will *follow* my study and meditation of the Word.

I worked for a manufacturing company and an advertising agency before joining the staff of a missionary organization two years ago. I had the idea that just because I was now in full-time Christian work, my finances, my social life, and my relationship with God would all "prosper." I didn't anticipate having to face financing a new car when my old one, not yet paid off, "died"; or having to work very hard at my friendships and working relationships. I'm beginning to realize that success for me may not mean security in material things and relationships. I am beginning to believe that God is achieving His purpose of making me more like Him, as I face the unexpected turns my life is always taking.

For Additional Reading: Psalm 48:1-3, 14; Philippians 1:9-11
Betsy, Age 25
Graphic Designer

DAY FIVE ■ Joshua 1:8

In Dallas, Texas where I live, "prosperity" and "success" are common everyday words. The mind-set is to drive that Mercedes or Jaguar with a car phone, to have a spacious beautiful home with the "nice" things, to wear the right clothes with those certain names on the label. What a contrast this culture was for me when I moved here after serving as a missionary in Haiti, the poorest country in the Western hemisphere. Of course, in Haiti, "prosperity" and "success" are common everyday words too, but have different meanings. For example, the majority of the population is successful if they own any make of car, and most people don't even have phones in their homes let alone their cars. Most people live in huts, and a step up is to have a concrete block house with a tin roof. And the clothes—who cares about style or color or brand name, just be thankful you have something to wear.

It is easy to get trapped into the cultural ideas of what "prosperity" and "success" mean, and it is a constant discipline for me to see those words from a spiritual perspective. It is difficult to not think in terms of materialism, but instead to consider my day prosperous when I meditate on God's good Word, when I share it with others, when I relate it to my life and when I am obedient to it.

It is a daily battle to keep my perspective straight, to not get caught up in the things around me. My hope is that I can accomplish what Joshua did in his life. My hope is to do the things that God has called me to do.

For Additional Reading: Psalm 119:9-16; Romans 12:1-2
Karen, Age 34
Missions Director

DAY SIX ■ Joshua 1:8

Have the gray areas of life given you another dull, mono-chrome day? Are you once again lost in that zone between right and wrong where we have so many choices to make? By focusing my eyes on the instruction the Lord gave to courageous Joshua I can see that there is life beyond the world of no contrast.

The Lord's provision for us is that we not leave the world of gray, but that we ever-increasingly renew ourselves in His Word. The Lord tells us that our unceasing priority is to take in the life-giving truths and precepts of Scripture: "Do not let this Book of the Law depart from your mouth; meditate on it day and night."

Though the Lord does not show us where to place each foot on the surface of the earth, He has given us His Word to come to know thoroughly, like a map and a set of coordinates to our destination. By doing this, we can be as courageous and as victorious as Joshua in marching through our gray.

For Additional Reading: Psalm 119:105-112; Luke 5:1-11
Joshua, Age 27
Librarian and Student

DAY SEVEN ■ Joshua 1:8

Walking in God's will took both Job and Solomon to the pinnacle of material wealth. Following God's will allowed Joshua and the nation of Israel to possess the Promised Land. Trust in God's will took Jesus to a rugged Roman cross and Paul to the insides of cold dark prisons . . . so much for the predict-able Christian life and my simple formulas for success. The varied experiences of these great and godly men is a challenge to me and my cultural view of success.

I find that I am forced to define success in relational terms rather than material terms. Success to me is experiencing a genuine and open relationship with God. Success is walking with God day-in and day-out. Success means pursuing personal holiness and integrity. Success is following that part of God's will for my life which is revealed in Scripture. Beyond that I must trust in the goodness of God and where He is taking me as I actively walk through life.

It is in my relationship with God that I find the only promise and assurance of true success and prosperity in life.

For Additional Reading: Psalm 119:129-136; 1 Peter 1:13-23
Karl, Age 30
Engineer

WEEK FOUR
■ ■ ■ ■

LEARNING TO WALK RIGHT

TEXT FOR THE WEEK: **PSALM 15**

KEY VERSES: PSALM 15:1-2   "Lord, who may dwell in Your sanctuary? Who may live on Your holy hill? He whose walk is blameless and who does what is righteous, who speaks the truth from his heart."

DAY ONE ■ Commentary on Psalm 15

Character—the word is seldom used in the Bible, and we don't see it very often in newspapers or on television. Yet we all know what it means, and we immediately recognize its absence. As someone has said, character is what you are when no one is looking. All too often we hear of government officials lying, businesses cheating, and scandals rocking the church. Too few have made it their goal to develop God-pleasing character. Psalm 15 is a call to character. It is worthy of study, careful attention, and memorization as I have done.

The psalmist begins with a question. The sanctuary here is no doubt the tabernacle, the dwelling place of God. The holy hill was Zion, the city of David (2 Sam. 6:10-12). The question is concerned with who was eligible to be a "guest" of the Lord and live in the place where His presence rested. It was a spiritual question: who can draw near to God and worship in His dwelling place?

Coming into the presence of God is what worship is all about. Think of it—actually coming into the presence of an awesome God! When Isaiah recognized he was in God's presence, he cried, "Woe to me! . . . I am ruined! For I am a man of unclean lips, and I live among a people of unclean lips" (Isa. 6:5). When Moses sensed he had come into God's presence, he was more than glad to respond to His command to "take off your sandals, for the place where you are standing is holy ground" (Ex. 3:5). What does the thought of God's presence cause you to do?

The acceptable person, the psalmist answers, is one who walks with *integrity* and whose actions are *righteous*. The metaphor of the "walk" is used throughout the Bible for one's pattern of life and conduct. "Blameless" means complete, sincere, or perfect. A person of integrity lives in obedience to God and maintains a life that is blameless. This psalm is a treatise on integrity. If you want to be regarded as a person of character, or integrity, join us in the quest for character. We invite you now to turn your attention to the 10 character qualities that follow in verses 2-5.

For Additional Reading: Isaiah 6:1-8; Romans 6:19-23

Richard P. Kennedy is the Singles Pastor at Big Valley Grace Community Church in Modesto, California. Six single adults from Big Valley write on the following characteristics of godliness.

DAY TWO ■ Psalm 15

On a cliff overlooking the rugged shoreline of Monterey, California grows a lone tree, a cypress. It stands as a testimony of endurance. The winds have ravaged it, the ocean storms have battered the cliff below, untold numbers of tourists' hands have caressed its bark — yet it stands firm, solidly established. It is gnarled and twisted, battered and scarred, but its roots are strong, and the tree healthy.

The Monterey Cypress has become a symbol of perseverance. Despite harsh, destructive external forces, it holds fast to life and is a partaker of the beauty surrounding it.

How about my character? Do I stand solid as the Monterey Cypress? Is there integrity in my life, my speech, my friendships, my business practices? Do my roots run deep in the strength of the Lord? If Psalm 15 characterizes my Christian walk I will never be shaken.

For Additional Reading: Isaiah 30:15-18; Ephesians 3:14-19
Ann, Age 35
Nurse

DAY THREE ■ Psalm 15

In our walk with the Lord, we sometimes find it difficult to always be sincere in what we say and do. In this hectic, fast-paced world we live in, we may not realize the image we portray to others. For instance, we might be in church or at a Bible study worshiping and praising the Lord and then the next day, we're at our jobs becoming angry with a customer or gossiping with the employees about one another. It is hard for me to believe that God sees our worship time as being sincere.

As a youth staff worker at my church, I see how teenagers struggle with sincerity on a daily basis. The challenge of not succumbing to peer pressure is something they face every day. They try to do what they believe is right but sometimes, as teenagers, they're apt to do what they need to do to be accepted rather than do what is right. I am there to let them know what the right way is and they should be able to not just hear it in my words and from God's Word but see it in my life. They should see that my walk is "blameless."

Whether teenagers or adults, we are to share the "Good News" of Jesus Christ with others through the humble sincerity and blameless walk of our everyday living.

For Additional Reading: Joshua 24:14-15; Ephesians 5:1-7
AnnMarie, Age 30
Travel Agent

DAY FOUR ■ Psalm 15

Sadly, it is amazingly easy to fake the "spiritual" Christian life by knowing the right words, saying the right things, and acting the part. We are almost forced to do the faking in a lot of Christian circles because certain sins and thoughts and hurts are the "unmentionables." We are far from the scriptural guidelines that God has given us.

While on staff at a church and Christian school in Anchorage, Alaska I saw the concept of "transparency"—being real—modeled in the pastor and other staff members, but not in me. In California, while teaching at a Christian school, the principal posted a statement around the school: *Reputation* is what people think you are; *Character* is what God knows you are. I had the reputation but I knew I did not have the character. I could not be real and speak truth in my heart. I was bound by sin, Satan, and self to "fake it." That only lasts so long—in my case, too long. As God's child, He required my confession, brokenness, and loss.

But praise God, the peace and joy He gives is worth it all! And now being able to "speak truth in my heart" has led to a close walk with God and the works of righteousness are through "Christ who lives in me." What a joy to be free in Christ—not a fake Christian.

For Additional Reading: Psalm 139:23-24; 1 John 1:5-10
Ken, Age 38
Teacher

DAY FIVE ■ Psalm 15

Sometimes it is hard for me to understand why God allows some things that happen in my life. When these trials occur it is difficult to always remember to count all these trials as joy. Why does God allow these trials and why are they necessary?

I have come to learn that God desires fellowship with me very much. I have also learned that there is a great deal about the way I live that is unacceptable to Him. I need to display in my life those character qualities that please God in order to enjoy the presence of God. Knowing these things, it is easier to understand that God will allow "character-building" trials to come into my life so that I will have the character I need to have fellowship with my Lord.

It is easy to count trials as joy when you know that they lead to the development of a godly character. We are called to character; a daily walk of integrity and righteousness. How gracious of our Father to help us develop that which He requires of us.

For Additional Reading: Psalm 32:1-7; Colossians 1:9-14
Scott, Age 25
Student

DAY SIX ■ Psalm 15

It came upon a midnight clear." Yet it wasn't that glorious song of old, it was that havoc-wreaking dream. Remember those nights? There you were in that compromising position; someone was drawing you into bed, or into crime. You did not want to go. You had never seen their faces, but your mind had created them. The place was unfamiliar, yet somehow you had been there before. And the colors, they were as vivid as if on a movie screen. It was so real; you needed to act, to risk, and be honest, to make a decision, and speak out the truth. And then you awoke and the dream was never finished. But, thank the Lord, it was only a dream.

Then again, let us remember that in life we don't get stopped from living out our true character. It is inevitable that who we are will be seen and heard. And what is that? As believers, it is desirable that from within us, "the image of the invisible God . . . the Firstborn from among the dead" would be seen. It is He, our Lord Jesus, who pulsates in our hearts and flows from us as truth.

Today is the day we can once again set our hearts to "speak the truth in love," helping not only ourselves, but others as well to overcome the bad dreams too often lived out in real life.

For Additional Reading: Deuteronomy 32:1-7;
Colossians 3:15-17
Carlton, Age 33
Paralegal

DAY SEVEN ■ Psalm 15

Recently I went to a dear sister with a problem. I was depressed and thinking negative thoughts toward myself. As I talked she occasionally interjected the question, "Where do you think those thoughts are coming from?" I told her I didn't know. She eventually got through to me. Whether the negative thoughts were from my heart or from the enemy was not the point. It was identifying that they were not from God.

One who enjoys God's presence speaks God's truth in his own heart, "His delight is in the Law of the Lord, and on His Law he meditates day and night" (Ps. 1:2). He sings and makes melody in his heart to the Lord (Eph. 5:19). In everything he gives thanks (1 Thes. 5:18).

When I began again to speak God's truth to my own heart and allowed it to rule my thoughts and the attitude of my heart, my depressive outlook could not abide; God was near!

For Additional Reading: Isaiah 55:8-11; Philippians 4:6-8
Wendy, Age 32
Student/Bookkeeper

WEEK FIVE

■　■　■

FORGIVEN AND HAPPY

TEXT FOR THE WEEK: PSALM 32:1-2

KEY VERSES: PSALM 32:1-2

"Blessed is he whose transgressions
are forgiven, whose sins are covered.
Blessed is the man whose sin the
Lord does not count against him."

DAY ONE ■ Commentary on Psalm 32:1-2

A religious person asked, "What is the most destructive thing a believer can do to his or her walk with Christ?" She thought I was going to say, "Stop going to church," or, "Drop out of the singles' group," or maybe, "Quit paying tithes," but after a few moments of reflection and prompting of the Holy Spirit, I said, "Unwillingness to practice the forgiveness of God."

Psalm 32:1-2 paints a vivid portrait of forgiveness from the eyes of God. It deals with the basic emotions of our being and evokes the nerve of happiness, acceptance, self-worth, guilt, rejection, and fear. The words of the psalmist are confronting but they are soothing to the soul.

Three different Hebrew words for sin are employed. Sin is more than just telling a white lie, for God's Word describes it as: specific sinful actions or habits, the ugly side of our sinful nature, and open willful rebellion against God. In spite of this bleak picture, God is portrayed as Forgiver. His tender mercies and love can heal the deepest pain brought by sin. The psalmist assures us that the person who has been forgiven by God is happy.

The word *happy* in Hebrew literally means, "to advance, or go straight forward." God's Word says that a person is on the right path in life when he or she is experiencing the forgiveness of God. To advance in the kingdom of God does not mean that the path of happiness is always smooth and easy. This is evident from the Beatitudes found in Matthew 5:3-12. Sometimes the "forgiven" may be poor in spirit, mourn, or be persecuted for Christ's name. The bottom line is that we are accepted by God. There is no good deed we can do to make God love us more. There is no hideous sin we can commit that would cause Him to love us less.

Are you truly happy or are you going down a dead-end street of despair trying to be perfect and resolve your guilt and pain yourself? God's way is best and for those who turn to Him, He will lift the guilt of their sin. He will not count or remember their times of rebellion. Never underestimate the power of God's forgiveness. Forgiveness is the doorway to true happiness and peace in God's kingdom. To walk through this doorway requires courage and transparency.

The end of Psalm 32:2 states, "in whose spirit is no deceit." The Hebrew word for spirit, *ruach,* means a person's total thoughts and innermost being. The "deceit" described here is a selfish and prideful kind. When we fail to repent of our sins and seek God's forgiveness, we allow deceit to rule in our hearts.

First John 1:8 sums up the matter succinctly: "If we claim to be without sin, we deceive ourselves and the truth is not in us." However, there is no greater joy in life than to feel and know we are forgiven. "Thanks be to God for His indescribable gift!" (2 Cor. 9:15) That gift is Christ and His forgiveness.

For Additional Reading: Psalm 84:1-8; Matthew 5:1-12
Rob Arp is the Pastor of Single Adults at Living Faith Fellowship in Athens, Georgia. Six single people from Living Faith Fellowship write the following devotional applications.

DAY TWO ■ Psalm 32:1-2

A child of God who requests forgiveness does more than ease a guilty conscience. He does more than set his priorities right before God. His life changes radically from the threat of wasted bones, groaning, and sapped strength (vv. 3-4), to the promise of protection, strength, and intimacy with the Lord (vv. 6-7).

An automotive breakdown can transform a vacation from joyful anticipation to boredom and frustration. Unconfessed sin is a breakdown in the life of a Christian. The unrepentant believer trades the fruit of the Spirit for the emptiness of the world (Gal. 5:16-26). The stranded vacationers must also spend one less day at their destination for each day they remain immobile. The Christian whose journey has been halted by sin also forfeits a future reward. It will take longer to reach future levels of maturity. Days that would have been spent as mature believers are instead spent making up for days of unrepentance.

For Additional Reading: Jeremiah 31:33-34; Matthew 9:9-13
Peter, Age 28
Graduate Student

DAY THREE ■ Psalm 32:1-2

No doubt we have all felt the horrible pain of guilt and condemnation gnawing away at our innermost being. This feeling of guilt brings about a sense of emptiness, isolation, fear, and confusion. These feelings, however, are but mere symptoms or results of the root problem—sin.

One of the greatest tragedies of our day and time, is how many of us either condone or justify (excuse) our sin(s). Whenever the Bible talks about sin, it does not joke about it. It is rather clear that sin in one's life causes spiritual, emotional, and even physical death. But thanks be to God. His Word tells us that He has provided a way out of this dilemma. The way in which God has provided an escape from this empty way of living is Jesus Christ. In the account of Jesus' birth we read, "And you are to give Him the name Jesus, because He will save His people from their sins." Isn't this fantastic? We can now experience and enjoy the gift of God's forgiveness through Jesus Christ.

For those of us who are immobilized by the weight of sin and guilt, we need simply call to God, confess our sins, ask Jesus to cleanse and forgive, and then cling to God's power and presence through obedience to His will.

For Additional Reading: Isaiah 43:24-28; 1 Corinthians 10:11-13
Doug, Age 29
Teacher

DAY FOUR ■ Psalm 32:1-2

I have been a single parent for two years because I chose to believe my marriage was hopeless. I truly believed I had done all I could—and perhaps I had, except turn it over to the Lord. While I had known the Lord since I was nine years old He was far from Lord of my life at that time. It was five months after my divorce that the Lord revealed my heart to me concerning the "hopelessness of my marriage." It came through a sermon my pastor gave one Sunday morning and I was under such conviction that when I got home I knelt by my bed and confessed my sin to the Lord. I had never done that before. Never have I felt such love and acceptance in spite of the ugliness of what the Lord revealed to me. In place of fear I felt peace, in place of condemnation I felt assurance that indeed nothing could separate me from the love of God. I experienced the double-edged sword as it cut away chaff and yet restored and healed me at the same time. Verse 5 of Psalm 32 is very meaningful to me because it was through confessing my sin that I not only received forgiveness but acknowledged my total dependence on God.

For Additional Reading: Psalm 103:1-13; James 5:16-20
Renee, Age 34
Registered Nurse

DAY FIVE ■ Psalm 32:1-2

Often as single adults we feel alone in life. We know deep down that our family and friends are out there "somewhere"—but that gives us little comfort when facing the reality of being alone. Sometimes we feel "alone" because we have sinned against God. God has not left us. The fact of the matter is that we have left Him.

It was only after coming out of the day-to-day crises of a difficult marriage that I realized the promise of steadfast love God made to Moses on Mount Sinai (Ex. 34:5-6). Not only did I learn about God's love but experienced His forgiveness. God forgave me of my divorce and has set my feet on the rock. I know that with God I am accepted and that He is faithful. The Lord never leaves us; even when we forget about Him, He continues to care for and about us.

When feeling alone, we can remember that the Lord's compassion for us never ends. "His compassions never fail. They are new every morning; great is Your faithfulness" (Lam. 3:22-23). What a joy it is each day to claim God's forgiveness. I know that those who come to Christ can have the assurance that He will hear and cleanse from all unrighteousness.

For Additional Reading: Psalm 19:9-14; Hebrews 8:8-12
Edith, Age 37
Quality Assurance Administrator

DAY SIX ■ Psalm 32:1-2

True happiness to me conjures up a mental picture of a young child running freely through a field of wildflowers with no limitations. To practice God's forgiveness on a daily basis is to run through life, so to speak, without the hindrances of sin to weigh us down. Hebrews 12:1 tells us to throw off anything that would hinder us . . . forgiven people are free people.

When I ignore a certain sin in my life that God is putting His finger on, I feel defensive and edgy. I may even do other things unconsciously which further encumber me. Sin seems to produce sin. The Bible clearly says that the way for a transgressor is hard. When we fail to face up to our sins, we make Christian living a burden.

When I stop to tell myself and God that I truly do *not* want to continue in this sin and repent of the sin already committed, God's forgiveness and grace flow into my life to give me a marvelous feeling of being totally free and happy. John 8:36 is the greatest statement on the forgiving power of God. "If the Son sets you free, you will be free indeed."

For Additional Reading: Psalm 51:1-10; John 8:31-36
Jan, Age 43
Homemaker

DAY SEVEN ■ Psalm 32:1-2

The forgiveness of God causes a person to live a godly life. Mr. "C" told me that I was a fool for declaring all the extra money I make typing for students on my taxes. He said that he never declared his extra money, the Lord allowed him to have extra work and didn't require the extra money. I told Mr. "C" that I tithe the extra money I made, and I didn't want to lie on my taxes. I quoted Matthew 22:21, "Give to Caesar what is Caesar's, and to God what is God's." I told Him Caesar is the government and if the government gets their money off the top, the Lord does also. "But Linda, you can't afford to tithe, much less declare it on your taxes." "I can't afford not to, Mr. 'C.'" There was a time when I gladly typed all the extra work I could get and never declared a cent to either the government or the Lord. Then I met Jesus—not the church, but Jesus—and now the government and the Lord receive the correct amounts. When you learn the love of Jesus and that He will take care of your every need, it's simple."

Psalm 130:4 says that "with You [God] there is forgiveness; therefore You are feared." In Christ we can have forgiveness for all sins. Then we live in agreement with the mercy of God.

For Additional Reading: Exodus 20:18-20; Matthew 10:24-33
Linda, Age 43
Secretary

WEEK SIX

■ ■ ■ ■

A GOOD FOCUS—FORWARD

TEXT FOR THE WEEK: **PSALM 37:1-8**

KEY VERSES: PSALM 37:3-4

> "Trust in the Lord and do good;
> dwell in the land and enjoy safe pas-
> ture. Delight yourself in the Lord and
> He will give you the desires of your
> heart."

DAY ONE ■ Commentary on Psalm 37:1-8

Yesterday I had a conversation with a woman whose husband wants to end their marriage; he's ready to bail out. Unfortunately, it's an attitude which is all too common in our world; it's a sign of some root problems in our society. My tendency when those situations arise is to get angry and want to "get even." I want to get a hold of the "abandoner" and set him down for a good "talking to." David's words help us get a perspective on situations like these. He says in verse 1, "Don't get heated up," or, "Be cool," "Don't blow a gasket" when it seems your enemies are getting the upper hand. Our tendency is toward a quick and sometimes vengeful response when we feel we've been unjustly treated or someone is taking advantage of us. It could be in the office, or your last dating relationship.

How do we deal with those emotions that well up within us? David says take charge and be focused. Where do we focus? He says, go back to the future, "For like the grass they will soon wither" (v. 2), or "A little while, and the wicked will be no more" (v. 10). Time is passing before us and sometimes we need to just plant our hope in the future. People and situations change and sometimes the best solution is patience—a very unpopular concept in our culture. Look to Job. Finally, after all he had been through, he is able to say, "My ears had heard of

You but now my eyes have seen You." That is also the second focus of David in Psalm 37—upward. He looks to the Lord and says, "Trust in the Lord," "Delight in the Lord," "Commit your way to the Lord." There is a certainty, a surety which the slippery ground of this world can't provide. David had ample opportunity to realize this as he began his descent down the slope with Bathsheba—temptation led to lust, led to adultery, led to murder. Our focus needs to be forward and upward. David also encourages us to put feet to our focus. "Refrain from anger and turn from wrath." There's some footwork to be done. We're responsible for the way we feel, act, and react. There are some choices to be made, not only with our thoughts, but also with our responses to that person that causes us to lose our cool.

For Additional Reading: Psalm 121:1-8; Ephesians 3:7-12
Lorin Staats is the Associate Pastor of Career Age, Single Adult, and Single Parent Ministries at Elmbrook Church in Waukesha, Wisconsin. The following six writers are members of the single adult ministry at Elmbrook Church.

DAY TWO ■ Psalm 37:1-8

Recently I've been learning that part of trusting the Lord is entrusting Him with my feelings, even the ugly and painful ones. It is not easy for me to always admit to myself, let alone the Lord, my anger, my longings, my fears, and desires. I don't like facing the fact that life isn't all I had hoped it would be. Yet admitting my feelings, accepting them as part of the human experience, and then entrusting them to God frees me to see life as it really is: difficult, yet rich.

When life doesn't seem rich and undesirable emotions well up, I need to stop and discover what I'm feeling. Then I need to tell the Lord. In telling the Lord how I truly feel, I discover what I'm truly believing about Him. Sometimes I'm believing that He really doesn't care about me, or He has a wonderful plan for everyone else's life but not for mine. Sometimes I'm believing lies.

When I find myself being honest with God it drives me back to His Word. In His Word I find the power to choose obedience over instant relief for unpleasant emotions, faith over doubt, hope over despair. I find the power to not only tell the Lord how I feel but to entrust Him with my deepest self. Entrusting happens in the presence of faith. In Genesis we learn that faith was counted to Abraham as righteousness.

May our righteousness be brought forth as light by the God to whom we entrust ourselves.

For Additional Reading: Genesis 15:1-6; Hebrews 11:11-12
Mary, Age 29
Educator

DAY THREE ■ Psalm 37:1-8

After 15 years of being a wife and mother, and assisting my husband with his work, I was forced to become a single parent, and go back into the marketplace. With few skills, and living in a rural area, it was difficult to find adequate employment. One morning, determined not to move until He answered, I prayed "Lord, show me where to find more work." But all that came to me was an impression to go visit Mary. I had learned her name from a friend who had spoken at the funeral of Mary's son who had taken his life. They lived near us, and I had decided to go over after school started in a few weeks. Now I was distracted by financial worries. After more waiting, no other directions came, so I decided to go and see Mary. On the drive over I said, "Lord, this isn't what I had in mind for today." But it was His mind. It is what He wanted me to do for another. His Spirit reminded me to "Trust in the Lord, and do good; so shalt thou dwell in the land, and verily thou shalt be fed" (Ps. 37:3, KJV).

For Additional Reading: Psalm 32:8-11; 2 Corinthians 8:1-5
Donna, Age 44
Massage Therapist

DAY FOUR ■ Psalm 37:1-8

It's easy to *trust* God for all your needs when things are going smoothly. Yet until we are brought to a state of having to rely on only our *trust* can we truly understand its meaning.

In the course of a career that seemed comfortable and promising, I suddenly found myself in a situation where my integrity and future were in "check." I had worked diligently to make the best decisions for the company and now those decisions were being questioned on the basis of false information and misunderstanding. The situation grew tense and I soon found my position in jeopardy. It was during this time that God showed Himself to be sovereign. Answers did not come quickly yet my vision was fixed on the Lord—I had nowhere else to look. For three months I persevered under less than pleasant working conditions. I waited on the Lord. It was during this time that I came to understand the meaning of the word *trust* and witness the impact that our Lord can have on others as we respond faithfully.

A new career was the result, but this one was far better than any I could have imagined. Of course . . . this is the promise of our God!

For Additional Reading: Proverbs 28:18-22; Hebrews 3:1-5
Scott, Age 25
Businessman

DAY FIVE ■ Psalm 37:1-8

It was less than a year after our divorce. We had not received child support for several months, and then one day the children (aged four and six) called their dad and were told that he had moved and left no forwarding address.

I was enraged. I couldn't believe God would let him get away with not supporting his children. My prayers were angry demands for justice that seemed to yield no results.

Then God's still voice seemed to tell me, "Be still . . . do not fret. I am your Provider . . . your Heavenly Father. You must let Me handle this."

I do not know how God handled my ex-husband's situation, but the children are almost grown now, and we're doing great. God has never failed to provide, but more important, He's allowed me to be free from the burden of bitterness.

For Additional Reading: Psalm 78:17-25; Ephesians 4:17-26
Pat, Age 43
Typesetter

DAY SIX ■ Psalm 37:1-8

If you are the King of the Jews, save Yourself," sneered onlookers at the Crucifixion. I wonder what feelings welled up in Christ on hearing that. After all, He was being executed for crimes that He did not commit. It's quite likely Satan was jabbing at Jesus, tempting Him to justify Himself before everyone. Jesus remained almost completely silent; the words He spoke are cherished to this day. He even asked God to forgive His unjust accusers.

Recently, I was accused of something that I did not do. Word of it traveled to others and the urge to clear myself was strong. Doing this would have meant accusing someone else. As I considered all of this, I realized that Jesus gave His life because of a false accusation. To refrain . . . to turn . . . and to be led by God is great joy.

For Additional Reading: Psalm 43:1-5; Luke 23:33-43
Beth, Age 29
Teacher and Travel Agent

DAY SEVEN ■ Psalm 37:1-8

Delighting in the Lord is the alternative to looking at the wicked and saying, "Why do they have _____ and I don't?" Or, as one of my friends often says, "Why doesn't

God give me a boyfriend when it seem all non-Christians have one?"

I ask questions like that myself. Sometimes it's easy to see only the shiny surface stuff in other people's lives and to envy them.

But God doesn't want us being envious of others and looking at their lives. He wants us to set our minds on Him, to trust in Him and wait, to commit our way to Him and to delight — take pleasure and joy — in Him.

But the reward is great. God promises abundant blessings, to help, uphold, and deliver us, to be with us through all our troubles, to give us the true desires of our hearts. The best thing is that God knows which desires are for our good and which ones aren't. And He won't do anything but what is for our ultimate good.

For Additional Reading: Proverbs 27:3-7; James 4:5-11
Nancy, Age 31
Training Manager

WEEK SEVEN

■ ■ ■ ■

STILL, WITH GOD

TEXT FOR THE WEEK: **PSALM 46:1-11**

KEY VERSES: PSALM 46:10-11

> "Be still, and know that I am God; I will be exalted among the nations, I will be exalted in the earth. The Lord Almighty is with us; the God of Jacob is our fortress."

DAY ONE ■ Commentary on Psalm 46:10

At the conclusion of my formal seminary training, I was required for graduation to attend a devotional retreat. During the eight-hour visit at the wilderness retreat center, each seminarian was required to spend 45 minutes alone in personal Bible study and prayer. It was a quiet 45 minutes in the sunlit wooded area next to the slow-moving river in the northwoods of Minnesota. I must admit, that 45-minute session alone with God was one of the most memorable and precious times that I spent in God's Word during my years of formal Bible and theological training.

Indeed, God has invited us to "be still and know" Him. He wants us to come before Him and acknowledge His holy loving presence.

In this passage from Psalm 46, the word "still" means "to loosen your grip, to let go." God wants us to let go of our tight hold on things around us in order to be able to hold His mighty and gentle hand. And He desires to hold our hand. He desires to hold us up. He desires to show His love. He desires to lead us along the way. But, our hand must be free and open to His.

Even as I sit and write this devotional, the noise of the traffic going by, the phone ringing, voices in the hallway outside my office plus the blowing of the air-conditioning unit fan are all reminders of a busy, noisy world that wants to have a grip on my life. We need to let go and let God! We need to learn to be still!

God also spoke through Moses, encouraging us to be still and let God have the victory in our lives (Ex. 14:14). He said, "The Lord will fight for you; you need only be still." It sounds so simple, doesn't it? Yet, in our busy world it is not easy to be still. We are encouraged from the first day of our lives to "hang on as tight as we can for dear life." We are afraid to let go.

In the northwoods of Minnesota, I did not have to hold on to anything but the hand of my Saviour in that brief quiet time. I did not have to hold on to my career, finances, relationships, or the next event on the calendar. I only had to hold on to my Jesus. It was just Jesus and me talking together while a few birds chirped in the background. The 45 minutes were "still" moments to let go of the busy routine and concerns of the last three years. It was memorable. It was too short. It has been often repeated. It has given much closeness and comfort with my loving Lord and Saviour.

So, let go! Know God. Experience Him apart from everything else around you. Experience His presence in everything you do. Take those things that are a constant bother that daily occupy your grip and get rid of them, even if only for 45 minutes. God is waiting for your free and open hand to join Him . . . hand-in-hand.

For Additional Reading: Psalm 4:1-8; Matthew 9:18-19, 23-26
Doug Fagerstrom is the Single Adult Pastor at Calvary Church in Grand Rapids, Michigan. Seven single adults from his former church in Muskegon, Michigan wrote the following.

DAY TWO ■ Psalm 46:10

The Lord Almighty is with us; the God of Jacob is our fortress." These are powerful words that the Lord has given us. There is nothing we do that the Lord is not with us. There is no situation we are in where we are not surrounded by the walls of God's love acting as our protection, our fortress.

As a student at a college in Michigan's Upper Peninsula, I had a long drive to my family's home in Muskegon. The horror stories about bad winter storms are true. I often found myself in the middle of a severe winter storm while driving home. Nothing is quite as scary as finding yourself enveloped in white with no sight of the road beneath you or the cars in front of you. It was during times such as these that I could really feel the "fortress" power of the Lord. I found myself praying without ceasing! And each time the Lord brought me safely home.

The Lord has used situations like this to teach me to let go of my self-trust, to rely completely on Him. I have to believe that God will do what is best for me. When I rely completely on Him, I have the courage and confidence to weather the storms, no matter how great or small. When blinded by the storms of life that I will face, I'll know that God is there as my fortress and I can be still with much comfort.

For Additional Reading: Psalm 46:7-11; Mark 4:35-41
Julie, Age 21
Mechanical Engineer

DAY THREE ■ Psalm 46:10

In this busy world of ours, I often have to tell myself to "stop and smell the roses." It gets harder and harder in this fast-paced, high-tech world to, indeed, take time to "smell the roses . . . to see the beauty God has created both within us and around us." To be "still" and silent long enough to see and hear this beauty sometimes appears to be "a thing of the past."

At the age of eight, during the bouncing years of childhood, I was diagnosed with leukemia. I learned all too quickly—sometimes not by choice—to be "still." My mother, a strong Christian lady, influenced me greatly and helped me to be "still." More important, during the most painful treatment, Mom helped me to find my fortress with God. You see, God and I built the highest and thickest walls against pain. **Together we** could get through **anything** and beat this cancer. I remember entering His fortress and asking Him to never leave my side.

He was then and always will be a source of comfort, support, and strength in my life. I never realized the POWER of the strength I received from God during my battle with cancer until I reached my adult years. Yes, I truly believe no human can ever build a fortress as wonderful as God's. Yet, why should we, when we are always welcome in God's mighty fortress?

It is a joy to curl up in my favorite chair, be "still" and let go and let God! It is a thrill discovering the comfort of His fortress!

For Additional Reading: Hebrews 13:1-5; Psalm 18:1-6, 16-19
Pamela, Age 26
Medical Assistant

DAY FOUR ■ Psalm 46:10

A fortress, no cars, no telephones, no bills, no employers, no favors to be done and schedules to be kept. A place where I can go to be with God alone. There is no way that I can place a price on this place with God. Besides, money cannot get one there. Power, possessions, and fame are all inadequate in bringing us to the fortress of God. But wait a minute. Where am I trying to go? Why am I looking for a fortress?

God, by His Spirit is within me. My body is His dwelling place. God has said to "be still and know that I am God." If He is in me and He indeed is my fortress, then I am in God's fortress. Wow! What a comforting delight to know that the fortress is here and now. Being still is being in the fortress. I am with God and God is with me (John 15:4-8).

It is in this incredible fortress that God has provided in my life that I find a place for strength and help in times of need. I can know that I am safe. I can know my God better and better as I dwell with Him in this wonderful place of safety.

For Additional Reading: 2 Samuel 22:1-7; Hebrews 4:14-16
Gary, Age 38
Lumber Company Manager

DAY FIVE ■ Psalm 46:10

Be still." It is hard to imagine a still moment in this busy world of mine. As a single parent who is going to school and working full-time, every waking moment seems crammed full of tasks to be completed and problems to be solved. My world is a busy and hectic world. It is a world full of pressures that never let up.

As I realize my needs, the Lord tenderly, yet firmly say, "Be still." My wise and loving Heavenly Father knows what is best for me, even if I think that what He is asking is nearly impossible. He knows that I need to slow down and turn to Him alone for strength.

I cannot get through this life on my own. That is obvious. And it is so good to know that the Creator is in charge. I realize more and more that I need to slow down and take time each day to give my hectic life over to my Lord. When day-to-day pressures seem to take over my life and overwhelm me in every way, I know that I need only speak His name. And when I do, I discover immediately that He is there. In fact, I now know that He has been there the whole time — through my entire day and struggle. Then He takes the burdens, all of them. And it only demanded a few quiet moments to be still and know my God and His desire for my life. Yes, it only takes a few moments from a busy life to know that I have a loving God who desires my presence and desires to give me the strength that I need.

For Additional Reading: Psalm 86:1-10; Matthew 11:25-30
Rhonda, Age 31
Student and Sales Personnel

DAY SIX ■ Psalm 46:10

Not again! My dog is hot on another scent. A chipmunk or field mouse, I hope. Lord, please not a skunk or a porcupine! He meanders in endless turns, often covering the same ground again and again. His yelps and squeals must mean excitement, or frustration. I call to him louder and with more intensity, but each time he fails to respond. His total instincts are so absorbed in conquering his prey that he doesn't even hear me calling him. My commands just echo through the woods unheeded.

"Lord, so many chipmunks cross my path each day. Tears are my yelps of frustration. I want, but cannot have. I need, but cannot work enough hours to buy. I long for everything this life can offer, but I fail to long for the One who alone offers life. Help me to stop chasing, to listen and know You as God. Teach me to be still. Now through my trust and contentment, may You be lifted up in my life. Amen."

For Additional Reading: Exodus 33:12-14
Carol, Age 35
Preschool Director

Psalm 46 means that I can have peace with God. I can let go and let God be God. He is with me all the way and He has promised never to leave me. It a great comfort to know that God has everything in control and that He works everything out for good.

I know that God is my fortress. It is only through Christ that I can have peace with God and know God in the stillness. And I thank the Lord Jesus Christ for what He has done for me.

For Additional Reading: John 14:25-27
Tom, Age 37
Custodian

DAY SEVEN ■ Psalm 46:10

Certain things in my life can easily get me uptight, nervous, worried, and more. And I always seem to want to handle them by myself.

I can remember moving back to Michigan from Texas. My biggest worry was finances. I worried about having enough money to move back. I worried about getting a good job. I worried about being a good provider and protector for my son. I soon learned that I was wasting valuable time and life by my worry.

Eventually, as always, the Lord subtly reminded me to give all of the things that I was worrying about over to Him. The Lord then reminded me to be still and know that He is God, in control! Then He told me to just leave those things there with Him. My job was to move away from those things that I left with the Lord.

Once I really stopped worrying and started resting and trusting God, the doors opened wide. The move was successful, the jobs came in line and I felt like I was doing what God was enabling me to do as a good mother. I have learned that everything that comes into my life, no matter how great or small, needs to be placed in the Lord's hands. It is then that I know that He does not just **give** solutions to the things that I worry about, but that He **is** the solution. It is there that I can rest and be still and know that my God is God!

For Additional Reading: Isaiah 26:1-4; Matthew 6:25-34
Gwen, Age 22
Receptionist

WEEK EIGHT

■ ■ ■ ■

WATER AVAILABLE FOR THE THIRSTY

TEXT FOR THE WEEK: PSALMS 63:1-11; 119:1-2

KEY VERSE: PSALM 63:1

"O God, you are my God, earnestly I seek You; my soul thirsts for You; my body longs for You, in a dry and weary land where there is no water."

DAY ONE ■ Commentary on Psalms 63:1 and 119:1-2

There is one principle challenge that surfaces from these Scriptures and seems to grip my heart with compelling conviction. It is this . . . to seek God with my whole heart, mind, soul, and strength, not for what He can do for me, but just to know Him.

I know of few Christians who pursue an intimate relationship with God the Father or Jesus His Son with the sole intent of knowing Him and His character, His goodness, meekness, holiness, etc. Much, if not most of the time, we approach the Lord with our wants and desires only, and then if we're considerate, our thanks. We ask, "Lord, give me strength . . . Father, please help me in my relationships . . . provide direction in this area."

It is not wrong to ask for these things, for His Word directs us to (Phil. 4:6; James 4:2). However, we need to seek God for more than what we desire and need!

God longs to have an intimate, deep relationship with each of His children. An earthly relationship would not be very fulfilling for two people and probably not last very long if one person usually asked the other for help, time, assistance, etc., and rarely took time to just get acquainted by enjoying a relationship that resulted from just knowing one another. One would wind up feeling hurt, used, and unappreciated for who he/she is. His/her thought would be, "My friend only wants me for what I can do and give."

I wonder, does God feel this hurt? Do we break His heart by usually asking Him for something (even with thanks), and rarely take time to know Him? Do we grieve our Lord by not pursuing a relationship with Him for who He is, to learn more of His ways and thoughts, to take on more of Himself, His love, joy, peace, and long-suffering. Do we seek Him more for what He can do for us than for who He is?

Psalm 63:1 says, "My soul thirsts for You, my body longs for You, in a dry and weary [thirsty] land where there is no water." The world is a dry and thirsty land. The sparkle, tinsel, excitement, allure, and charm of the world and its activities does nothing to permanently satisfy the deep hunger and yearning within the spirit of man for meaning, fulfillment, purpose, and lasting relationships.

Nothing can fill the void inside of a man or woman except the presence and goodness of God Himself. Nothing can satisfy the God-given spiritual longing but the love and life of the very Life-giver! Oh, my soul, seek God!

The end result and benefit of seeking God and pursuing Him for His presence and anointing in your life is that your spirit becomes filled with His spirit. He increases and you decrease. "Blessed are they who keep His statutes and seek Him with all their heart" (Ps. 119:2).

For Additional Reading: Psalm 27:4-14; Matthew 19:16-29
Dennis Franck is the Singles Pastor at Bethel Church in San Jose, California. Six single adults from his church share the following devotionals.

DAY TWO ■ Psalms 63:1; 119:1-2

When I was a young girl and recovering from a serious illness, my parents gave me a spot in the family garden for my very own to grow anything I desired. This was to get me out into the fresh air and sunshine. I chose to grow a flower garden from seeds.

It was during this time that I learned what "thirsting for You in a dry and weary land" really meant for my home was a dry, warm climate where the wind was always blowing. The soil dried out quickly, the plants wilted and died if unnoticed.

It is the same in our spiritual lives. If we fail to notice the winds of the world blowing on us we will become dry and brittle. If we fail to water our souls with frequent prayer and Bible reading, not only will the soil of our souls dry out, but also those whose lives we touch will not be watered and nurtured.

After a few of these experiences, I have learned not to wait for the signs of dryness to appear, but to drink regularly from the fountain of life which is Christ Jesus.

For Additional Reading: Psalm 130:1-5; Matthew 13:1-8
Geri, Age 58
Personnel Manager

DAY THREE ■ Psalms 63:1; 119:1-2

Have you ever heard these words, or perhaps found yourself saying them? "I'm bored."

My son, age 14, often says these words to me. I find myself asking God, how do I, a single parent with no time to be bored, respond to his boredom?

Satisfaction comes from much more than just having material possessions, food, clothing, and activities of life. True, lasting satisfaction comes from seeking God. The inner man is at peace when he finds time to put God and His Word first in life. "If My people who are called by My name will . . . seek My face then I will hear from heaven" (2 Chron. 7:14). Oh, that my soul would be full of the peace and joy of God, that's everlasting satisfaction!

When I'm feeling bored, I begin to praise and worship the Lord. The peace and joy He gives starts to fill the empty void and this is part of the medicine I prescribe for my son. I suggest that he listen to Christian music and then involve himself with his friends by serving them in some way . . . repairing bicycles, playing catch, etc.

Praising God, seeking Him, and serving others brings a change of attitude within. These are the cures that our spirit desperately needs.

For Additional Reading: 1 Chronicles 28:8-10; Philippians 3:12-16
Karis, Age 41
Human Resource Coordinator

DAY FOUR ■ Psalms 63:1; 119:1-2

Webster defines the word "seek," to perceive, explore, inquire to acquire, pursue, investigate. To seek God means to invest time and energy, using all mental, emotional, and physical resources to capture fully His dimension and character.

I see a process developing in the verses of these psalms. First, we are told to seek God earnestly with all of our heart . . . to pursue Him and His goodness, love, and nature. Second, our seeking God will result in a life of obedience and ultimately, complete transformation.

I can utilize my singleness now! I can fill the empty hours learning to know and obey God, for the more I know Him, the more I trust Him. In trusting, I am able to yield to His sovereignty. I can better cope with the loneliness of singleness knowing that calamity and good things come from the mouth of the Most High (Lam. 3:38).

Blessed am I! In dying, I live. (What a paradox!) As I seek Him, my aspiration, my will, my "self" begin to decrease, while His presence, His will, and His love increase in my life. I melt into Christ and behold "my Father and I are one."

For Additional Reading: Jeremiah 24:4-7; Philippians 3:7-10
Catherine, Age 60
Community Volunteer Worker

DAY FIVE ■ Psalms 63:1; 119:1-2

In a society based on competition, we are lonely. I feel isolated from my peers. Why? They are all my brothers and sisters, the children I grew up with, played with, the people I trained with and work beside. But our relationships, based on worldliness, have come and gone without leaving a lasting impression except on those they have hurt. Our hearts wither as we age, never getting enough to fill the void within us.

I hated the impermanence of my life for years and yet I drifted, not finding a place to rest. I've been slow to listen, but now I hear the call. I feel it. The emptiness that I've always felt can be filled.

It is God who makes the lasting impression and the only permanent relationship is with God. My sanctuary and place of rest is my church. With God's help I will find the lasting relationships that I need. Living under God I find nourishment for my soul. I am blessed with a new drive and meaning.

For Additional Reading: Exodus 33:12-17; John 7:37-39
Phil, Age 36
Writer & Computer Programmer

DAY SIX ■ Psalms 63:1; 119:1-2

As I look at my daily life, I see very clearly the desert that David describes. I live in a world where many times it seems that there is no water to quench parched souls. I see areas of desolation in the newspaper, on the television, and with my own eyes as I drive the streets in our fast-paced world. I used to believe the assumed reality that the world was arid, void of truth and hope.

But I have come to realize that when we look to our Lord, the Living Water, we can see through His promise that we need not go thirsty. Even in our driest, most desolate moments, we can be satisfied by earnestly seeking God and His cup of strength and comfort.

God desires that we turn to Him, staying on the obedient and right-wise path that He has provided for us. In return, He has promised us an eternal well, Jesus Christ, who will never leave us alone in the desert.

For Additional Reading: Isaiah 30:23-26; John 4:7-14
Mike, Age 29
Purchasing Manager

DAY SEVEN ■ Psalms 63:1; 119:1-2

I can relate to David in Psalm 63 because I lived most of my life feeling spiritually dry and emotionally thirsty. Everywhere I looked I saw pain, suffering, hunger, war, immorality, and loneliness . . . especially in the singles scene. It seemed that people were always searching for other people to meet their needs.

At 28, I ended my searching and stopped looking for people to meet my needs. I asked Jesus into my life and found an oasis . . . complete with living water. He met all my needs then and continues to now, according to the riches of God's glory.

While in a desert one must travel early in the day to beat the heat. Likewise in Psalm 63, we're encouraged to seek God early, before we feel the heat of a potential problem.

We're assured in Psalm 119:1-2, that if we will seek God and His way with our whole heart, He will bless us. What an encouragement to give your life to Jesus and be like David. Seek God. You'll find an oasis.

For Additional Reading: Isaiah 33:13-16; Philippians 4:14-19
Bob, Age 34
Airline Mechanic

WEEK NINE

■ ■ ■ ■

A FATHER AND FAMILY
FOR ALL

TEXT FOR THE WEEK: PSALM 68:1-35

KEY VERSE: PSALM 68:5   "A Father to the fatherless; a Defender of widows is God in His holy
dwelling."

DAY ONE ■ Commentary on Psalm 68:5-6

Psalm 68:5-6 is filled with promises and resources which single adults can claim in their daily lives. Half of the children born today are destined to live in a single-parent home before their 18th birthdays. God promises to be "a Father to the fatherless." He will provide guidance, protection, and love for those children who are without a father. Christ was very clear with His disciples about how special little children are to our Heavenly Father.

God also promises to be "a Defender of widows." When faced with overwhelming challenges and attacks from every side, what security and safety we can find in God's strength and unconditional love for us. I believe that this promise is not just for those who are single again due to the death of a spouse.

The death of a marriage through divorce creates millions of new relational widows/widowers every year. Single adults must never forget or doubt that God loves those of His children who have experienced the traumas and transitions of divorce.

One of the most specific promises for single adults in all of Scripture is that "God sets the lonely families"(v. 6). "Family" is one of the most emotionally powerful words in the English language. God ordained families to provide protection, nurture, and encouragement. Many of our families are sadly deficient if not clearly dysfunctional in meeting these basic needs. God promises that through His church and His people the "solitary" single adult can find a protective, nurturing, and encouraging family of believers. Here is a place for healing, guidance, and the resources to meet life's challenges.

God also promises to "bring out those which are bound with chains" (v. 6, KJV). No longer do we need to bind people with iron chains. However, the chains of fear and addiction are still alive and devastatingly active. How many of us suffer under the bondage of a life of fear. How many of us struggle to free ourselves from addictions both chemical and relational. God's promise is not just to free us from these chains, but to bring us out into prosperity. God promises those who believe on His Son the prosperity of a life overflowing with peace, joy, contentment, and fulfillment!

For Additional Reading: Genesis 16:6-11; 1 John 3:1-3
John R. Etcheto is the Singles Pastor at Reno Christian Fellowship in Reno, Nevada. Six single adults from his church share the following devotionals.

DAY TWO ■ Psalm 68:5-6

When God says He will be "A Father to the fatherless," He means exactly what He says. Both of my children have been raised without the love and support of their dad. I used to see them watch the mailbox for birthday cards or Christmas gifts. None came. It broke their hearts as well as mine. What could I do to make it up to them or help them understand? The answer was found in Romans 8:15: "Abba, Father!" I could help lead them to Jesus!

With Jesus we have a future and a hope. Broken hearts are mended. Yes, there are still hard times, but our Heavenly Father is always there to comfort, protect, and give assurance of His unchanging love.

Now as my children are practically grown and on their own, "I have no greater joy than to hear that my children are walking in the truth" (3 John 4).

For Additional Reading: Lamentations 5:1-21; Ephesians 6:1-4
Connie, Age 41
Single Parents Network Coordinator at Reno Christian
Fellowship

DAY THREE ■ Psalm 68:5-6

Family. As a single mother raising two small boys that word was no longer in my vocabulary. We weren't a family anymore. And it seemed everywhere I looked there were perfect families of four: mom, dad, two children. I was looking everywhere except to God. I was "rebellious . . . in a sun-scorched land." Eventually, I was miserable. My sights were set solely on myself and my situation. I knew for sure that I was *the only* single parent on the face of the earth.

Then I became involved in ministry, reaching out to others who were feeling or hurting like I had. I was finally seeking God's will for my life and the healing process began within me as I allowed God to use me to His glory.

By doing so, I became part of a family like none I'd ever thought possible. My boys are often in the company of "big brothers" who see that they get the male companionship they need. Repairs are done at my home. "Family" outings are regular, and other needs of a single mom are met. There is a sense of love and bonding that could *only* come from God the Father.

So take a chance and reach out to those around you. Allow God to use your experiences to help others. You'll be blessed beyond measure—and there's a family just waiting to happen.

For Additional Reading: Psalm 51:11-15; Luke 11:11-13
Carol, Age 30
Legal Assistant

DAY FOUR ■ Psalm 68:5-6

Father to the fatherless"—how many, many times have I gone to Him as my Father for comfort and guidance. Though recovered now, my natural father was an alcoholic during my childhood and into my young adult life. "Father-daughter" talks were not a part of my life. However, since accepting Jesus as my Saviour nearly seven and one half years ago, He has become my Protector, Provider, Counselor, Friend, and Father.

When my 16-year-old son was killed over three years ago, it seemed as though my world had collapsed. Friends and relatives were of great comfort and strength, but only Jesus could soothe my aching heart . . . only Jesus could *totally* understand my brokenness. He was ALWAYS there to share my tears, to talk to, to comfort me, and to restore my shattered life. Gently, He nurtured me; lovingly, He gave me guidance; slowly, faithfully, He put the pieces of my life back together and gave me the courage and desire to share His never-ending, never-failing love with others. He was then and is now my loving Father.

For Additional Reading: Psalm 61:1-8; John 12:24-28
Marialice, Age 44
Legal Secretary

DAY FIVE ■ Psalm 68:5-6

Well, we've just about given up on Jim, he'll probably never marry."

"Your great uncle never married; he was always a little strange."

"You'd better find a wife before the rest of your hair falls out."

Not long ago I allowed comments about my singleness to put distance between my family, friends, and me. I found myself very unhappy about being single and devastatingly lonely. I had withdrawn into a nearly solitary life and contacted friends and family only when I wanted to.

The key to climbing out of the cold pit of loneliness, for me, was to find contentment and completeness in being single. Contentment came through prayer and fellowship with Christ. I was suddenly free from searching for a mate, and feeling like an incomplete person because I hadn't found one. I was free to join in with other singles where I found fellowship and love with my new family, my brothers and sisters in Christ.

Our precious Father in His infinite wisdom and perfect timing, set this lonely man in the most loving family of all.

For Additional Reading: Isaiah 58:1-6; 1 Timothy 5:1-8
Jim, Age 33
Geologist

DAY SIX ■ Psalm 68:5-6

In Matthew 12:50 Jesus says, "Whoever does the will of My Father in heaven is My brother and sister and mother." Does He call you His brother or sister—does that sound like family?

In Psalm 68:4 are more directions for receiving the promise of verses 5-6: "Sing to God, sing praise to His name, extol Him who rides on the clouds—His name is the Lord—and rejoice before Him."

Our love for a family member is something Jesus knows we all understand, yet He asks for *more.* Knowing that, as we give God His rightful place in our lives and rejoice in that knowledge of Him, an "outworking" begins in our lives. We need to learn to thank Him for the "family" He *is,* and for others He brings into our lives. He is more than sufficient in all ways to provide for *all* our needs—try it!

The personal P.S. to this is that in applying the sovereignty of God to my life, the Lord gave me a friend who sometimes has some of the same (annoying) characteristics as a close family member. I had to laugh at His sense of humor as I learned tolerance and patience in another area while gaining one of the best "sisters" in the world. My life is living proof that by His power you can be alone, but never lonely!

For Additional Reading: Psalm 17:1-7; Matthew 12:46-50
Sandy, Age 55
Office Manager

DAY SEVEN ■ Psalm 68:5-6

Having suffered through a painful divorce early in life and now becoming a widower after 28 years of marriage, how comforting to hear the Word of God that He will indeed be the mother of my motherless children, that He will give me the strength and His love as I attack all of life's tribulations without my wife. "God sets the lonely in families" and through the church I have found a new family. While not forsaking my own immediate family, I have been encouraged, nurtured, and allowed to help others in their healing process.

It is the drawing together of single people and the demonstration of the caring, understanding, and love that helps us heal and feel a part of the family. God is fulfilling His Word through this church family!

For Additional Reading: Psalm 36:6-10; Matthew 6:9-15
Frank, "Sixty-Something"
Self-Employed

WEEK TEN
■ ■ ■ ■

A BRUTE BEAST. WHO, ME?

TEXT FOR THE WEEK: **PSALM 73:1-26**

KEY VERSES: PSALM 73:21-22   "When my heart was grieved and my
spirit embittered, I was senseless and
ignorant; I was a brute beast before
you."

DAY ONE ■ Commentary on Psalm 73:21-26

"What kind of an animal are you like?" Someone once compared me to a collie; loyal and friendly. That's neat! The truth is sometimes this collie feels like a pig or turkey. In all of our lives there are times when we'd like to think of ourselves as a stallion, but we feel like a donkey! The author of Psalm 73 remembers such a time, "When my heart was grieved and my spirit embittered; I was senseless and ignorant. I was a brute beast before You."

What made the psalmist feel this way? As the psalm opens he states the problem, "I envied the arrogant when I saw the prosperity of the wicked" (v. 3). When he compared his life with those who cared nothing for God, he sank into self-pity; "Surely in vain I have kept my heart pure. . . . All day long I have been plagued, I have been punished every morning" (vv. 13-14). His mental state almost led him to deny his God (vv. 15-16).

Imagine the tune for the early verses of Psalm 73 as an original blues piece — reflective and remorseful. But with verses 23-24 comes a brighter note, "Yet I am always with You: You hold me by my right hand. You guide me with Your counsel, and afterward You will take me into glory." What brought this change? It started when the psalmist realized he had only been viewing the wicked temporally. In verses 17-20 he begins to see them eternally. "Till I entered the sanctuary of God; then I understood their final destiny."

A "brute beast" experience can be beneficial, if through it we discover life's true worth. Listen to the psalmist's discovery, "I'm always with you. My flesh and my heart may fail [death], but God is the strength of my heart and my portion forever" (vv. 23, 26).

"Pie-in-the-sky" thinking? No, the psalmist's experience produced in him a deep dependence on God. His thoughts might have been like this: "And to think I almost gave up on One who refuses to give up." YOU UPHOLD ME WITH YOUR RIGHT HAND. "I almost gave up on the only One who can make life purposeful." YOU GUIDE ME WITH YOUR COUNSEL. "My resolve . . . " WHAT HAVE I IN HEAVEN BUT YOU? AND EARTH HAS NOTHING THAT I DESIRE BESIDES YOU!

For Additional Reading: 2 Samuel 22:29-37;
Matthew 14:25-33
Larry White is the Single Adult Pastor at Skyline Wesleyan Church in Lemon Grove, California. The following applications come from the lives of six single adults in Larry's ministry.

DAY TWO ■ Psalm 73:21-26

Sometimes I slip back into old, familiar behavior. Without really knowing how or why it happens, I find myself muddling around. I realize one day that I've done it, even though intellectually I know better, and spiritually I am warned of the danger. But there I am, feeling a little lost, lonely, out of control, and depressed. I'm unmotivated to do much of anything and worst of all, I feel there is nothing I can do about it except ride out the low wave that has hit me.

Like a caged lion waiting to be fed, I feel bored and the prospect of being "really" happy seems far away. I focus on my next meal or wait for those outside the cage to notice me, to give me value or worth, or to rescue me from the cage. Even if I'm not ignored, the depression can continue and I can feel more confined and "locked up."

But then I finally hear the still small voice inside me. "I love you. I give you worth. You are valuable to Me. The cage you are in is of your own making. You closed the door but it is not locked. Push open the door and I'll set you free."

Who is this voice? Why does it call me? It is my Lord, the voice of truth calling me, and missing fellowship with me. I don't really know why the King of kings and the Lord of lords even bothers with me, but He does. And who am I to question this King, the knower of all? He says I have value to Him. He has work for me to do, and for some reason He delights in the time we spend together. So, why should I stay in the cage of darkness when the Light calls me to come out to be with Him — the One who really loves me so completely — who always has my interest at heart — who asks so little of me, yet gives so much. My heart is filled with gratefulness and joy that He has chosen me at this time and place to be with Him. He fills me up, dries my tears, and makes me joyful.

For Additional Reading: Job 13:15-18; Ephesians 2:4-10
Gail, Age 43
Professor at SDSU

DAY THREE ■ Psalm 73:21-26

The comfort a Christian has lies in the realization that God has hold of our hand and nothing can break that hold! Paul says in Romans 8:35, "Who shall separate us from the love of Christ?" and he answers, "Nothing!" God has hold of *our* hand, and that makes all the difference.

I have a four-year-old son who likes to run ahead of me whenever we are out. However, when I do not want him to run from me, I grasp hold of his hand and hold onto him. No matter how much he struggles to get away from me, he cannot. However, there are times when he is holding onto my hand, he can break away whenever he wants. That is the way it is with God. *He* is holding onto *us* and nothing can break His grip.

I was recently unemployed for a month. What kept me going

during that time was the comfort of God being in control of my life. During that time, I was constantly hearing the voice of the enemy trying to get me to blame God for my unemployment. However, I was able to see the light at the end of the tunnel because I know God has hold of my life.

As singles, we sometimes struggle from paycheck to paycheck, but we need to remember that God has hold of us. He will never let us out of His grip and *He* will meet our needs.

For Additional Reading: Psalm 5:1-12; 1 Corinthians 9:22-27
Dale, Age 38
Mechanical Draftsman

DAY FOUR ■ Psalm 73:21-26

At first it was not easy, this separate lifestyle that I was subjected to. Who would guide me? Who could I depend on for support in time of need?

Frantically I searched and foolishly turned to others with my questions and inner desire for closeness, but others were also lost, shallow, and artificial or had no time nor care to hear me. Ultimately, I was left alone again.

Friends passed out multiple wrong answers they did not abide by. Answers became detours and disappointments. Yes . . . it took awhile to find the "trusted few," the older and wiser ones who took the time to explain how they made it through and lived to tell about it as I have now.

As I reflect back on day after lonely day, with each problem unsolved, I drew closer to the Lord, while helping others forget their ills in a rehabilitation center. And as I sang the old, beautiful hymns to them, I realized I would never be alone again because of Him.

Lonely ones, hear me now! With God's guiding light there is direction, meaning, strength, and understanding. Search me no more. Fear not. Single is only a word and not a situation or condition, for with God as your Counselor, you will never be alone again.

For Additional Reading: Genesis 32:24-26; Luke 15:3-7
Marlys, Age 57
Administrative Assistant in Nursing

DAY FIVE ■ Psalm 73:21-26

I can really relate to the psalmist's sense of confusion as he watches the wicked prosper. I've been single for nine years and a believer for seven of those years. And life as a single adult can be hard and life can be unfair. I go through periods of time when I feel very lonely. At these times I find myself envying my single acquaintances who are not believers. They are free to live "the good life" that the psalmist describes. Ask them why they do it and they will say "because it feels good." "If it feels good to have one-night stands, then do it. If it feels good to become involved in live-in relationships, then do it. After all, everybody's doing it so it must be right! Right?"

But something doesn't ring true. And as I enter the sanctuary of God, when I get back on my knees and into His Word, I get my perspective back again. They're trying to find fulfillment apart from an obedient committed relationship with God. And compared to the holiness of God their relationships are nothing more than shallow fleeting moments of narcissistic self-gratification that ultimately end in empty, meaningless despair. My relationship with God is the standard for all other relationships.

Like the psalmist, as I enter again into the sanctuary of God, my heart is renewed. "But as for me, it it good to be near God. I have made the Sovereign Lord my refuge" (v. 28).

For Additional Reading: Psalm 9:1-10; Luke 15:11-27
Flo, Age 44
Singles Intern

DAY SIX ■ Psalm 73:21-26

I met him when I was 15 years old, I was engaged at 18, and I married him at 20. I had my first child at 24, second at 26, third at 27, and fourth at 28! I was married to a wonderful man and had a wonderful family. Being an Air Force family, we lived many places—some terrible, some OK, and some great. Just when the children were ready to leave the home and retirement was approaching so my husband and I would be able to spend some time together, he decided he needed to "be his own person" and "do his own thing." My feeling of rejection was total!

Being a Christian from childhood and being raised by Christians, divorce was not in my vocabulary. What was I to do now? Who was I now that I no longer was Mrs. _____? Several years of soul-searching passed before I was able to accept this situation. I found great comfort in Psalm 73:23. Just because one man had rejected me and no longer loved me did not mean that other people did not love me. I realized just how much God loves me and it is an unconditional love. It did not matter how much I had failed Him or what I had done to displease Him; He still loved me with that special love of His. I could go forward from that point and make a new life for myself. I kept recalling God's words: "Yet I am always with you." This can also be your affirmation today; say it over and over until it becomes your special verse.

For Additional Reading: Psalm 91:14-16; 1 John 4:7-12
Charlotte, Age 55
Executive Secretary

DAY SEVEN ■ Psalm 73:21-26

My heart has occasionally grieved as I observed the success of wicked people around me. I have experienced the psalmist's dilemma. Promotions which I have earned were awarded to genuinely wicked peers. I didn't understand; but I chose new goals and increased the pace because I am a survivor.

Then God, my wise Counselor, assertively entered the picture. He lovingly reminded me that these observations weren't all of the truth, even though all were true. My thinking had been brutish. How easy it is to reason "logically" to a conclusion without considering all the evidence.

I started life in the same condition as those around me. Growing up as a compliant child in a Christian home only caused the volume to be turned down. It did not change my condition. I had been identical to them. *Lost. Hopeless. Isolated.*

Then Jesus came! He surrounded me with His love. He reconciled me to God. He established me on the solid rock of His truth.

I am beginning to understand. God finds us where we are. Along the way, He allows encounters with the wicked to remind us what we would be like without Him.

What hope in heaven do I have without God? Whom on earth could I possibly consider to replace Him?

For Additional Reading: Isaiah 8:13-17; 1 Peter 2:4-9
Gene, Age 53
Paralegal Student

WEEK ELEVEN

■ ■ ■ ■

IS ANYONE LISTENING? YES!

TEXT FOR THE WEEK: PROVERBS 1:33

KEY VERSE: PROVERBS 1:33   "Whoever listens to Me will live in
                                 safety and be at ease, without fear of
                                 harm."

DAY ONE ■ Commentary on Proverbs 1:33

I've discovered that when I start to feel frantic, anxious, and "off-center," it's time to do some "prayer repair." Usually, it's because I have been doing more *talking* to God and less *listening* to God speaking to me. I've found that it's not easy to hear someone else when you're the one doing the talking.

Jesus told the Jews, "My sheep listen to My voice; I know them, and they follow Me" (John 10:27-28). Isn't it wonderful assurance to know that we have nothing to fear — *if* we are quiet long enough to listen. Jesus didn't say, "My sheep talk to Me." He said they listen.

A devout Christian man sat on his porch in the middle of one of the worst storms of the century. Rescue teams scoured the town, attempting to evacuate everyone from the rising floodwaters. Two men in a motorboat spotted the man and yelled to him to get into their boat so they could take him to safety. He calmly refused, saying "God will protect me. Thanks anyway."

As the water continued to rise, he was forced to sit on top of a stepladder. Sometime later, a National Guard team saw him and tried to get him to go with them, but, over the roar of the raging water the man yelled, "No thanks, God is watching over me and will keep me safe."

The water rose higher, and he had to move to the roof, where, fortunately, he was spotted by a helicopter crew who lowered a rope to him. But he refused to climb up, yelling to them, "No thanks, I'll be fine because God will protect me."

Soon the water rose higher than the roof and the man drowned. When he arrived in heaven, he asked God why he hadn't been saved. After all, hadn't he shown incredible faith? He said, "I told everyone that You would protect me and You let me down."

God answered, "Apparently you weren't listening to Me. I sent two men in a motorboat, a National Guard rescue team, and a helicopter and you told them all to leave! What more could I have done to get your attention?"

Psalm 4:3 assures us that "the Lord will hear when I call to Him." That's incredibly comforting. However, I suspect that we all need to remind ourselves that God *always* hears, and also always *speaks* to us. Sometimes God speaks loudly and sometimes softly. But we must always be both *alert* and *listening* for His message.

Wouldn't this be a good day to do less talking and more listening—for God? The promise and rewards are great: "Whoever listens to Me will live in safety and be at ease, without fear of harm."

For Additional Reading: Psalm 37:5-7; John 10:27-28
Ron Hagberg is the Director of Single Adult Ministries at Hennepin Avenue United Methodist Church in Minneapolis, Minnesota. The following applications to Proverbs 1:33 are written by six single adults at Hennepin Avenue U.M.C.

DAY TWO ■ Proverbs 1:33

I was in a job that could go nowhere and fear was mounting that I would always be right where I was. I had been searching for another position for some time, but nothing was the proper career move. Depression was starting to set in when my job was eliminated due to budget cuts.

The next Sunday morning our minister gave a sermon titled "Earthquake Living." Suddenly his words caught my attention— "What do we do when the stones of our business, family, or friendships are reduced to rubble? What happens to our self-esteem and our lives? What do we do when our world falls apart? When a job is lost or a marriage fails?"

I knew I was not alone! "In the middle of earthquake living, keep on praying." There is nothing to fear, for God will take care of us.

The next week I accepted a new position in the company and city I had only dreamed of before.

For Additional Reading: Luke 21:5-19; Deuteronomy 26:1-11
James, Age 45
Director of Marketing

DAY THREE ■ Proverbs 1:33

When he left, I was devastated. Daddy was gone, I was only 12 years old and left with an invalid mother to care for. She was just barely out of the wheelchair and on crutches after her accident 3 years earlier but we knew there would not be any further improvement in her condition.

There was really no place to go for support other than a wonderful minister and the church. I'll never forget his words, no matter how long I live, "If ye have faith as a grain of mustard seed, nothing will be impossible unto you. June, you must have strength because your mother needs you, Jesus needs you, and I need you. Believe me, if you listen to God and heed Him, you will always be secure and free from harm."

No one will ever know how those words helped in later years when my husband left me with two babies, after a second marriage failed, and through the years that I fought depression and love addiction.

He has always been beside me and often *carried* me through the hardships of life. I know that if I continue to listen, He will lead me without fear.

For Additional Reading: Psalm 56:1-13; Matthew 17:14-23
June, Age 48
Secretary to Director of SAM

DAY FOUR ■ Proverbs 1:33

Why do we have so much trouble believing in God's all-encompassing love and care? Psalm 23, which frequently comes to mind, says it all: "The Lord is my Shepherd, I shall lack nothing."

Seventeen years ago, the sudden death of my beloved wife caused me to lose many of the values I had held essential. Within three weeks after the funeral, I had a stroke causing speech difficulty and some paralysis in my left side. This did not stop or slow my descent into alcoholism. For four years, I was exposed to treatment and therapy galore — unfortunately without the desired result.

Finally, one day while completely alone, with just the Lord as my companion, I asked for help and guidance. It was that very moment, when I started to truly listen and believe. His message came through loud and clear to stop blaming alcohol, to look in the mirror and listen up.

More than 14 years have gone by and my life with God is good — very full of love and contentment, as long as I continue to listen.

For Additional Reading: Psalm 23:1-6; 2 Corinthians 7:5-7
Donald, Age 71
Construction and Real Estate

DAY FIVE ■ Proverbs 1:33

Listening requires effort. I finally realized this after a recent career transition. Nearly 10 years out of college, in a seemingly successful career, I did not *hear* anyone around me.

Only after nurturing by Christian friends, did I absorb some nuances of what listening was about — that it didn't involve quickly giving advice, solving a problem, or talking or doing anything but simply hearing. If I were to be a Christian or Christlike, I must listen as He does; without prejudgment. As I began to practice this, it became easier and more often that I could hear the Lord. (He could get a word in edgewise at this point!) And with this new communication and attitude, the fear and uncertainty of a career change became manageable. Indeed, the Scripture says, "He who listens to Me will live in safety."

It seems ironic that only by releasing my grip on the security of things seen and learning to listen to the Lord—the things unseen, did fear lose its grip on me.

For Additional Reading: Proverbs 1:5-7; James 1:19-25
Frank, Age 34
Graduate Student

DAY SIX ■ Proverbs 1:33

I'm very fortunate to be in my present position—Food Service Director for a large downtown church. Daily I meet and serve members, staff, and guests of the congregation. Traditionally the breaking of bread has been a large and vital part of the Christian doctrine and in being privileged to be a part of that service, I feel I am serving God in my own small way. It is a very challenging job to handle the frustration and problems involved when dealing with human foibles and personalities. I'm fortunate to have supportive clergy and staff members who truly are my friends.

As hard as it is for me to write these words, this past year has been very trying and sad for me because of an intensely unhappy and unresolved problem with my eldest son. Through it all I keep hearing "whoever listens to Me will have safety and be at ease, without fear of harm." I am able to overcome my feelings of hopelessness and helplessness by sharing with my friends and remembering these words. By listening, believing, and following His words, I can attain the peace of mind God intends for all His children.

For Additional Reading: Psalm 111:1-10; Mark 4:1-12
Rachel, Age 69
Food Service Director

DAY SEVEN ■ Proverbs 1:33

Have you ever climbed a mountain, flown an airplane, or swam in the ocean? I think all of us are confronted with challenges — things that take us beyond that which we feel fit our capabilities. The only thing that can carry us through these experiences is a belief in One who is far greater than all. I believe the words in this passage are telling us all to believe in the Lord and He will calm our fears. I feel if we believe in Him, that belief will strengthen our self-image and help us to grow as people who can shoulder more and more of life's trials as time marches on.

For Additional Reading: Deuteronomy 30:15-20;
John 20:24-31
Rodney, Age 46
Airline Simulation Instructor

WEEK TWELVE

■ ■ ■ ■

A NEW PATH, A GOD WE CAN TRUST

TEXT FOR THE WEEK: **PROVERBS 3:5-6**

KEY VERSE: PROVERBS 3:6   "In all your ways acknowledge Him, and He will make your paths straight."

DAY ONE ■ Commentary on Proverbs 3:5-6

I would estimate that in any given audience, 60 percent of the people are wrestling or struggling with an extremely difficult need or problem for which they themselves can see no answer or end. Perhaps you have been disappointed, discouraged, dissatisfied, or depressed in the last few weeks. You may even have been disenchanted with life. Just because you are a Christian does not mean that you will not have any problems. There is a difference, though, in problems besetting us and problems begetting us. Christians have a source of power and strength to draw from that can give peace in the midst of the storm.

Proverbs 3:6 is one of the great answers and truths of the Christian life. God has promised that if you will acknowledge Him "in all your ways," then "He will make your paths straight." The preceding verse gives a key on how to acknowledge Him in all your ways. It begins with a complete trust in the Lord. The word "trust" in verse 5 expresses the sense of confidence that "the rug will not be pulled out from under you." Then you must not lean on your own understanding but on God's understanding. By placing absolute trust and confidence in Him, no matter how difficult the situation, you leave the situation in God's hands. You must wait on God to see you through. Just remember that God's understanding is often the opposite of what seems to us the most logical or normal thing to do.

God will direct your paths in different ways. Sometimes He may place obstacles in your way to lead you in another direction. To keep you from getting ahead of His plan for your life, God will place an obstacle in your way to slow you down, then He eventually removes it. Often, He keeps you waiting after you have sensed His guidance in a particular direction. This divine discipline of delay is where great men and women of God are molded as they learn to lean completely on the Lord.

So obey God and trust Him no matter what you are facing and leave all the circumstances up to Him. When you have a need, God knows it. If you will wait on Him, He will supply your need. Acknowledge Him in everything you do by putting God first, making Him known, and obeying Him. Then He has promised that He will direct you where you are supposed to go.

For Additional Reading: Proverbs 3:1-18; James 1:5-8
Bobby Mullins is the Minister of Singles at Ridgeway Baptist church in Memphis, Tennessee. Six single adults from Ridgeway Baptist respond to Proverbs 3:5-6.

DAY TWO ■ Proverbs 3:5-6

To trust with all of our hearts can be difficult. I find the hardest time comes when I cannot see God's hand at work.

When I was searching for a new job I asked for God's guidance and direction. However, when progress seemed slow I took things into my own hands. This left me frustrated and miserable. When I fully gave control to God I received a peace and my prayers were soon answered. Once the doors opened I could see how God had been working in my life for over a year to prepare me for the job He had for me. The words to a song have become dear to my heart as a reminder, "When you can't trace His hand, trust His heart."

For Additional Reading: Isaiah 57:10-13; John 14:1-6
Beth, Age 28
Registered Nurse

DAY THREE ■ Proverbs 3:5-6

Will you marry me?" Though these beautiful words are familiar, they are seldom spoken or heard. For most, one will only speak or hear this question once in a lifetime.

I asked this very question to a beautiful, Christian young lady. I had prayed for months that she was part of God's will for my life. Both she and God had the same answer, no.

Why? The answer is simple. In God's matchless wisdom and love, He did not put us on the same path. As I acknowledged God by asking for His choice, He directed my path for me.

The path we would take is not always the path God wants us on. It may hurt sometimes to be on God's path, but whose path do we want to travel, God's or ours? Simply acknowledge God and He will keep you on the best path possible, His.

For Additional Reading: Psalm 16:7-11; Luke 12:27-32
John, Age 27
Ministerial Student

DAY FOUR ■ Proverbs 3:5-6

It is always difficult to leave friends and familiar surroundings. I believe God had arranged a job change in my life to remind me that I need only trust Him to help me through. As a single adult, I looked to my church for companionship and support. God used this job change to take away that support making me totally dependent on Him.

I do not fully understand why I had to move, but I do know without a doubt that God moved me for a purpose. I sometimes question God's direction for my life, but that is because I sometimes forget that He alone knows what is ahead of me and He alone knows what is best for me.

For Additional Reading: Exodus 15:11-13; Philippians 2:12-18
Harold, Age 31
Medical Technologist

DAY FIVE ■ Proverbs 3:5-6

When my husband had a heart attack that caused his death, my children and I were in shock at losing someone we loved dearly. We had been married for over 30 years and I had taken seriously my wedding vows where I had promised to love, honor, and obey my husband.

What do you do when the head of the household is gone? I had depended on him to provide my every need. Then a friend who had lost her husband earlier shared some Scripture verses with me, but one in particular was special. In Isaiah 54:4-5 the Bible says that for the widow, God becomes the husband. I claimed that verse and made the same vows to Him that I had made to Lyle. I promised to love, honor, and obey Him. By trusting in the Lord, I no longer had to do things in my own strength, but I let God have control. My dependence on an earthly husband has been transferred to a heavenly Husband. Now He directs my path.

For Additional Reading: Isaiah 54:1-8; Romans 8:28-32
Dot, Age 65
Education Secretary

DAY SIX ■ Proverbs 3:5-6

The truths set forth in Proverbs 3:5-6 were proven in my life about a year ago. When I became dissatisfied with my job, I began praying that the Lord would guide me to a new one. A few months later, I was offered a great opportunity in a growing company. Anyone in my position would have jumped at the opportunity. I committed it to the Lord; His answer was no.

About six months later, I was "let go" from my job. I began wondering why the Lord told me not to take the previous offer. I thought that it would be better than not having a job at all.

Finally, I was offered a job which was and still is the ideal job for me.

I definitely would not have chosen this route to change jobs, but nothing has strengthened my faith more than seeing God say "wait" and then providing the perfect answer.

For Additional Reading: Psalm 37:23-29; Philippians 4:10-13
Kristi, Age 27
Certified Public Accountant

DAY SEVEN ■ Proverbs 3:5-6

We can't trust the Lord if we don't know Him. The more we get into His Living Word and know who He is, and what He has done and is doing, the easier it will be for us to trust. God's desire for your life and mine is that we know Him. The more time that is spent at His feet, the easier it will become to trust Him who is trustworthy and put our confidence in Him who never fails.

If we as Christians cast our eyes on Him, come to Him, and trust Him as a child, the fear will disappear. Having spent time with the Lord God Almighty, the natural by-product is that we will acknowledge Him for who He is. We will not be able to hold it back. We will have to proclaim His greatness.

Won't you take Him at His Word today?

For Additional Reading: Job 42:1-6; Hebrews 10:19-23
Warren, Age 28
Student

WEEK THIRTEEN
■ ■ ■ ■

A BALANCED LIFE OUT OF WORSHIP

TEXT FOR THE WEEK: **ISAIAH 6:1-8**

KEY VERSE: ISAIAH 6:5   " 'Woe to me' I cried. 'I am ruined! For I am a man of unclean lips, and I live among a people of unclean lips, and my eyes have seen the King, the Lord Almighty.' "

DAY ONE ■ Commentary on Isaiah 6:1-8

It had only been a year and a half since I had seen John. He had graduated from seminary and had gone to his hometown to work as an associate pastor at his home church. I asked him how his church work was going. He recounted the excitement with which he had begun his ministry, the demands put on him by a growing church, and the zeal with which he had pursued his work. Within one year he was burned out and forced to take a six-month rest and reevaluation time.

It was not very long into my first ministry position, the one I hold now, that I began to exhibit some of the same traits and tendencies John had manifested in his ministry. Fortunately, it was also early in my ministry here that I had an experience that would define my future ministry, give me a gauge to measure my drivenness, and provide a way toward health and balance between my life and my responsibilities.

"The year that King Uzziah died" (v. 1) sets the stage for this passage. It was a time in the nation of Judah of great fear and apprehension concerning the future. The people of Judah had seen the anarchy that had broken out with the death of King Jeroboam in Israel, and there was little reason to think that the same would not happen to them. But there is movement in this passage from discouragement to productive service that comes about by an encounter with God. A vision of God leads to despair (v. 5), but despair opens the door to needed cleansing (vv. 6-7) and strengthening for service (v. 8).

No, God did not appear to me in a vision, but I was encountered by Him in worship. Through a series of events and the help of an old friend I came to recognize that my heart and my whole self had not been involved in worship for a long time. I began to pray that God would break down the barriers that surrounded my heart. As He did, my first response was a need for confession and repentance. With that came peace and a new sense of purpose. I wish I could say that I am no longer a driven person, but I can't. (It is now midnight, I'm in my office writing this, and I'm on vacation!) But the gauge is the peace with which I carry out my responsibilities. My way toward health and balance is in a heart-engaged worship and prayer life that helps me sort out the responsibilities and empowers me to do that which I am called to do.

You may be overwhelmed and discouraged by the demands on your life this day. But don't forsake your personal and corporate worship and prayer life. Ask not that the demands be removed, but that God give you the wisdom to discern His call on your life — those responsibilities that are truly yours — and the strength to carry them out.

For Additional Reading: Exodus 34:10-14; Revelation 22:7-9
H. Henry Williams is the Director of Singles Ministries at Westlink Christian Church in Wichita, Kansas. Six Westlink Christian singles write the following from their experience in worship.

DAY TWO ■ Isaiah 6:1-8

Could you imagine me in Jamaica?" Those were my words to a friend of mine as I went to the front of the church to get more information about a short-term missions opportunity. After visiting with the speaker, he said, "The trip to Jamaica will be July 12–22. I think you should pray about going and see what God wants you to do."

As I prayed, I tended to present God with all the reasons why I could not go. He did an excellent job of answering them. First, I said, "Lord, I do not know the language." I found out they spoke English. Next, I said, "Lord, I do not have enough money." My grandmother helped finance my trip. Finally, I said, "Lord, I do not have a place to stay or a job for the summer." I was able to live in an apartment with three other girls for only $50 per month and work at the university library.

I did take the trip and it was interesting to observe how God continued to guide me and provide for all my needs in every situation during the trip. Since then, I have seen God's faithfulness as He has guided me and equipped me for every new opportunity of service. At times, I still feel inadequate, but I have learned to trust the Lord and say, "Here am I, send me." I look with anticipation into the future and wonder, "Lord, what new adventures and opportunities of service do You have planned for me?"

For Additional Reading: Jeremiah 1:4-8; Mark 1:16-20
Mary, Age 26
Christian Bookstore Sales Clerk

DAY THREE ■ Isaiah 6:1-8

All of us have had less than satisfying employment experiences. From the time we are old enough to accept responsibility, work is a very important part of our lives. Looking back, I think I had my worst jobs as a teenager—with one exception. Recently, I accepted a position in management in a local convention hotel. I was very excited about the opportunity and was full of enthusiasm. However, my excitement and enthusiasm soon faded. I had to work many long hours and I could tell this was really taking a toll on my relationship with Christ. In my interactions with coworkers, I sensed that many of them were unhappy with their lives and without hope for the future. Without really realizing it, I slowly began to feel many of those same feelings. I resigned after only four months among feelings of failure, despair, and hopelessness.

Isaiah must have felt much the same way when he cried out, "Woe to me! . . . I am ruined! For I am a man of unclean lips, and I live among a people of unclean lips, and my eyes have seen the King, the Lord Almighty" (v. 5).

Through this experience, I have been reminded of the faithfulness, mercy, and grace of God. And just like Isaiah, God has atoned for my sin and freed me of guilt. Now I stand ready for His service once again.

For Additional Reading: Psalm 36:1-5; Romans 7:22-25
David, Age 29
Student, Mental Health Counselor

DAY FOUR ■ Isaiah 6:1-8

Have you ever seen a cocky teenager sass a respected teacher and felt an overwhelming desire to shake his shoulders and yell in his face, "Just who in the world do you think you are?" Sometimes we need that kind of slap-in-the-face treatment to awaken us to the reality of God's awesome holiness.

Having just completed my bachelor degree in violin performance, I experienced a kind of slap back into reality as I awaited surgery to remove an elusive congenital tumor in my cerebellum.

As I sat in my hospital bed contemplating giving up my future as a symphony violinist, I was confused and nearly devastated. I tried to hide my tears and my profound sorrow as a sweet older lady from church walked in to visit me. The majority of time was consumed with talk of my present concerns, and then I discovered that this woman was currently suffering from her husband's tragic deterioration from Alzheimer's disease. What a slap! I was humbled to recognize that perhaps someone else had a burden even worse than mine! God allowed me to see that my attitude was just like a sassy teenager. Like Isaiah, I could only repent of my sin and then accept God's gracious cleansing and strengthening for service. So often I forget that I am here to serve Him!

God graciously let me retain the musical abilities I once thought He would demand that I give up. And I know that He will use these to His glory for His service. A humbling reprimand is actually a wonderful way God reaches out to draw us to Himself.

For Additional Reading: Job 5:17-21; Hebrews 12:7-13
Joan, Age 28
Violinist, Instructor

DAY FIVE ■ Isaiah 6:1-8

I've often envied Isaiah for the clearness of his call to service. I've struggled to find my place of service for God and often fall into the trap of thinking that I need a certain type of career in order to be effective for God. Recently, I got my teaching certificate and I thought I had it all figured out. Then God showed—through the lack of a job—that perhaps His plans were not the same as my plans. I was forced to give up my own expectations. This was the first step in learning to take Isaiah's approach. He may also have had to give up his own plans, but he just said, "Whatever You want, Lord, here I am." As I've been learning to do the same thing, God has given me unexpected opportunities to serve (such as writing this devotional) and opened new doors I'd never dreamed of. All He was waiting for was my willingness and surrender.

For Additional Reading: 1 Samuel 3:1-19; Ephesians 3:20-21
Eileen, Age 30
Investigator, Defense Investigative Service

DAY SIX ■ Isaiah 6:1-8

Tension. We hear a great deal today about its causes and effects. There have been books, magazine articles, lectures, and television programs on the subject. It seems that even though we have generated a wide array of material, we have done very little to prevent the problem.

We need look no further than the example of Christ Himself to find insight into the problem of "tension prevention." His ministry was enveloped in prayer. Time and time again He withdrew to pray (Luke 6:12). The great Christian reformer Martin Luther considered prayer so important that the more work he had to accomplish, the more time he spent in prayer. When once speaking of his plans for the following day he said: "Work, work from early till late. In fact I have so much to do that I shall spend the first three hours in prayer."

We can see in verses 1-8 the strengthening that can occur as the result of an encounter with God. Isaiah was cleansed of his sins and was then willing to say, "Here am I, send me!"

"Tension Prevention" begins with prayer. It is through these daily encounters with God that we are enabled to deal with the pressures of daily living. It is only here that we can lay our sins and troubles on the altar and walk away strengthened and renewed. Maybe we need to think less about dealing with tension and more about how we can daily encounter God in a personal way.

For Additional Reading: Exodus 19:3-8; Luke 9:28-36
Brett, Age 29
Maintenance

DAY SEVEN ■ Isaiah 6:1-8

A vailable — qualified or willing to do something or to assume a responsibility; present, accessible.

Accessible — capable of being reached. (*Webster's New Collegiate Dictionary*)

Struggling? — Take heart! There is a Saviour who's sacrifice on the cross has made a holy and loving God accessible and available to you. First Timothy 2:5 states, "For there is one God and one Mediator between God and men, the man Christ Jesus."

Discouraged? — Take hope! There is an Intercessor who is for you, not against you. One of my favorite verses is Hebrews 6:19-20: "We have this hope as an anchor for the soul, firm and secure. It enters the inner sanctuary behind the curtain, where Jesus, who went before us, has entered on our behalf."

Lonely? — Take Christ as your Saviour and Lord! He will *always* be there for you!

Make yourself accessible and available to God and see what incredible wondrous things He can do!

For Additional Reading: Exodus 15:1-6; Hebrews 7:24-28
Sharon, Age 37
Secretary for Oil Company

WEEK FOURTEEN

■ ■ ■ ■

SOARING, NOT FALLING

TEXT FOR THE WEEK: ISAIAH 40:28-31

KEY VERSE: ISAIAH 40:31   "But those who hope in the Lord will
                                     renew their strength. They will soar
                                     on wings like eagles; they will run
                                     and not grow weary, they will walk
                                     and not faint."

DAY ONE ■ Commentary on Isaiah 40:28-31

Do you ever feel really exhausted? I don't mean just physically, but emotionally and spiritually as well. Maybe you are feeling that way even now as you read. In our high-performance culture many Christians have succumbed to the temptation of judging our own worth on the basis of activity and accomplishment. If you are a growing Christian, you may well be up to your ears in "wonderful ministry opportunities" in addition to your job, family, financial, and social commitments. But instead of feeling refreshed and energized, fatigue and apathy are setting in. Perhaps you are one of those who has already been a Christian "burn-out" victim, and you are frightened at the prospect of getting involved in ministry again. Then again, maybe you have never volunteered for Christian service because you are over-taxed by the demands of "ordinary" living.

Isaiah 40 was written to a people who were, like us, in need of renewed strength. The Northern Kingdom of Israel had already been conquered and exiled by the brutal Assyrians. The Southern Kingdom of Judah lived in fear of the same treatment, first from the Assyrians and later from the Babylonians. In fact, Isaiah had already affirmed that Jerusalem would eventually fall to Babylon (Isa. 39). Thus, even those Israelites who were faithful and obedient could only look forward to future hardship and difficulty during their lifetimes. No wonder Israel complained (40:27), "My way is hidden from the Lord; my cause is disregarded by my God." They were tired of the hassles and it seemed like God didn't care. Don't you feel like that too sometimes? I do.

But then God speaks through Isaiah some of the most encouraging words found anywhere in Scripture. Here we see the Lord's true nature and strength: He is the everlasting God, the Creator, He never tires, His understanding is unfathomable. Better still, the Lord strengthens His weary and weak people who keep their hope in Him. In fact, "they will soar on wings like eagles"!

On what or whom are you placing your hope today? If you are waiting for circumstances to get better or relying on your own strength or the strength of others, your chances for renewal are slim. As the saying goes, "It's hard to soar with eagles when you work with turkeys." Compared to the Lord and His Word, all other hopes are "turkeys" at best.

For Additional Reading: Psalm 42:1-5; Luke 18:1-8
Scott F. Last is the Pastor with Single Adults at Emmanuel Faith Community Church in Escondido, California. Six single adults from his church write the following devotionals.

DAY TWO ■ Isaiah 40:28-31

It can be so hard to wait on God. We spot a goal and eagerly rush ahead. We frantically wear ourselves out trying to keep up with our responsibilities and desires.

Wouldn't it be wonderful to soar above the daily grind? You could look down below and see that there are no household quarrels, the laundry is done, your next meal is already prepared, your boss has given you the day off and all your obligations are met.

God tells us to wait on (hope in) Him. He WILL renew our strength. We can walk. We can run. We can soar like eagles. He promised! And now: You look down and observe the ongoing struggles at home, the laundry pile that grows daily, the dinner that is still frozen, the grueling hours at work, the numerous obligations that are humanly impossible to accomplish, and in your soul. . . you are at rest.

For Additional Reading: Psalm 63:1-8; 2 Corinthians 4:1-6
Cindy, Age 33
Receptionist/Secretary

DAY THREE ■ Isaiah 40:28-31

Several years ago I began dating someone who seemed to be responding warmly to me. Our times together were very enjoyable. I started to envision a home, kids, dogs, fish, and a family van in our future!

One day I confidently decided to express my feelings to her. She listened closely . . . but didn't respond. "So what about you?" I asked expectantly. "Are you feeling any inkling whatsoever of emotion for me other than friendship?" She thought, paused, thought again, and finally responded, "No, not really."

Ouch! What a disappointment! Talk about discouraging! I felt more like a slug than an eagle! Of course, God could always change her heart. But He didn't.

I needed encouragement! I found it in Isaiah 40. As I place my hope in Him, God renews my strength to be faithful and obedient in relationships . . . in spite of disappointments!

For Additional Reading: Proverbs 3:11-17; Romans 15:5-7
Mike, Age 35
Optometrist

DAY FOUR ■ Isaiah 40:28-31

The world looks different through tired eyes. As a full-time student and working on the side, it's easy for me to feel exhausted and focus on my own discomfort. Instead of letting the Lord take care of my needs and keeping Him the center of my life, I find myself being self-centered and trying to take care of those needs alone. Thus, I end up being a very poor substitute for the One who so powerfully meets needs in ways that surpass what I could ever ask or think. After all, it is He who promised me abundant life!

As the weary hope in the Lord and wait on Him, He becomes the source of increased power and new strength. Instead of turning tired eyes inward, I need to turn them upward in anticipation that He will do as He promises.

For Additional Reading: Habakkuk 3:16-19; John 10:7-10
Dave, Age 28
Student

DAY FIVE ■ Isaiah 40:28-31

Fatigue is a by-product of anxiety. When I'm anxious about tomorrow, I become weary. And it's my nature to be anxious.

That's why I adapt so well to the work ethic. That's even why I chose a career in a stable industry like utilities. But, in reality, who am I trusting for my future? My employer and my abilities?

Enter a merger! (Today's tiger at the cave door.) Rumors of layoffs. "My job, Lord!" Of moves to unknown places. "Me, Lord?"

"But those who hope in the Lord." "Do not worry about tomorrow" (Matt. 6:34). Thank You, Lord. You renew my strength, my hope. Instead of anxiety, I'm thankful that You have new experiences saved for me. New places, jobs, and friends! They sound exciting instead of threatening. And guess what? Instead of fatigue, I feel adrenaline flowing.

For Additional Reading: Psalm 6:6-10; Luke 10:38-42
Nancy, Age 45
Customer Account Coordinator

DAY SIX ■ Isaiah 40:28-31

Lord, what does it mean to hope in You? I feel physically exhausted and spiritually dry. I know You can help. I've seen

You provide me a coupon for a free loaf of bread when I had no money, comfort me when I poured out my hurt to You, lead me to service with, "Now begin the work and the Lord be with you." I told You of my discontent and You said, "Never will I leave you; never will I forsake you." Then I realized that if I had You, all else paled in significance.

So, is this waiting on You, Lord? Taking time to tell You how I feel and remembering all You've done for me? I do feel refreshed and refocused. It's amazing what spending time with You can do *in* me. Thank You, Lord. I love You.

For Additional Reading: Psalm 91:1-11; John 15:1-8
Wendy, Age 41
Secretary

DAY SEVEN ■ Isaiah 40:28-31

Did you know that the wings of an eagle are uniquely designed for soaring? The eagle can soar at great heights (2,400 ft.) with very little effort on his own part. Also, because of his special wing configuration, the eagle can fly in turbulent, hurricane-force winds.

God offers us this choice—to spread our spiritual wings and be lifted up by the thermal winds of His Spirit, or to keep trying to fly by madly flapping our own wings. I've often tried to fly on my own power with madly flapping wings of my own design. But today I'm wearing the wings of an eagle by hoping in the Lord. My trust, my hope, my eyes are on Him. I'm soaring higher. The earth is growing strangely dim. Those problems I was worried about down below have created some turbulence which seems to be giving me more lift. I'm soaring faster. Wow! I really have a bird's-eye view from up here. What's that light ahead? I think I see a glimpse of His glory and grace.

For Additional Reading: Psalm 33:18-22; Hebrews 2:10-13
Lynn, Age 45
Church Secretary/Piano Teacher

WEEK FIFTEEN
■ ■ ■ ■
GOD'S LOVE FOR REAL

TEXT FOR THE WEEK: ISAIAH 54:1-10

KEY VERSE: ISAIAH 54:10

" 'Though the mountains be shaken
and the hills be removed, yet My unfailing love for you will not be shaken
nor My covenant of peace be removed,' says the Lord, who has compassion on you."

DAY ONE ■ Commentary on Isaiah 54:1-10

The first words in this passage don't seem to go together:
"Sing, O barren woman!" Isaiah uses the image of a Jewish
woman who doesn't even have a chance of becoming a Jewish
mother; she's barren. There is no greater tragedy in the Hebrew
culture! Sing! he says. Cheer! Go crazy with hysterical joy! It
makes you ask, "Why?"

The answer comes. I've got something for you that is even
greater than all the children any one Jewish mother could ever
bring into the world. Life may not be going the way you hoped.
But I've got some news for you that is going to overwhelm your
barrenness, your shame.

Isaiah is speaking to some people who need to hear some
good news. Long ago God selected Israel to be His chosen bride,
His special servant people; but they did not live up to their
privileged position. They left Him. So, He enforced the separation that they were living and they were carried into Exile.
Separation from the living God threw them into barrenness,
guilt, and shame; a people with no country and no honor. A
bride without her husband.

To this sad and desolate, rejected people Isaiah says, "Sing, O
barren one." Why? Because your Maker, your Husband, the
Lord of Hosts, still loves you and He wants you back. Yes, He
was really, really, really mad at you, but His anger only lasts for a

little while, just long enough to teach you the lesson of separating yourself from Him. But the incredible thing is this: His love for you, His favor, His compassion, His devotion to you lasts for all eternity.

Your Maker loves you with an everlasting love. How lasting? " 'Though the mountains be shaken and the hills be removed, yet My unfailing love for you will not be shaken nor My covenant of peace be removed,' says the Lord, who has compassion on you." Nations come and go; money comes and goes; buildings and cities come and go, people come and go—wives, husbands, children, parents; even the mountains and hills, which were the most permanent thing that Israel could think of, they may "be shaken," they will "be removed." There is only one thing that does not come and go, the one thing that can bring you deep, abiding joy: the everlasting, committed love of your covenant Partner, "He is called the God of all the earth."

For Additional Reading: Psalm 30:1-5; 1 John 4:13-18
Mary Graves is the Associate Pastor at Solana Beach Presbyterian Church in Solana Beach, California. Six single adults from Mary's church write the following.

DAY TWO ■ Isaiah 54:1-10

Sing, O barren one! Why? Because your Maker, your Husband, the Lord of hosts, still loves you and He wants you back. How could God ask me to do that? How could He expect me to shout for joy? Doesn't He know that through my divorce, I have lost everything? I am a ruined man, I have lost my wife, my kids are 2,000 miles away, financially I am struggling to just stay afloat, my friends have abandoned me, and I feel like I have been walking in the pits of despair, depression, and hopelessness. I thought of ending it all, and then, God, You told me to shout for joy. What is there to be joyful for? I have felt that You, O Lord, left me, You left me to die. Oh, how could anyone live through so much pain?

But, He never did leave me. He was always there for me. He

walked through the shadows of death with me. He felt my pain, my sadness, my loneliness, my desire to give up. He had compassion for me, He cared. "I am here by your side, Dana. I will wait. I love you. You are worthy, you are special. What I have for you, Dana, is greater than anything you could ever imagine. I give you life."

God has spoken to me when I was in the lowest days of despair, and I am aware that He will still give me a choice, to see His joy or to wallow in my misery.

For Additional Reading: Isaiah 57:14-15; 2 Corinthians 4:7-12
Dana, Age 37
Water Works, Utility Person

DAY THREE ■ Isaiah 54:1-10

How often I run after my work, my exercise, my money, my social life, and even my church work, to the exclusion of the One who makes all these possible. I run after these, just as the Jews of Isaiah's time ran after "other gods." The Jewish woman's identity seemed as synonymous with numbers of children (what she does) as my identity gets confused with what I do. Has anything changed? Ah, thankfully, yes! I, as a child of God, have the indwelling Spirit as a constant Companion who draws and woos and loves me back to God. The God, who will not let me go; who may weary of my failures, yet never ceases to act on my behalf. He finds ways, as gentle as possible, to remind, and encourage me to keep my eyes on Him as the priority which makes all the other issues of life manageable. For longer than the sun will continue to rise and set, He will love me with a love I can only vaguely comprehend. On the days that I *really believe* this, I make time to spend with my Lord, the God of all eternity.

For Additional Reading: Psalm 57:1-3; John 3:16-18
Dottie, Age 60
Real Estate Appraiser

DAY FOUR ■ Isaiah 54:1-10

Singleness is not easy—there are times when I feel alone, barren, and desolate just like the nation of Israel. I feel separated from love, from love of any kind—family, friends, partner. And there are times when I engage in a frantic search for Mr. Right, keeping busy and becoming involved in lots of activities. But then I turn to God right here beside me, feel His love encircling me like a husband or a father, and I know that His love is steadfast and I need search no farther. Unlike human love, which may depart or be removed like the hills and mountains, God's love for me is everlasting and unchanging and unconditional—I may do things that separate me from God but He loves me anyway. When I let the love of God enfold me, He gives me a peace, a peace "which transcends all understanding" (Phil. 4:7).

For Additional Reading: Deuteronomy 7:11-14; 2 Thessalonians 2:13-17
Jane, Age 42
Librarian

DAY FIVE ■ Isaiah 54:1-10

In my translation, God promises "I will" 9 times in 10 verses. That's amazing when I realize that even one promise from a person can't be absolutely, 100 percent for certain, simply because of our imperfect nature—even with the best of intentions (I mean, Peter *swore* that he'd never renounce Jesus, didn't he?). But God says it not just once, but 9 times. He's the only One whose promises are absolutely certain. And I love what He promises—to draw near to me when I'm overcome by loneliness or shame or disgrace or humiliation, wondering where in the world He could *possibly* be. He promises to lift me beyond all of that into a life of lasting joy and peace and unshakable love. He speaks directly (v. 6) and lovingly, and says, "It doesn't have to stay like this. I love you too much. You're worth too much. No,

I haven't left you: My love and compassion toward you *will* set you free—I promise." In a world which is so full of broken promises and unfilled hopes and all of the "barren" feelings which accompany them, how wonderful it is that I can count on God's promise to draw near—in unshifting love—bringing joy and hope.

For Additional Reading: Psalm 103:13-18; John 17:23-26
Ellen, Age 24
Singles Associate, SBPC

DAY SIX ■ Isaiah 54:1-10

The first four verses talk about a widow or an abandoned woman. Strangely, the advice to her is to be encouraged, rejoice, enlarge her tents! She's also told that though she is desolate, she shall have more children than the woman with a husband!

When I was a student at the University of Washington, I was part of a very committed group at the Baptist Student Center. Many of them refrained from dating or marrying early in order to commit more time to knowing God and sharing Him with others. As a result, many of them waited too late to marry and have children. Sadly, they are barren. But as a result of their lives, many people have become Christians and are walking with God. Of the core of 53 of us, 12 are missionaries today. Seventeen more entered pastorates or full-time Christian work. The rest of us, laymen, continue to lead men to Christ in small group Bible studies throughout the world! So, yes, I've seen it's true: the desolate woman has borne more children and has enlarged her tents, as ordinary men and women were willing to sacrifice the present for the eternal.

For Additional Reading: Psalm 86:11-17; 1 Corinthians 7:32-35
Bob, Age 37
Entrepreneur

DAY SEVEN ■ Isaiah 54:1-10

Six years ago I found myself divorced from the man I had expected to love forever. At the time, the tragedy and despair seemed impossible to endure. While my faith in a loving God was badly shaken, our church family surrounded my children and me with love and encouragement. There were seemingly endless problems to solve and the pattern of our life felt tragically rearranged. By living life in small segments we survived the early days. Eventually we even found moments of peace and love.

The mountains still come, but with thoughtful prayer the problems become more manageable. There have been many relationships for me during this time, but the real constancy and strength come from the love of God and His presence in my life.

For Additional Reading: Zephaniah 3:14-17; 1 John 3:16-20
Laura, Age 42
Educator

WEEK SIXTEEN

■ ■ ■ ■

GOD ANSWERS PRAYER IN ADVANCE

TEXT FOR THE WEEK: ISAIAH 65:17-25

KEY VERSE: ISAIAH 65:24   "Before they call I will answer; while
                                 they are still speaking I will hear."

DAY ONE ■ Commentary on Isaiah 65:24

It was Thursday afternoon and on arriving at work I received a phone call from my wife Marcia. In a very nervous voice she began to tell me that my three-year-old son, Todd, had just had an accident while visiting my mother.

When Todd entered the house he saw a friend in the backyard through what appeared to be an open patio door. As he made a dash for the backyard, he hit the closed glass door with such great force that the glass literally shattered. He did not fall forward or back, but he was caught by a large piece of glass protruding up into his abdominal area. Panic struck.

My mother had just moved into this new house and the phone was not working. What can only be described as a miracle took place. The phone installer had just arrived a few minutes before Marcia and the kids. It was not possible to receive calls; however, within just a few moments, using his equipment, a call was made by the installer to the paramedics.

The paramedics arrived and took Todd to the hospital. On hearing this I hung up the phone and headed to the hospital. On the way my thoughts turned to Isaiah 65:24, "Before they call I will answer." God knows our need and will not fail to hear and answer my prayer. When I arrived at the hospital Marcia and Todd were already there. We stood in the middle of the emergency room and prayed. "God, You know our son and what has happened to him, please help him to be calm and thank You for his healing." When we went in to see him we spoke to him of Jesus and how He would help him. Todd was calm and without pain. Todd looked at us and said, "Jesus loves me." We knew then that God had already met Todd's need and ours. After an hour in the emergency surgery room, the doctor came out and reported that the inner walls of his abdomen had not been cut, nor was there any sign of glass. "Thank You, Father, for hearing and answering prayer."

When you are walking with God you have the confidence to know that His answers to our prayers are on their way before we pray. God desires for you to know Him intimately, so you can come to Him without hesitation, knowing He is always close by when you need Him, and His answers are already on their way.

For Additional Reading: Psalm 70:1-5; Matthew 6:5-8
Kim Johnson is the Singles Pastor at the Community Church of Joy in Phoenix, Arizona. Six adult singles from Kim's church write the following personal applications.

DAY TWO ■ Isaiah 65:24

A few months ago, I was really struggling with the desire to be a mother. Since marriage wasn't in the picture for the next several years, things did not look good. Reading books for Christian singles, reading the Bible, praying, and talking to friends didn't seem to help. In 1 Corinthians 7 Paul says it is better to remain single, but at that time, I didn't exactly agree with him.

After several weeks of struggling, I began to feel at peace with my singleness. I told God that I knew He was in control and I would accept whatever He had in store for me.

A short time later, I found out that my sister was pregnant. Not only was I going to be an aunt for the first time, but I was going to be the godmother! Maybe someday God would answer my prayers and let me become a mother, but until then, being able to show my love as an aunt would bring great joy.*

---

*Just today my nephew, Nathan Lawrence, was born.

When I was struggling, my sister was already pregnant, but I didn't find that out until I stopped trying to be in control. It would have been much less painful if I had trusted God from the beginning.

God loves each of us dearly and wants the best for us. We need to believe that God is in control and that our prayers are being answered even though we might not be aware of the answer at the present time.

For Additional Reading: Isaiah 30:19-22; Romans 8:26-27
Rachel, Age 25
Computer Scientist

DAY THREE ■ Isaiah 65:24

No prayer is too small. It is OK to pray for red slippers. God hears all our prayers.

The pastor said these words the first Sunday I attended church after many years of absence. Feeling a great need to make peace with God about my attitude, these words seemed too simple. Surely God couldn't be bothered with such small matters as my feelings; the small things that are a part of my routine, everyday life.

My hectic daily life made me unhappy with myself. Misplacing things, forgetting important details, and losing a grip on my housekeeping caused me to doubt my ability to effectively function in the world around me.

One particular morning I couldn't find my car keys. Looking behind the couch, under cushions, and through yesterday's pockets seemed futile. I searched through the blankets thrown on the bed and the dishes stacked on the kitchen counter but the keys could not be found.

Feeling completely out of control, I thought, "This is the fifth time this week you have done this. You are really losing it." In discouragement, despair, and desolation, I muttered, "Oh, God."

I looked down and the keys were at my feet. Praise God! He wanted so much for me to acknowledge Him, to realize that He is available anytime we ask. The Lord answered my prayer before I knew it was a prayer. I smiled. "OK," I said. "I know now You are real."

As I continue to walk with Jesus, I become more and more aware of how He blesses His children. Our lives are filled with little and big miracles every day. He indeed answers before we call and hears us as we are speaking.

For Additional Reading: Psalm 34:1-7; John 11:1-6, 14-23, 38-44
Alberta, Age 43
Registered Nurse

DAY FOUR ■ Isaiah 65:24

My cup of joy would have been overflowing except for a relationship problem at work. I had recently been appointed Program Director at a residential facility for people too handicapped to live unassisted. It had been a God-inspired idea and there was a lot of love, joy, and hope within the residents and staff alike. Why, then, did He allow discord?

A man who had been on the staff before my arrival was the Cottage Director. Our functions often intertwined, so a spirit of cooperation between us was essential.

Very early on, a chance meeting turned into a confrontation and I felt that I was attacked verbally by this man. Our relationship steadily worsened till we were barely speaking to one another. Our attitudes hardened and God was not honored. I became caught up in something I could not see how to change.

I prayed about it often; in fact, many times daily. Perhaps, because I felt that I was the one wronged and innocent, my prayers were amiss. Nothing changed!

After a few weeks, I devised a plan to bring about a meeting to either settle the issue between us or to see that one of us left the staff. I assumed that it would be my adversary who left. My plan made sense to me. I thought it had God's blessing.

Suddenly, a thought came to me. It said, "Praise and thank

Me for him." I knew that this was a message from God and it was exactly the opposite from what I was thinking.

The words came out of my mouth haltingly, and it was as if a great weight was immediately lifted. There was an inner peace as my old plan of action was discarded. Now I had no plan! I knew that whatever God had in mind was definitely better.

Shortly after arriving at my office, the Cottage Director came to see me. The Holy Spirit had done a work in his heart that I could never have done. He came seeking reconciliation and forgiveness. By then, we both needed forgiveness. I was over-joyed as I saw how God fulfilled His promise of Isaiah 65:24.

For Additional Reading: Psalm 34:8-16; 2 Timothy 3:10-15
Bill, Age 64
Physical Therapist

DAY FIVE ■ Isaiah 65:24

For almost 25 years I was a homemaker and mother, living mostly in small towns and traveling around the United States with my Air Force husband. Sheltered from a lot of today's world and its problems, the Air Force was the only life I knew. Then I found myself alone in a city of a million and a half strangers, with my closest relative 14 hours away.

I prepared myself to be on my own in the "real" world with a real job by completing my bachelor's degree, but I found that this did not prepare me for the push and shove of the business world. The stress of the job sometimes got me down, but it was good to know that God was always there with me.

My boss has been in the business world for over 20 years and has a difficult time understanding where I am coming from. She has been pushing me to be more firm. Working in a position where, at times, I am in an adversarial position with the public has been hard for me. I care about their problems and try to understand when they need to have more time to comply with my requests. My boss does not always understand or approve of this attitude.

Recently, I had an especially stressful day in store for me. My boss was to review my work for the past several months. Since she had already expressed dissatisfaction with my lack of firmness, I told one of my dear friends about my concern and we prayed that God would be there beside me through this difficult day.

I felt His presence all day long. The office was especially quiet. I went to lunch alone instead of with my usual two friends, and the restaurant seemed unusually quiet. He reminded me of the Bible verse, Isaiah 65:24, to assure me that His love never ends.

That day, I was convinced that if things got especially rough, I could reach out and take His hand and He would be there to help me. I did not have to reach for His hand that day, but I know that He was there.

I know that if I need Him tomorrow, I will reach for His hand and He will be there. He will answer before I call. Even before I am done asking, He will meet my needs.

For Additional Reading: Psalm 34:17-22;
1 Corinthians 12:7-10
Bobbie, Age 42
Accountant

DAY SIX ■ Isaiah 65:24

One evening a few years ago, during a period when my wife was having serious medical problems, I was driving past a church when a voice called to me. It said, "My son, I have missed you. This is where you belong."

I had been raised in a Christian environment, but I had drifted away from the Lord. I did not understand why this voice was speaking to me. I continued home and gave no further thought to this event.

A month later, my wife — my companion, my best friend — was taken from me. For a brief period I withdrew from reality and felt I was being punished. I became like a turtle who had retreated into his shell. I was hurting, alone, and lonely. At times, I felt like ending my life.

One Sunday morning, for what reason I did not know at the time, I arose, got dressed, and drove my car to that very same church. As I walked through the door, I heard that voice again, saying, "Welcome back, son."

I now know that the voice was the Lord assuring me that He was there for me. He is our greatest Comforter. I know that without Him by my side I would not feel as I do now. I am at peace with myself and my life. I am no longer lonely and alone.

Praise the Lord.

For Additional Reading: Psalm 95:6-11; Hebrews 10:24-25
Eldow, Age 59
Senior Programmer Analyst

DAY SEVEN ■ Isaiah 65:24

Another night out. Another embarrassing scene in front of friends and relatives. As I walked home that night, the words "I'm getting out . . . I'm getting out . . . " went through my head every step of the way.

With no job, no college degree, and only a few part-time jobs to claim for a work history, I was alone and afraid. What would happen to me now? How would I survive?

Two weeks after that walk home, I received a phone call from the office where I had done volunteer work for the previous two months. It was an opportunity for part-time employment.

I worked 15 hours a week while attending night school at a nearby college. Eventually, my hours were increased and after a year and a half I was offered a full-time position with an excellent salary and benefit package.

Being told that I could never make it on my own by those I loved had hurt, but not anymore.

I was working in a personnel department where hundreds of applications were taken in at a time for the same classified position that I held. Reviewing applications of people who had many more years of education and experience than I had helped me to realize that God had already been at work as I walked home that night many months before.

Remembering the long walk home on that eventful night made this Bible verse very real to me: "Before they call I will answer; while they are still speaking I will hear" (Isa. 65:24).

For Additional Reading: Psalm 93:14-19; 1 John 5:13-15
Betty, Age 43
Office Assistant

WEEK SEVENTEEN
■ ■ ■ ■

THE PRESENT PLAN,
A PLAN OF PRESENCE

TEXT FOR THE WEEK: **JEREMIAH 29:10-14**

KEY VERSES: JEREMIAH 29:11-12

" 'For I know the plans I have for
you,' declares the Lord, 'plans to
prosper you and not to harm you,
plans to give you hope and a
future.' "

DAY ONE ■ Commentary on Jeremiah 29:11-12

He will gather me. . . . He will return [restore] me. . . . and He will show me riches beyond measure or understanding.

In my pilgrimage from mountaintop to green valley, from desert wasteland to refreshing, cool, clear waters of refreshment, never has He withdrawn from me. In the wasteland of grief and seeming desolation in experiencing the removal from my presence of a most significant other . . . never has He not been there for me.

Experiencing the sudden death of my husband and the instant single-parenting role thrust on me, I anticipated the fears, the anxieties relating to loneliness: the physical, the emotional, and the spiritual. Yet there in the times of my deepest needs His presence became more and more real to me.

There came an exciting and challenging job opportunity where He could be served, rewarding relationships both personal and corporate. He knew, He had plans for me, Mary. He was, is, and always will be "there all the time!"

For Additional Reading: Jeremiah 8:11-15; Luke 9:57-62
Mary Randolph is the Director of the Singles Ministry at As-

bury United Methodist Church in Tulsa, Oklahoma. Day 2 through 5 applications are written by members of Mary's ministry. Days 6 and 7 are written by members of Larry White's (Week 10) and Dennis Franck's (Week 8) ministries.

DAY TWO ■ Jeremiah 29:11-12

CARAVANS

A caravan of human souls
Marching forward
Going nowhere

Motions automatic
Nonthinking

Silently moving
Toward uncertainty

Too painful
To break free

Hundreds not hearing
Thousands not seeing

Hearts hardened
To the pain of knowing

Compromised fears
For illusions growing

Down endless roads
Too tired to question

Peace with a price
A nonchanging stance

Relief from life's shadow
In a brief glance

A caravan of human souls
Marching forward
Going nowhere

For Additional Reading: Jeremiah 5:18-25; Matthew 10:5-16
Ginger, Age 45
Company General Manager

DAY THREE ■ Jeremiah 29:11-12

I sat in my room staring out the window feeling all alone, wondering what went wrong. We had it all, a marriage made in heaven that seemed so strong.

Then walls were built between us and words were said that could not be erased. And our love slowly died without leaving a trace.

Hoping that through reading His Word a turning point I could find, I turned to the Lord with an open heart and mind.

And as I turned the pages a verse caught my eye, " 'For I know the plans I have for you,' declares the Lord, 'plans to prosper you and not to harm you, plans to give you hope and a future.' "

Upon reading this I began to see that the Lord's love was directing me. I was never alone. He was by my side guiding me toward a brand-new life.

I will be all right.

For Additional Reading: Psalm 103:1-12; John 15:9-17
Linda, Age 40
Administrative Assistant

DAY FOUR ■ Jeremiah 29:11-12

RAINS ON MY DESERT

Like the hawk
Soaring
Searching

I survey my desert
Scorched and dry

Hope forsaken
A solitary cry

Raw hunger to remain
Throughout my barren domain

Yearning
Burning
For the rain

Then gentle showers
Release fragile flowers

Planted long ago
With full intent
To answer my lament

Sweet surrender
Yields
Fertile fields

Alive
Awakening
The hidden seed

Completing the season

As the rains come to my desert

For Additional Reading: Genesis 9:12-17; 1 Corinthians 3:1-9
Ginger, Age 45
Free-lance Writer

DAY FIVE ■ Jeremiah 29:11-12

MY SOUL THIRSTETH

My soul thirsteth
Hunger so deep

I barely keep
Time from enveloping

Like a foggy mist

Covering the emptiness
For an eternity

Emotions exploding all around

No words to tell
Describing the spell

My soul thirsteth

Will the rains ever come to the desert

Giving life
To the death hidden within.

For Additional Reading: Isaiah 32:1-8; Revelation 22:12-17
Ginger, Age 45
General Manager and Free-lance Writer

DAY SIX ■ Jeremiah 29:11-12

Have you ever had a year you would like to forget? I have just finished one that I hope I never see again. I truly experienced failing health and that is devastating to a person who is rarely sick. Every three months during the year I was sick with something different and some ailment that I had never had before or not had for a long time. It seemed I could never get well and get on with my life. I had to put many social activities and ministries on the back burner because I had no energy to get anything done.

"God, what are You doing in my life? Why can't I stay well long enough to do what You have called me to do? Why do I feel like I'm in a holding pattern? What are Your reasons for all of this?" I found myself reading God's Word more and more and spending more and more time with Him in prayer. I have come to realize that when God wants to get my attention, it is usually by putting me out of commission physically for a while. Then I have to stop and take account of my life. What is He trying to tell me? Does He want me to go in a new direction? Take a new job? Move to a different location? Become involved in a new ministry? Sometimes it is all of these and at other times it is just one or two. Eventually, you will come out of the winter of your life and find new vitality and energy to follow a new path or the old one with new insights.

For Additional Reading: Proverbs 28:25-28; Luke 12:13-21
Charlotte, Age 55
Executive Secretary

DAY SEVEN ■ Jeremiah 29:11-12

As David must surely have started each new day, "Earnestly I seek You" (Ps. 63:1), we should ask God for His guidance and blessings each day. As David prayed, "My soul thirsts for You," we must spiritually thirst after God and His Word just as our bodies thirst after water. Even more so, because the water for our bodies is temporary—we thirst again—the water for our souls is eternal so we thirst no more.

The Lord expects us to walk uprightly before Him, keeping a pure heart and clean mind. "Blessed are those whose ways are blameless" (119:1). God wants us to obey His Word and His laws. Verse 2 reminds us to keep His statutes. God sent His Son Jesus, not just as a sacrifice for our sins, but also to be an example for us in our daily living. By seeking and communing with Him every day, we can receive the strength and direction needed to obey Him and know Him more and more.

For Additional Reading: Psalm 143:5-12; Titus 2:11-15
Rocky, Age 42
Lab Technician

WEEK EIGHTEEN

■ ■ ■ ■

GOD'S FAITHFULNESS IN AN UNFAITHFUL WORLD

TEXT FOR THE WEEK: LAMENTATIONS 3:19-24

KEY VERSES:
LAMENTATIONS 3:22-23

"Because of the Lord's great love we are not consumed, for His compassions never fail. They are new every morning; great is Your faithfulness."

DAY ONE ■ Commentary on Lamentations 3:19-24

Everywhere he looked there was devastation. His hometown was a pile of smoldering ruins. There was little food, little water, and little shelter. The city had just been totally destroyed by the enemy. In every direction there was pain, brokenness, suffering, and death. The city he loved was nothing more than a refugee camp. How do you go on in the middle of such devastation? When everything that you value has been wrenched from you and your life seems like "a pile of smoldering ruins" how do you continue? When pain, discouragement, and disillusionment paralyze you, how do you go on? When dreams, hope, and prayers seem to fade away like a puff of air on a cold morning, where do you get the strength to live?

The man described above wasn't a Vietnam war refugee but rather Jeremiah, the prophet of God. Jerusalem had been devastated by the Babylonians. Jeremiah looked around the city and clung to the only thing remaining, the character of his God. Trusting in the mercy, compassion, and faithfulness of God gave him the courage to go on.

There are times in our lives when important precious things are stripped away from us: friends, homes, jobs, spouses, and children. During these times we must cling to that which can never be taken away, our God. When we seek Him He will make Himself known to us. There may be times when all we can say to Him is, "Lord, help," or "God, I don't understand, I'm so confused," or "God, I'm so tired of all this." In our honesty we will find a gracious, compassionate, and faithful God who never leaves us, a God who works in the midst of the rubble and smoldering ruins.

If you feel like Jeremiah, take heart this week. Don't focus on the external circumstances as much as you do on your Saviour. Seek His face, His mercy, His compassion, His faithfulness. Draw close to Him in your pain, confusion, and disillusionment. The Word of God promises you will find a Saviour who will care, who will listen, and who will be a faithful friend.

For Additional Reading: Jeremiah 23:3-6; Luke 10:25-37
Chris Miller is the Singles Pastor at Southern Gables Evangelical Free Church in Lakewood, Colorado. Six single adults from his church write the following devotionals.

DAY TWO ■ Lamentations 3:19-24

Recently I went through a time when both my health and my marriage failed simultaneously. I was left as a single mom facing physical disabilities which made it difficult to care for my young children. Over and over I came to the Lord seeking to find solace through worship and music. He gave me songs which spoke of His great love in the midst of great pain.

SAFE IN THE FATHER'S ARMS

When you're all alone
And only God can know
The depths of what you feel
Then know His love is real.

When you bow your knees
And for His grace you plead

Cry out from your heart
For He knows every part.

When your emotions run wild
Know that you're His child.
No storm is beyond His command
And He will help you stand!

Know whatever comes,
When this race is run,
He'll keep you from harm
Safe in the Father's arms.

God is *faithful*. However insurmountable the problems may look from our perspective, we can find comfort as we pour out our hearts before Him. We can trust our God to be compassionate. He has promised that His loving-kindness and His mercy will be there for us at the start of each new day.

For Additional Reading: Psalm 89:13-18; Luke 7:11-17
Kathy, Age 39
Musician

DAY THREE ■ Lamentations 3:19-24

Compassion can be defined as love in action. God will respond with compassion when we ask. Yes, He already knows what our needs are, but He wants us to vocalize them in prayer. When we do this, He can display His love in action by forgiving us, by restoring us, and by blessing us.

Many times I have gone to the Lord asking for compassion. Sometimes it was for not doing something that I should have, for a sin that I thought He would not forgive, for restoration of my dignity, or for a blessing of patience to get through a trying situation. Each time He has displayed His love in action. I've learned that no sin is so great, no need for restoration so large, or no desire of blessing unanswerable by the compassionate God.

For Additional Reading: Isaiah 49:8-13; Mark 9:17-24
Hugh, Age 32
Landscape Architect

DAY FOUR ■ Lamentations 3:19-24

How many times in our lives do grudges go unchecked against us? Perhaps it was something we said, or some little action which seemed insignificant to us but was a time bomb to someone else.

When I was attending undergraduate studies in Greeley, Colorado I had a very good friend who I will call Paul. Paul and I did much together, both as friends and as cohorts in a campus ministry. For about one year we shared in trials and joys and grew together in our walk with God. I held my relationship with Paul to be one of the most precious things in my life. I couldn't imagine us ever being at odds. However, one day, I can't remember when or how, our relationship went sour. Due to a misunderstanding and lack of communication, where there was once friendship and encouragement, there was now only bitterness and pain. For whatever reason Paul never forgave me, despite numerous efforts to make things right.

What a frightening thought it is to think that our most precious relationships could crumble with a slip of the tongue or an unintended gesture. Yet, what an extraordinary comfort it is, that though we often hurt and disobey a perfect and blameless God, we can always turn back to Him and be unconditionally received into His loving arms. Despite Israel's outright disobedience and resulting discipline, Jeremiah could see the hope at the break of a new day embraced by God's overwhelming compassion and faithfulness. How awesome it is to think that every new day shines forth with hope in the presence of a forgiving and holy God.

For Additional Reading: Psalm 119:84-88; Romans 9:14-18
Rich, Age 27
Student and Industrial Tool-setter

DAY FIVE ■ Lamentations 3:19-24

What an example Jeremiah is for us! Standing in the midst of the rubble of Jerusalem he was able to speak of God's love, His compassion, and His faithfulness. During the periods in our lives when we feel our world has been reduced to rubble we would do well to remember Jeremiah's steadfastness.

In the past year, the world as I had known it was destroyed. My wife of 16 years walked away from our marriage and our family. In the wake of that event, I lost my job and have struggled emotionally, financially, and spiritually. Through it all, God has revealed Himself as a loving, compassionate, and faithful God.

In those times of despair He has always provided something which has given me hope. The greatest gift I received from Him this year was when my sons gave their lives to Jesus Christ. With His help we are rebuilding our world. Praise God, for great is His faithfulness.

For Additional Reading: Psalm 119:137-144; 2 Thessalonians 3:1-5
Kelly, Age 36
Certified Public Accountant

DAY SIX ■ Lamentations 3:19-24

I find that the Lord's wisdom and faithfulness come in ways I never expect but it is so perfect.

About a week before Christmas 1988, I fell while ice-skating and broke my knee cap, requiring surgery. For the next 10 weeks, I found my independence taken away. Everywhere I went I had to have someone take me. Even the simple tasks of carrying things and getting through revolving doors became almost impossible (and sometimes humorous). During that time, the Lord poured out His loving-kindness through His faithful servants.

It seems that life is so fast paced that I often don't stop to see the love and concern the Lord pours out on me every day. When my independence was taken away, I was forced to stop and take a good look around me and realize that God is with me in everything I do and say. He is there when I cry out to Him in frustration. He is there when everything seems to be going just fine.

I have been challenged to look for God in everything that happens to me. Through this, I have found that "because of the Lord's great love we are not consumed, for His compassions never fail. They are new every morning; great is Your faithfulness."

For Additional Reading: Psalm 40:8-12; 1 Peter 4:12-19
Bonnie, Age 29
Secretary

DAY SEVEN ■ Lamentations 3:19-24

Have you ever felt like the *last* thing you want to do is sing praise to our loving Lord? How can I sing of His justice? Is God really in control? Is He out there at all?

I remember moving from Texas to Colorado—from the known to the unknown. I stayed with my brother and his family while looking for a job. I knew no one else. I went to church with them—a church that was rapidly dying. My living situation was pulled right out from under my feet then. Now what? No job, no home, no friends! Is this justice?

As I sat in a restaurant, I anxiously read Psalm 101. My prayer was similar to David's in verse 2:

I have tried to be careful to lead a blameless life—
When will You come to me?
Come to me and heal my bitterness and hurt.
Come to me and help me *live* again.
O Lord, please come to me!

I have made myself vulnerable with no one
knowing all strife—

When will You come to me?
Come to me and change my heart and mind.
Come to me and help me *love* again.
O Lord, please come to me!

I have tried to be hopeful if only just a trifle —
When will You come to me?
Come to me and show me laughter and compassion.
Come to me and help me *trust* again.
O Lord, please come to me!

It will take a lot from You — I'll try not to stifle —
When will You come to me?
Come to me and help me give and grow.
Come to me and help me *run* again.
O Lord, please come to me!

I'm tired of being used, abused, misread, half dead —
When will You come to me?
Come to me and bring that abundant life and
faithfulness I've heard so much about.
Come to me and help me remember my first love
again.
O Lord, please come to me!

He often works when our hands are totally empty. That way, He is able to fill the hands with Him and Him only. He knows and understands our most inward parts. He loves us and is still very much in control!

For Additional Reading: Psalm 101:1-6; Ephesians 1:17-23
Gwen, Age 31
Elementary School Teacher

WEEK NINETEEN
■ ■ ■ ■

HOPE — A DOOR TO BE ENTERED

TEXT FOR THE WEEK: **HOSEA 2:14-23**

KEY VERSE: HOSEA 2:15

"There I will give her back her vineyards, and will make the valley of Achor a door of hope. There she will sing as in the days of her youth, as in the day she came up out of Egypt."

DAY ONE ■ Commentary on Hosea 2:15

I confess, I like words. Oh, don't get me wrong, I'm not hung up on esoteric conversation. It's the capricious efficacy of words woven into the fabric of thought, and spilled on the page that intrigues and beguiles me. Yet, I admit it's "oxymorons" that I love the most. Oxymorons are those delightful, yet absurd quirks of our daily conversation that defy logic; phrases like "jumbo shrimp," and "cruel kindness." These are oxymorons because they are incongruous to themselves and self-contradictory. Some would add to the list, only in jest I'm sure, "airplane food" and "military intelligence."

Oxymorons are often just a word or two, but equally often whole phrases that are self-contradictory. That is exactly the case with Hosea 2:15. Hosea says, "I will give you the Valley of Achor as a door of hope." English unfortunately camouflages the oxymoron. In Hebrew, the word "Achor" means trouble. Thus Hosea's words become, "I will give you the valley of trouble as a door of hope." There's the oxymoron; a "valley of trouble" is, at least in my mind, inconsistent with a "door of hope."

The Valley of Achor, as recorded in Joshua, was the first encampment of the Israelites inside the Promised Land. It terminated 40 years of desert wanderings. From that camping ground the first campaigns were launched to possess the land. There too, the sin of Achan was uncovered, judged, and severely punished. That is, in fact, how the valley became known as the "valley of trouble." Yet, Hosea calls it a door of hope. Why?

Let me draw a simple parallel. We, like Israel, have by our faith in Jesus Christ entered into the kingdom. We are encamped in the Promised Land. Yet, ours is a valley of trouble far afield from God's full promise. Jesus reveals in His parables that the kingdom will come gradually, and that as it grows, good seed (Christians) will grow up alongside of tares (unbelievers). We know this is true. But Jesus, by virtue of our relationship with Him, also provides us the enabling power to live as kingdom subjects in our valley of trouble.

Our hope is more than a matter of perspective, however. It is true that we need to see our present life as a slice of the kingdom, and that perspective is in itself a door of hope. But, our greatest hope is in the person of Jesus Christ. Here, in our valley of trouble, Jesus discloses Himself to us (John 14:21). Here, He has given us the Spirit of power (2 Tim. 1:7). Here, Jesus Himself defeated death and the power of Satan (Heb. 2:14). Here, we strip ourselves of the garments of sin. And, here, we taste "the goodness of the Word of God and the powers of the coming age" (6:5). That's a door of hope, oxymoron or not.

For Additional Reading: Psalm 39:7-13; Romans 8:22-25
Jim Millermon is a Director of Singles Ministries in Denver, Colorado. Six single adults from his ministry write of their experiences in the following devotionals.

DAY TWO ■ Hosea 2:15

On a glorious summer day, walking alongside one of Colorado's great rivers, the steep walls of the canyon rising on either side, I could not help but reflect on the wonder of God's creation. Then, I heard a deep rumbling sound. Thinking it to be thunder, I looked up only to see a high rock slide plunging toward me. In seconds, tons of rock had fallen, but bounced over my head into the river just yards away.

Shaken and trembling, I thought of God's not speaking through the "earthquake, the wind, and the fire." I had heard Him in the beauty of creation, and now in the still small voice. The journey of life has its periods of calm and peace and then, quite suddenly, God often gets our attention, by the unexpected; through things like loss of a job, sickness, sorrow, and broken relationships. Whatever they be, a valley of trouble is where God speaks and seeks our attention, and our response. Remember that God's revelation has often come in unlikely places and through unlikely events. Hear God's Word, "listen to His voice, and hold fast to Him" (Deut. 30:20).

For Additional Reading: Psalm 29:1-11; Revelation 3:19-22
Allan, Age 55
Counselor

DAY THREE ■ Hosea 2:15

L et's not be naive. Life doesn't always deliver what it promises. No matter where you are in your journey through life, I can safely assume that somewhere along the way you too have experienced disappointment. Perhaps even today you're feeling the grief of losing something you've longed for, or of living through something that you had hoped to avoid. Your disappointment may be insignificant, or it may be tragic.

Whatever the disappointment, we need to know that God is able to meet us in the pain of our disappointment with a comfort that produces hope. Disappointment is not final. It hurts, but it's never the end. I must add, however, lest this sound too trite, that God's comfort is not always a salve to assuage our pain, or a windfall that reverses our circumstances. Our own experience tells us it doesn't happen that way. Rather, God's comfort comes to us as an inner strengthening, giving us a deep, divinely empowered ability to persevere.

In Romans we read that, "suffering produces perseverance; perseverance, character; and character hope. And hope does not disappoint us" (5:4-5). Disappointments in life are inevitable. But, through our disappointments, God is able to refine our character with the ability He gives us to persevere. Painful as it is, that makes disappointment "a door of hope."

For Additional Reading: Jeremiah 17:5-8; Ephesians 2:11-13
Scott, Age 28
Seminary Student

DAY FOUR ■ Hosea 2:15

Camped in the Valley of Achor is the entire nation of Israel. Imagine, if you can, all the Christians you know camped together and committed to a common goal. To me the Valley of Achor is a picture of the church body, huddled together, yet committed to Jesus Christ. We live in a world of "trouble." Sickness, sin, and pain surround us. We find in the church a place of refuge and solace. We enter and find a place to lay aside our burdens. There we receive the healing and nurture that we need to go back out and do battle.

Even in our valley we encounter seasons of trouble. Sadly, our response is often up and down. To the many things and pleasures God provides, we, for the most part, respond favorably. They make us feel "up." Yet, we know how quickly we can go from "up" to "down." Too many live "up" and "down" kind of lives, without ever finding the "in" and "out." We need to learn to go "in" to find refuge and refreshment in the Rock (Jesus). We need to go "out" to exercise the gifts and the talents He has given us. We find Him in the Valley of Achor, a door of hope for "in" and "out" living. We can do nothing without Jesus, and we find Him always there for us.

For Additional Reading: Psalm 9:7-10; Romans 15:1-4
Martha, Age 59
Artist

DAY FIVE ■ Hosea 2:15

Understanding hope necessitates defining hopelessness. Hopelessness is finding myself in the midst of despair and confusion, with a lack of will to go on. It's when everything looks impossible and there is no expectation of accomplishment. We find it among the Children of Israel wandering in the wilderness without God's perspective and unwilling to be obedient to Him. We find it as well in ourselves.

If this is hopelessness, what are the ingredients of hope? Hope is Jesus. Hope produces courage, joy, assurance, and stability. Hope is the anchor of my soul. He is sure and steadfast, a refuge, a source of possibilities, and the only spring of constancy in an ever-changing world. The degree that these qualities of hope are evident in my life is dependent on how willingly I abdicate control of my life, and allow God to reign.

For Additional Reading: Malachi 3:6-7; Hebrews 6:17-20
Trish, Age 32
Personal Banker

DAY SIX ■ Hosea 2:15

When the cares of life press in on me, there is a part of me which clings to the hope that things will get better. It can only go up from here! Is that the indomitable human spirit speaking, or am I just too stubborn to accept the fact that there could actually be a hopeless situation?

No! My hope comes from God's promise that He will never leave nor forsake me (Deut. 31:6). I may not understand *what* is happening, or *why* it is happening to me. But, I can be confident in God's ability to work all things according to His will in all situations (Rom. 8:28).

For Additional Reading: Deuteronomy 31:6-8; 1 Thessalonians 4:13-18
Jody, Age 30
School Social Worker

DAY SEVEN ■ Hosea 2:15

I am comforted by the experiences of David. On the *Myers-Briggs Personality Inventory* David would undoubtedly be classified as a "feeling" person. Strong, virile, and confident, David reflects qualities of leadership all admire. Yet, we find him weeping in caves, confused, and discouraged. As he intimately shares his bumps and bruises, both physical and emotional, he meets God. There the transporting power of God lifts him from the pit of despair, and enables him to fulfill his calling.

The Valley of Achor is most of all a place of personal exposure. It is there we ought to weep over the circumstances of our lives, and over the subtle sins so much a part of our behavior. In doing so we meet God, just as David did. We find the same power not only to persevere, but to live abundantly in this present age. That's the hope: God has made available the resources of the kingdom to live triumphantly now. They are ours through confession and commitment.

For Additional Reading: Isaiah 31:1-5; Hebrews 2:14-18
Jim, Age 41
Computer Consultant

WEEK TWENTY
■ ■ ■ ■

HAPPINESS — GOD'S DESIGN FOR LIVING

TEXT FOR THE WEEK: **MATTHEW 5:1-12**

KEY VERSE: MATTHEW 5:1   "Now when He saw the crowds, He went up on a mountainside and sat down."

DAY ONE ■ Commentary on Matthew 5:1-12

We are living in a fast-paced world that puts a premium on getting things done right away. No doubt you feel the constant pressure to do more and to be more. The Sermon on the Mount provides us a balance to the messages we hear in the world we live in.

That portion of the Sermon on the Mount we refer to as the Beatitudes helps us focus on eight essential truths that will not only redirect us, but renew us daily. They give us Christ's agenda for our lives. Each one of them relates to the others; they are to be understood together as the complete picture. It is not enough to conform to just one of these truths, we must strive to conform to them all. Yet we live in a world that says, "Don't worry about anyone but yourself," and, "If you slow down or draw away for even a moment, you will lose the race." These are lies; but Jesus Christ gives us a model and direct teaching to the contrary of the messages we hear from our fast-paced society.

Matthew 5:1 states, "Now when He saw the crowds, He went up on a mountainside." Jesus drew away. In this case, He was withdrawing from a very successful situation. Can't you just hear the people who were left behind, waiting for Him: "Jesus, You're so wonderful! Perform another miracle!" Do more, be more! That's the message. Yet, Jesus withdrew into the mountains to be quiet and still.

The narrative continues with the words, "and [He] sat down." Many of us desperately need to stop and sit down and listen to our Saviour's loving words, the words that give His agenda for our lives.

After He sat down, Jesus shared with His disciples these eight truths. (We too are His disciples when we hear His voice and obey His teaching.) The first four were inward and the last four were outward characteristics of living the faithful life. He used the word "Blessed" each time He told them about a truth, which translates, "Happy are those who hear these words and heed them." Reading these verses, we get the sense that Jesus means our lives will be worth living when we strive to live by these truths.

Who are the blessed ones, according to the eight truths described by Jesus? They are the poor in spirit, those who sense how much they need God. They are those that mourn, those who are grieved by the evil in this world. They are the meek, the ones who have a confidence that God is God. They are those that hunger and thirst for righteousness, those who are hungry for real faith and not dead religion (vv. 3-6).

The blessed ones have these outward qualities (vv. 7-10): They are merciful, people who are not blind to the broken world they live in, the new Good Samaritans. They are pure, people-builders, not people-destroyers. They are peacemakers looking for opportunities to practice peace, not merely hoping someone else will do it.

Finally, Jesus says, "Blessed are those who are persecuted." Life is tough. It was hard for Christ and it will be hard for us, but when we strive to live our lives by Christ's model and teaching, we will slow down and hear His agenda and it will change us.

For Additional Reading: Deuteronomy 28:1-11; Luke 6:17-22
Rich Hurst is the Vice-President of Christian Focus Ministries. The following personal applications follow the Beatitudes from the "Sermon" Christ gave His disciples. They are written by adult singles living in the area surrounding Seattle, Washington.

DAY TWO ■ Matthew 5:1-12

B lessed are the poor in spirit, for theirs is the kingdom of heaven" (Matt. 5:3).

It is so easy to get involved in acts of service "for" God while forgetting to spend time "with" God. It seems difficult to believe that God can still love and forgive me even when I am concerned more about the glory that comes from being in the spotlight. But He does. And He is the ultimate Friend and Parent, always patient, always there when I need Him.

Being poor in spirit means knowing that I need God. I do! He is my best Friend, I can trust Him. Not long after I moved to Seattle, the agency I was working for went broke, leaving me without a job. At the same time I broke up with the man I was dating. I felt extremely lost and alone. It took awhile, but I finally gave up trying to do things my way and told God that it was His turn. It wasn't long before I began to feel peaceful, and in a short time things turned out for the better. It happened when I realized how much I needed God, and I needed Him to be in control. He brought me through that time and many others. When I stop and realize how much I need God, it is then I learn about God. He comforts my soul, creating a desire to know Him more. Often, it is difficult to admit I need God, but I do.

For Additional Reading: Psalm 46:1-6; Colossians 3:12-14
Suzanne, Age 27
Marketing Promotions

DAY THREE ■ Matthew 5:1-12

B lessed are those who mourn, for they will be comforted" (Matt. 5:4).

Two years ago, my grandfather passed away as I held his hand. We shared a remarkable friendship and my sense of loss and grief when he died was profound. I was very familiar with Christ's promise of comfort for those who mourn, and had always thought it to be an incomprehensible paradox. If "blessed" means "happy are those" how could those in mourning be "blessed" even if they were to be comforted.

I experienced what He meant before I understood it. In the midst of my mourning, I was overwhelmed by an almost tangible sense of God's presence. The sensation is difficult to explain, but I felt held—hugged, really—by the God of the universe. Months later, while reflecting on the experience, I began to understand it. I remembered that Christ referred to the Holy Spirit as a "Comforter" He promised to send His disciples in His absence. So, while life still provides plenty of opportunities for sorrow and mourning, I respond to them differently knowing that God is present and available in a special way in their midst.

For Additional Reading: Isaiah 40:1-8; John 14:15-21
Ken, Age 28
College Instructor

DAY FOUR ■ Matthew 5:1-12

"Blessed are the meek, for they will inherit the earth" (Matt. 5:5).

When I think of people who are meek there is one key underlying trait: a quiet, calm confidence that God will be God. Confidence in God and His desires for the best in our lives sounds easy. In day-to-day practice it isn't easy. Many times I have said, "Sure, I trust God," then turned right around and done what I wanted. I do it out of fear and doubt that God really cares about me as an individual. Other times it is just "ego" that says, "I can do it myself." As I grow in my relationship with Jesus I am beginning to trust Him more, and be less afraid.

Being meek means I have confidence that God is with me through everything I go through. He is there in my fear, just as He was when David was being pursued by Saul. He is there in my doubt, just as He was when He said to the Apostle Thomas, "See for yourself, I am for real." Since God will not abandon me

138

to fear or doubt, today I can choose to trust Him!

For Additional Reading: Psalm 118:1-9; Hebrews 10:35-39
Kris, Age 28
Skier

DAY FIVE ■ Matthew 5:1-12

Blessed are those who hunger and thirst for righteousness, for they shall be filled" (Matt. 5:6).

What are some of the things we hunger and thirst for and why are they so important to us? I am a great believer in keeping a journal to serve as a reminder of the issues I struggle with. As I look back over my entries, I discover there are recurring themes: the search for a successful career, more money, more clothes, to be more attractive, and a better social life. These are the things I thought could bring me happiness. But I have learned that none of these external things could ever fully satisfy me. In life, God calls us to set our priorities straight. He wants us to make it a priority to develop a deep passion, not for things, but for holy living. When we have a passion for holy living, we discover the greatest secret of all: God will satisfy and fulfill us.

For Additional Reading: Isaiah 55:6-11; Matthew 8:18-22
Laurie, Age 32
Dentist

DAY SIX ■ Matthew 5:1-12

Blessed are the merciful, for they will be shown mercy. Blessed are the pure in heart, for they will see God" (Matt. 5:7-8).

To show mercy is to withhold punishment from those who deserve it, to forgive or pardon them for their wrong. Christians are told to be merciful and forgiving. To the degree we show mercy and forgive others, God will be merciful and forgive us. God will treat us in the same manner we treat others.

I'm not so sure I like this, since I do not feel like forgiving many of the people who have wronged me: "friends" who have gossiped about me and others who have lied to me or deceived me.

Now if I do not forgive others, I not only disobey God, but lock myself in the past. I keep scorecards against others, who end up keeping scorecards against me.

Forgiveness is the starting point of having a pure heart. Pure is defined as something that is clean, complete, full-strength, undivided, unadulterated. A pure heart, then, would be one that is wholly dedicated and directed toward God, when one's mind, will, and emotions want and seek to glorify and honor God!

For Additional Reading: Numbers 14:17-24;
2 Timothy 1:13-18
Brian, Age 32
International Business Development

DAY SEVEN ■ Matthew 5:1-12

Blessed are the peacemakers, for they will be called sons of God. Blessed are those who are persecuted because of righteousness, for theirs is the kingdom of heaven" (Matt. 5:9-10; also read verses 11-12).

Persecuted. Insulted. Accused falsely because of Jesus. This is what Christ's followers can expect in life from many who do not know Him. We note that the word "if" does not appear in this passage. But the word "when" does (v. 11). It is not "if" these things happen to us, but "when." We must be prepared.

And the Word tells us what our response must be. There are two activities that should characterize the followers of Jesus. First, we are to be peacemakers. Peace is defined in the dictionary as "calmness of mind and heart; harmony in human relations." Such are the gifts God's people offer in return for persecution, insults, and false accusations.

Second, Jesus tells us to rejoice and be glad. The word *rejoice* is defined as "to feel great delight." The verb is in the imperative mode, meaning it is something within our power to do, not

merely a feeling that comes to us, but an activity that we ourselves initiate. Jesus looks both backward and forward in time to
explain the reason for our rejoicing: we are like God's faithful
prophets of old, and our reward in heaven will be great.

For Additional Reading: Isaiah 51:1-8; James 3:17-18
Jim, Age 57
College Professor

WEEK TWENTY-ONE

■ ■ ■ ■

ORDINARY GIFTS –
EXTRAORDINARY RESULTS

TEXT FOR THE WEEK: **MATTHEW 14:13-21**

KEY VERSE: MATTHEW 14:20   "They all ate and were satisfied."

DAY ONE ■ Commentary on Matthew 14:13-21

This astounding event in the ministry of Christ is a fascinating lesson in the stewardship of life and ministry. In this wondrous account, Jesus calls on His disciples to minister to the needs of an overwhelming multitude. Their resources are meager – impossibly inadequate. But Jesus takes their resources, blesses and multiplies them, and gives them back to His disciples to distribute to the hungry crowd. An astonishing miracle occurs – there is more than enough to meet the needs of the people! What lesson is the Master teaching His novice followers?

Certainly, Jesus is demonstrating to His disciples that they must never underestimate the power of God – He admonished them on more than one occasion that "with God all things are possible" (19:26). At the same time, I believe He was also teaching them that they ought never to underestimate the resources of man! The point He was making to His disciples is elegantly and profoundly simple: God is in the business of using ordinary human resources with extraordinary divine power. Notice that Jesus used only the very limited resources the disciples were able to supply. He used the "materials at hand," so to speak.

Jesus continues this same method with us – He uses whatever talents, abilities, or resources we have; whatever we dedicate to

His purposes. Unfortunately, most of us remain a bit skeptical about this whole business: Are our meager means really of value to God? Sadly, many Christians today live in a false frustration, believing that God cannot use them in a mighty way, because they do not possess "mighty" enough resources, talents, or abilities. The thinking goes something like this: "If only I had the musical ability of that great soloist, or that talented instrumentalist, then God could really use me in ministry through my music." The logic is dastardly! God can certainly use *any* talent or ability. But He cannot use (in us) an ability we do not possess! If we want to be used by God in a powerful way, we must dedicate to Him whatever it is we *do* have! God will never taunt us by putting an unrealistic expectation on us.

I have seen God use humble resources in a mighty way, time after time after time! One young woman I know was the victim of incest while growing up. What a terrible and tragic wound! Yet, she has turned this "setback" into a "comeback" by sharing her own journey of healing with others in a ministry she developed, consisting of strong support groups and informative seminars. A divorced single adult I know has shared his recovery from alcohol with other "fellow pilgrims" through a dynamic support group based on principles from the Alcoholics Anonymous movement.

What do you have that you could dedicate to Christ? Do you have a little time each week, like the people I know who visit a convalescent home? Do you have a car, like the young man in our church who provides transportation to shut-ins? Can you cook, like the young woman who organizes meals for over a hundred single adults each month as part of a special outreach program at our church? Can you use a telephone, like the single woman I know who calls shut-ins and disabled members of our fellowship and offers a word of encouragement and prayer? Maybe you don't think much of the resources you have at hand—but you and your meager means just might make all the difference in the world in the life of another human being. Think for a moment of what you have; and then consider how you might use those resources in ministry right where you are!

For Additional Reading: Deuteronomy 15:7-11; 2 Corinthians 9:6-15

Jim Dyke is the Single Adult Pastor at College Avenue Baptist Church, San Diego, California. Six single friends from Jim's ministry write the following.

DAY TWO ■ Matthew 14:13-21

It is my deep desire to see a divorce recovery group started for children. In our country we offer a lot of help for adults, but nothing for our hurting, bleeding children. They are crying out in pain, but we can't hear them because our own pain drowns them out. I believe God hears their cries, sees their bleeding, aching hearts, and longs to heal them just as much as He desires to heal the parent. It takes people who are willing to do the work and pour their hearts into these little ones, who long to be told this devastation is not their fault. We need to find people who have God's heart of love and understanding, who are willing to stretch out their hands to a sinking child. All of this could take place only if people are surrounding their own will in the will of our Lord Jesus.

Through my own divorce, God has taught me a lot about myself and my heartbroken son. What do I have to give? Myself, my free will to become ensconced in His will. God has put my torn heart back together, so that I am able to reach out and help other broken, bleeding hearts. Where does God begin with such a big task? I believe it all begins with each of us, and me.

For Additional Reading: Deuteronomy 24:18-22; Matthew 10:40-42

Debi, Age 25

Church Secretary

DAY THREE ■ Matthew 14:13-21

What struck me most about this passage was not only the obvious—that God uses what we have and multiplies it for

His purposes—but also, how much we are like the disciples! They had been with Jesus for some time, during which He healed the sick and even raised a young girl from the dead! Yet they still had no faith that He could take care of this situation.

How often has Christ worked powerfully in our lives? How fast do we forget and struggle through the next crisis without trust and faith in God? The disciples seemed to forget as quickly as we do, yet they walked with the Master, and witnessed all His miracles! Let us not lose sight of the miracles worked in our lives, lest we forget that Christ is sufficient in every way and in all situations.

For Additional Reading: 2 Chronicles 31:20-21; Galatians 3:1-9
Greg, Age 35
Land Engineer

DAY FOUR ■ Matthew 14:13-21

I am constantly in a state of being overly critical of myself—selling myself short. I call it "humility," or "honesty"—disdain of "blowing my own horn." The results are crippling in all areas of my life. The fact of the matter is, I have much to offer in many areas: the ability to listen; the ability to be self-taught; attention to detail, quality, and completeness; the ability to analyze and present an intangible idea in an easy-to-understand way.

If I allow myself to be used, I will touch the lives of many people—be it professionally in my insistence for detail and quality; personally, with my ability to listen; intellectually, with my ability to teach a difficult concept; or spiritually, with my ability to comfort or to encourage someone in their relationship to God. The point? To be used of God and God alone.

For Additional Reading: Psalm 149:4-9; Matthew 23:1-12
Howard, Age 42
Technical Designer

DAY FIVE ■ Matthew 14:13-21

It is so easy to compare myself with others to see what gifts and abilities I don't have. It's also easy to see the hindrances or shortcomings that I have that others don't have to deal with.

I should not look at what I don't have, and then say, "I can't do anything for God." The little that I do have can be used greatly if I invest it wisely, and allow God to use it. God doesn't just take the little I have and use it—instead, He gives it back to me to invest in the lives of others. The returns of this venture and my spiritual journey will depend on how wisely I "invested" what God has given me.

For Additional Reading: Proverbs 4:5-13; 2 Peter 1:5-11
John, Age 31
Accountant

DAY SIX ■ Matthew 14:13-21

DEAREST FATHER

Write upon my life this day
The plans and events that lead Your way
All scheduled and purposed to shape and mold
To create me into a vessel of gold.

Help me bend my will to Thine,
Make me this day loving and kind,
Help me accept what You bring this day
And to react in love and a godly way.

Thank You again for a brand new start
And I pray, upon me—more of You impart,
May I not resist, what You've planned for me,
Knowing it's for now and through eternity.

Tina Miller

Your resources are never adequate to serve the Lord on your own. Even if you don't have faith that God will multiply your resources, but dedicate them to His service, He will produce results for His glory.

For Additional Reading: 2 Chronicles 20:18-21; John 2:1-11
Chris, Age 28
Naval Officer

DAY SEVEN ■ Matthew 14:13-21

LIFT

As I elevate Him and lower me
  I see more clearly what He'd have me be,
And that is to be a walking light,
  That tells so clearly the Way that's right.

Yes! Be bold in Him and back not away,
  For we need not shrink from the weights of the day
But march ahead and possess what's there,
  Prepared already, with His personal care.

Oh, lift Him high for all to see
  That there is deliverance and liberty
And may we become ever dim in view
  As we let His glory and love shine through.

Tina Miller

In Matthew 14:13-21, God emphasizes that He uses whatever we make available to him. It does not matter how great or how small. The important point in my life is to be available.

For Additional Reading: Deuteronomy 13:3-4; Philemon 8-21
Ray, Age 31
Hydro Engineer

WEEK TWENTY-TWO
■ ■ ■ ■

IF GOD SAYS, "COME," THEN COURAGEOUSLY GO

TEXT FOR THE WEEK:	**MATTHEW 14:22-33**

KEY VERSES: MATTHEW 14:27-29   "But Jesus immediately said to them: 'Take courage! It is I. Don't be afraid.' 'Lord, if it's You,' Peter replied, 'tell me to come to You on the water.' 'Come,' He said."

DAY ONE ■ Commentary on Matthew 14:22-33

Jesus had been trying to find time to be alone. His cousin and friend, John the Baptist, had just been killed by King Herod. Jesus had just ministered to the 5,000. He desired to be alone. Therefore, He instructed the disciples to go on ahead of Him in the boat while He went up into the hills to pray.

Later that night, the winds being against them, the disciples had still not reached the other shore. In the middle of the night, Jesus came to them, walking on the water. At first, they thought it must be a ghost. After all, people cannot walk on water. When Jesus spoke to them and told them not to be afraid, Peter said to Him, "Lord, if it is You, tell me to come to You on the water." "Come," said Jesus.

If you had been Peter, what would you have done when Jesus invited you to come to Him on the water? I remember wrestling with that question one night during a Bible study group. Without thinking, I quickly said, "I'd go. It sounds exciting." Almost immediately, however, I realized that this was not a hypothetical question. It was a real one, and inside myself I heard Jesus beckoning me, "Come."

For some time, I had become more and more dissatisfied with

my role as pastor at the church I was serving. After my divorce, I did not seem to "fit" anymore. When I heard that inner voice inviting me to get out of my boat, I knew what Jesus meant. However, I had no idea of what to do or how to do it. All of my training and all of my experience was as a pastor. Did Jesus really mean for me to give that up? Yes, I was sure that was what He meant, and if He could call me into the ministry, I knew that He could also call me out of it. As for me, like the disciples in the boat, I was terrified.

Nevertheless, I got out of my safe boat. At first that meant going back to school to study journalism. The very first article I tried to write was about the needs of singles in the church. That led me into something I never knew existed—singles ministry. Instantly, I knew the essence of the invitation that came during that Bible study. This is where I needed to be, but I also realized that I never would have found it if I had not left my boat.

Jesus is constantly inviting people to give up the security of the boat, venturing out with Him onto the water. How will you respond?

For Additional Reading: Exodus 3:1-10; Matthew 10:37-42
Dick Dunn is the Minister of Singles and Stepfamilies at Roswell United Methodist Church in Roswell, Georgia. Six single adults from the church wrote the following thoughts.

DAY TWO ■ Matthew 14:22-33

My life had spiraled down—divorce, death of my parents, dissatisfaction with where I was in my life, and deepening depression. I felt empty. Sometime during all of this, I began to experience feelings that I needed to get out of the boat. I know now that Jesus was calling to me, "Come!"

Here I was, a backsliding Christian, looking for something but not sure what it was. Slowly, however, I began to listen to the Lord's voice. His message to get out of the boat was getting louder as events progressed. Life was beginning to go two steps forward and one back. I decided to see what a singles group at the United Methodist Church was all about. On Sunday morning, before my first singles meeting, I spontaneously decided to go to the church where the group met. Strange thing for me to do! The church loomed up before me that Sunday morning. My feet walked up the steps and I entered the sanctuary. A wonderful feeling of utter peace came over me. Jesus beckoned and my feet began walking on the waters of faith.

For Additional Reading: Jeremiah 3:21-25; Luke 17:12-16
Gene, Age 49
Communications Planner for Telephone Company

DAY THREE ■ Matthew 14:22-33

CHALLENGE: Jesus said, "Come" when Peter saw Him walking on the water.
RISK: Peter got out of the boat.
REALITY: Peter began to sink.
FEAR: Peter said, "Lord, save me."
ASSURANCE: IMMEDIATELY Jesus reached out . . .
ACTION: . . . and caught him.

The greatest challenge of my life was to parent two teenagers as I began single life after 20 years of marriage. My well-constructed boat was adrift and the shore far away when the pain in my chest sank me to my knees and I forgot how to walk or breathe.

Slowly, however, I moved forward. Everything seemed a RISK. Financially and emotionally I was drained, as though I had been tipped over and poured out. REALITY. Where was God? FEAR. A singles group in our church opened their hearts and pulled me along with their prayers, friendship, and love. ASSURANCE AND ACTION. Why did I doubt?

For Additional Reading: Psalm 102:12-17; Galatians 6:1-10
Pat, Age 44
Associate Director Singles Ministry
Roswell United Methodist Church

DAY FOUR ■ Matthew 14:22-33

In this passage, we are impressed that Jesus walked on water to meet His disciples at sea. The Sea of Galilee and its shoreline were well known to Jesus and His followers. It was central to their environment.

After grieving the death of His cousin John, Jesus found a new way to traverse familiar territory. Amidst turbulent seas, He walked.

Two years ago, my fiance died unexpectedly shortly before our wedding day. I found myself amidst stormy emotional tides. Though I continued to live in the same house, work at the same place, and hang around the same crowd, I felt ill at ease. I too had to find a new way to survive and then grow in familiar surroundings. As time has passed, I see that walking, taking patient deliberate steps, is the best way to travel. Moving ahead, reaching out to others, as Jesus did to Peter, gives direction to my path.

For Additional Reading: Psalm 55:1-8; 1 John 2:3-6
Sandy, Age 29
Computer Systems Analyst

DAY FIVE ■ Matthew 14:22-33

Several years ago, I was challenged in a similar way that Peter was when Jesus invited him to walk on the water. I was comfortably adjusting to living alone with a secure job that allowed me the freedom to make my own schedule as a management consultant on a client's site. When I had completed my assignment for the client and returned to the home office, I was told that there was not another assignment for me as a consultant. However, I was given some technical writing to do. While this was certainly not my forte, I did manage to survive at the same salary.

Two months later, the vice president came into my office and said, "Nancy, we are cutting your salary 40 percent effective in two weeks. You will be going on commission selling consultant services and recruiting consultants." My first reaction was panic. How could I possibly survive a 40 percent pay cut as a single parent with one child in college? I had never sold anything in my life. Where would I begin? I searched for the strength to say, "Thank you for not telling me that I have no job."

I recalled every thought I had ever had regarding my industry and used every journal I could locate for hints about sales. For two months I reluctantly called on everyone and every company I had ever known in the field. I was determined that I would survive. In the third month, after many rejections, I finally made my first sale. Three years after that first sale, I have tripled my salary. Many times I said, "I can't do this job," but each time, God has enabled me to go on.

For Additional Reading: Isaiah 41:10-14; James 2:14-23
Nancy, Age 47
Technical Consultant

DAY SIX ■ Matthew 14:22-33

Peter wanted further proof of the Lord's identity and asked Jesus to allow him to walk to Him on the water. Stepping onto the lake, Peter experienced doubt and fear and it was his own faith that was found to be wanting as he began to sink.

In midlife and recently single, I sometimes participate in interaction with other singles who also very much want friendship and companionship. Often, however, we quiz and test one another warily. Trust and faith in other people has been broken. Therefore, each of us in our own little boat, like Peter beckons for others to prove themselves by stepping onto the waters first. Faith and courage to leave the sanctuary of our own boat is found wanting, making the new relationship begin to sink before it really begins.

Jesus reached out to Peter and lifted him to safety. What an example! With faith and trust bolstered, we too can reach out and help find the firm ground of faith in each other.

For Additional Reading: Deuteronomy 1:29-36; John 13:13-17
Jim, Age 50
Real Estate Consultant

DAY SEVEN ■ Matthew 14:22-33

In a heartbeat my husband was gone. Our singles minister approached me a few months later about starting a widowed support group. Me? I CAN organize. Yes, I can do that. But stand up in front of a group and say anything—well, I CAN'T do that. The more I thought about it, however, the more determined I was to help others who became widowed. I knew that my experience could indeed help others. I have been there and I have so much to share.

"O God, I want to do this, but You know I am scared to death." God put His arms around me, and I knew that with His help anything was possible. Didn't Philippians 4:13 say, "I can do everything through Him who gives me strength"? "OK, God, I want to do this, but I need Your help."

I struggled with stage fright. The blessings I have received over the past three and one half years far outshine what I have put into the group. Getting widowed people together to share their thoughts, find out that their grief is similar to those in the same situation, and to see them grow in their "new" life has given me courage to venture out of my boat and try other things as well.

For Additional Reading: Exodus 3:11-15; 4:1-11; 1 Corinthians 2:1-10
Wanda, Age 49
Financial Secretary

WEEK TWENTY-THREE

■ ■ ■ ■

RESULTS COMING. PRAY

TEXT FOR THE WEEK: **MATTHEW 21:18-22**

KEY VERSE: MATTHEW 21:22   "If you believe, you will receive
whatever you ask for in prayer."

DAY ONE ■ Commentary on Matthew 21:22

According to Matthew 21:22, "If you believe, you will receive whatever you ask for in prayer." That's *whatever* you ask in prayer—not just some of those things or a part of them, but all of them according to God's will and in agreement with His Holy Word.

When we depend on Jesus Christ and on His Word, and seek Him in prayer, we can't help but renew our minds. When our minds are renewed, we discover God's will because we come to know His mind and heart. We are then able to ask for those things which we know are in His will; and since they're in God's will, we can believe that He will provide. And He takes great pleasure in giving to us when we have this kind of faith.

A few years ago I made the decision to search for a church in Marin County and to leave the church I loved attending across the bay in Berkeley. Initially I had concerns. Which church should I join? Which church group? Will I make any friends? I expressed these fears to the Lord in prayer and it became clear to me that because it was His will for me to change churches, He would take care of my needs. I trusted in this, and asked Him to take care of me. He did not let me down.

"Everyone who trusts in Him will never be put to shame" (Rom. 10:11). He knows what is best for our lives, so seek Him and His will in prayer, and He will take care of your concerns. His answer will be more than what you asked or even thought to ask!

The Apostle Paul has written, "Pray continually" (1 Thes. 5:17). Let us do the same and not miss an opportunity to seek God in prayer. He wants you to. He longs to fulfill your needs and to bless you. Trust and acknowledge Him in all areas of your life, and you will experience life to its fullest.

For Additional Reading: Psalm 37:1-4; Romans 12:1-2
Mary Consolacion is a Registered Nurse and the Career Group Director for Marin Covenant Church in San Rafael, California. The six applications are written by single adults from Marin Covenant Church.

DAY TWO ■ Matthew 21:22

The concept of having to ask for something has always been difficult for me. I always thought that it was better to give than to receive. For me, asking displayed signs of weakness. I had the attitude that I could do it by myself and that I needed no assistance from anyone. How foolish I must have been.

Prayer is making your needs known to God. When we know the will of God, then we can ask and receive graciously. It has been comforting for me to know that when I ask God for something with the right intentions, He will hear and answer my prayers. All that God requires of me is that I seek His will and am obedient to His Word.

I still wrestle with the idea of asking; but knowing that God commands me to pray and loves me has made the task easier.

For Additional Reading: Psalm 20:1-5; James 4:1-3
David, Age 27
Stockbroker

DAY THREE ■ Matthew 21:22

I am challenged by the question, "What's the biggest thing you're trusting God for?" Too many times I confine the power of God within the parameters of my natural abilities.

To overcome this, I started a page in my prayer journal and listed the five biggest things that I am trusting God for. I listed a variety of requests ranging from a computer, to revival in my church, to the salvation of my parents.

An exciting transformation has taken place as the weeks have passed since the formation of this "faith page." A conviction has developed in my heart that God can answer every request on that page. Also, I am learning to trust Him more in my everyday activities. It is a great challenge to look anew at Matthew 21:22 and to increase the magnitude of the "whatever."

For Additional Reading: Ezra 8:21-23; Luke 17:1-6
Gary, Age 25
Youth Pastor

DAY FOUR ■ Matthew 21:22

Jesus promises to be faithful to those who truly believe in Him. October 17th, 1989 represents a personal landmark in my life. It was also the day the earth shook in San Francisco. My studio apartment in the Marina was my little haven. I decorated it and it contained everything I owned and loved. Unfortunately, my building collapsed during the quake and it was the first one demolished the following day. I lost "everything."

I remember thanking God for keeping me safe and unharmed and then praying for strength and comfort in the days to come. I felt such peace during this chaotic time and I had no doubts that God was already taking care of all my needs.

Sure enough, He provided a temporary home and the love and support of family and friends. On October 17th, I trusted Jesus to meet my needs—I hate to think what might have happened if I hadn't.

For Additional Reading: Deuteronomy 32:8-11; Colossians 3:1-4
Kristi, Age 26
Sales Manager

DAY FIVE ■ Matthew 21:22

The heart of applying Matthew 21:22 lies in giving back to God what was His in the first place, namely control—the authority to complete the work He started without my interference. I simply need to seek Him first, tune in to His plan, pray and wait for Him to bring about His design.

In 1984 I prayed for a wife believing that *if* He desired, it would come about. Neither prepared for marriage, nor anxious, I concentrated on learning all I could about God and developing myself accordingly. For six years, I trusted that His goals followed His timetable and not mine.

Recently, God initiated my contact with a young woman, still many years before I'd anticipated. All the while, He'd been preparing her for the same purpose. The meeting, courting, and the culmination of the friendship were His idea. Seven weeks remain before our wedding date.

For Additional Reading: Psalm 138:1-3, 8; Philippians 1:3-8
Rich, Age 27
Radio Sales

DAY SIX ■ Matthew 21:22

In 1982, before I was a Christian I visited Japan for two weeks. Afterward I longed to live in Japan among the people. At 29 I turned my life over to Jesus. So like a well-planned puzzle the Lord put the pieces of my life together.

In 1989 He led me to a new church. Without knowing my desire, the people at this church introduced me to some missionaries in Japan. As a result of this meeting, I spent four and one half months living in Japan teaching English and the Bible to the Japanese people.

Even when I did not know Jesus, He knew me and my desires. How fortunate I am to now be led by Him. God has a plan for every life. If we believe, if we ask, He will guide us to and through this plan. He will give us the desires of our hearts.

For Additional Reading: Isaiah 65:17-25; Acts 14:8-15
Therese, Age 34
Property Manager

DAY SEVEN ■ Matthew 21:22

This is an age when we can take nothing for granted. We must toil for every accomplishment, every need. Sometimes it is hard to remember that Someone is on our side.

However, when I read Matthew 21:22 my response is that we receive the desires of our hearts when our requests are in line with God's will. And when I can be totally honest, I realize that God's will is always focused on my best interest and truest happiness.

Currently, I am in the process of seeking a job. As I conduct my search, I think about future job responsibilities, living situations, new friends, etc. What a relief to lean on God's promise. He understands my needs and has the power to make miracles happen! I will continue to do my part in this job hunt, but I'll leave the results to Him.

For Additional Reading: 1 Kings 3:3-14; Matthew 7:7-12
Karen, Age 23
Youth Ministry Intern

WEEK TWENTY-FOUR

■ ■ ■ ■

BURNED OUT? CHOOSE
THE BETTER!

TEXT FOR THE WEEK: LUKE 10:38-42

KEY VERSE: LUKE 10:42   "But only one thing is needed. Mary
                                 has chosen what is better, and it will
                                 not be taken away from her."

DAY ONE ■ Commentary on Luke 10:38-42

Are you doing more and enjoying it less? Does busy as a bee sound like a vacation to you? If so, you are not alone. Workaholism has been added to the list of social disorders in the last 10 years. Burnout is rampant, even among Christians.

Does Jesus Christ call you to a pace of life that pushes you to the edge of your physical and emotional health? Luke 10:38-42 provides an answer.

The setting is described in verse 38. Jesus is heading toward Jerusalem to complete His earthly mission. As He goes, He is given hospitality by two women disciples.

The story introduces us to two sisters, Mary and Martha. The contrast between them is dramatic. In verse 39, Mary is pictured as actively listening to Jesus who is sitting down, teaching. To "sit at Jesus' feet" is to take the position of a student or disciple. This expression is used to describe Paul, who sat at the feet of the great rabbi, Gamaliel (Acts 22:3). Mary is portrayed as the loving disciple who listens to her Master's instruction.

In contrast, while Mary sits listening to Jesus, Martha is preparing a great meal (Luke 10:40). The context suggests that Martha also would like to be sitting, but she is distracted by her service. The term *service*, in the original biblical language, is the word from which we get *deacon*. Service is tremendous. But even Christian service can become an obstacle to intimacy with Jesus.

Martha is the portrait of a workaholic: crazy schedule; performance hangup; perfectionistic; inability to say no; inability to relax; and critical (expresses anger easily, but not warmth). Martha is angry with her sister for not joining in her level of performance. Frustrated, Martha asks Jesus to intervene on her behalf: "Jesus, tell her to help me!" (v. 40)

Jesus responds with a loving rebuke: "Martha, Martha . . . you are worried and upset about many things" (v. 41). The term "worry" reflects inner turmoil or an agitated state of mind. This kind of anxiety is one by-product of busyness. Paul declares that single Christians can be worry free compared to their married counterparts (1 Cor. 7:32-35). Martha allows the preparations for a meal to rob her of the joy of Jesus' presence. Jesus tells Martha that, among all the many things for her to do, there is only one real need. Instead of demanding that Mary enter into Martha's anxiety, Jesus commends Mary's understanding of the options. Jesus says that Mary had chosen for herself the best portion. Some think Jesus is making an allusion to the meal. Mary had eaten a spiritual portion, consisting of the teachings of Jesus. Jesus concludes by stating that the portion which Mary had selected would never be taken from her. Jesus' words are eternal. Mary's choice has lasting benefit.

Sometimes we must choose between genuine discipleship and busy activity. Martha was the perfect hostess; Mary, the perfect disciple. Which one characterizes you? What one change could you make to become more like Mary?

For Additional Reading: Ecclesiastes 2:17-23; John 13:31-35
Dwayne Adams is the Minister to Singles at Northwest Bible Church in Dallas, Texas. Six adult singles write the following. Days Two—Six are from the ministry at Northwest Bible Church. Day Seven is from Tina in Lynden, Washington.

DAY TWO ■ Luke 10:38-42

We, like Martha, can become so caught up in the preparations that have to be made in our lives, that we forget our focus. Our focus should always be on the Lord. The most joyous time I have found with my son, Nicholas, is when I am walking *daily* with the Lord. Every morning, I wake up before Nicholas and spend time with the Lord. I know I need to start breakfast, feed the dog, and get ready for work, but before I start each day, I study the Word and pray. I want to listen to what the Lord has to say. I pray that the Lord will make me the mother He wants Nicholas to have.

Mary was focused! She sat at the Lord's feet and listened. We should follow her example daily. In doing this, we become an inspiring role model to our children.

For Additional Reading: Deuteronomy 11:18-21; Titus 2:1-8
Laura, Age 29
Secretary

DAY THREE ■ Luke 10:38-42

What was she to do? The Lord had come to her home. There was so much to be done — fresh linens to lay out, water to draw, food to prepare. "Now, where is Mary? I *really* need her! Well, of all things, there she sits doing nothing!" I can feel Martha's frustration and identify with her. The pressure of service had robbed her of the joy of being in the presence of the Lord. Her focus was on work — not worship.

Like Martha, without warning, I find myself shortcutting the time I spend with the Lord, caught up in activities which, while worthwhile, keep me so preoccupied that I fail to take time just to be still before the Lord, reading His Word, praying, and really meditating.

Jesus' answer to Martha's plea reminds me that time spent at His feet, learning from Him is never wasted and that nothing is as significant for eternity as my relationship with Him.

For Additional Reading: Psalm 132:4-10; John 4:21-24
Darlene, Age 54
Paralegal

DAY FOUR ■ Luke 10:38-42

My job as a bank officer demands a lot of time. In addition, I am chairman of my Sunday School class of 150 singles. I am taking a class at the local seminary, and play in a weekly racquetball league. Since I also try to have an active social life, my social calendar frequently fills up weeks in advance.

I've always had problems scheduling "additional activities" into my life. This passage stresses to me that I need to make sure my spiritual life takes priority. I cannot afford to consider my quiet time or church as "extra" activities. Those things need to be the platform on which the rest of my schedule is built. I need to make sure that all of the many things that I am involved in do not overshadow what is the most important—my walk with the Lord, and those things that will help me keep my eyes on Him.

For Additional Reading: 2 Chronicles 15:1-7; Hebrews 11:5-6
David, Age 29
Bank Vice President

DAY FIVE ■ Luke 10:38-42

Distractions. Decisions. Demands on my time, energy, emotions. Confusion sets in as I attempt to organize and prioritize my ever-mounting list of "to-do's." When will it end? How much can I hope to accomplish as a single parent, responsible not only for myself, but also for those others living under my roof? This moment in time seems fleeting and, yet, so significant.

I temporarily stop watching the clock, purposely put away all thoughts and activities, and quietly sit at the feet of Jesus. Peace prevails over the storm, sanity conquers chaos. My perspective clears, hope returns. I am refreshed! Around me, nothing has changed, but inside there is a newness, a calm that defies description. Energized and content, problems now become challenges, offering opportunities to see God at work. At His feet, I am accepted and made whole. Before, caught up in the rat race of life, ironically I served alone. Now, having taken time-out to sit and know Him, more is accomplished and we, God and me, operate as a team!

For Additional Reading: Ezekiel 36:24-30; Luke 19:11-17
Sandy, Age 39
Social Worker

DAY SIX ■ Luke 10:38-42

Recently, I have become increasingly involved in our Career Singles Class. I have found that serving God by serving people is very satisfying and fulfilling. As music coordinator and chairman of our Steering Committee, I can spend every spare minute trying to improve our music, handling administrative details, or encouraging others. Like Martha, I struggle with balancing ministry and my personal relationship to God.

From this passage, I realize that the most important thing in life is to know God. If I (like Mary) spend plenty of time alone in prayer and Bible study, I will accomplish this most important task. If I let myself be consumed by ministry, I will miss knowing God and be less effective in ministry. In light of this, I now take Monday nights away from class responsibilities and delegate more tasks. This allows me to spend time with God.

For Additional Reading: Deuteronomy 6:4-9; Mark 12:28-33
Charles, Age 36
Computer Systems Analyst

DAY SEVEN ■ Luke 10:38-42

THE TIMING OF GOD

He's never too early
And He's never too late
So why is it that

SINGLE TO SINGLE

I so often hesitate
To rely and relax and
Trust completely in Him
To deliver me from
The spot I am in?

You would think I would learn
After all of this time
That He knows the answers
For this heart of mine.
But what do I do
But I fuss and I fret
And go about in circles
To get no place yet.

Do you ever or
Do you suppose
That I will learn
On Him to repose
And trust in His timing
And in His great way
To deliver me by Love
Every hour of my day?

Well, try harder, I will
To believe what He said
And I just know for certain
That He'll take away dread,
That oft times I have
As I stumble my way
Because I failed to relinquish
To Him, my day.

Why don't you join me
And walk in His Way,
Knowing in His Word
That He's prepared your day,

Keeping the time as you
Give it to Him,
Knowing what's best
For the victory to win.

For Additional Reading: Hosea 10:12; Mark 4:13-20
Tina, Grandmother
Radio Broadcaster

WEEK TWENTY-FIVE

■ ■ ■ ■

GET READY FOR REALITY

TEXT FOR THE WEEK: LUKE 12:13-53

KEY VERSE: LUKE 12:35   "Be dressed ready for service and
                                        keep your lamps burning."

DAY ONE ■ Commentary on Luke 12:13-53

"With a smile of Christian charity great Casey's visage shown;
he stilled the rising tumult; he bade the game go on."

Casey at the Bat, Ernest Thayer

Every June old Casey celebrates another birthday. He's been
immortalized for over 100 years (an interesting note for trivia
buffs is that it's the only poem Thayer ever wrote). Why has this
hero of disappointment survived for so long in our culture?
Because as a society we tend to thrive on myths and legends
more than on truth and reality.

It's easier to live thinking you already believe the right things
than it is to strive to discover what the right things really are.
We like to imagine Casey as the quintessential baseball hitter.
We see him tall, muscles popping as he strides to the plate, an
ancient Ruth, Mantle, and Canseco with the power to bring
victory with one mighty blow! It becomes easy to create a vi-
brant visual image as the person leaps off the page into our
mind. It's great fun.

As a Christian I don't want to live my life according to
Christian legends about Christ. In Luke 12:13-53, the Bible is
clear, the words of Christ are clear, and there is no room for
myth or legend. In these verses Jesus talks about three myth-
crushing realities of truth which guide us through each day's
onslaught of self-perpetuated legends. Myth-crushing reality #1

is "Live managing well the money you have" (v. 21). One of the most difficult issues I ever had to face in my life was managing money. Since money didn't seem "spiritual" to me I ignored its cry for management to a point where it managed me. After a caring financial planner set me on track I began to see how "spiritual" money is and how an astute management of money brings peace of mind. It's easy to say, "I don't have much money." It's difficult to grasp the implications of how managing what I do have affects my growing spirituality.

Myth-crushing reality #2 is "Live preparing for Christ's return" (vv. 35-37). I'll admit it. I do not carry around a chart of Revelation in my back pocket. *He will come again,* but *when* He comes back is not as much a concern to me as what I'll be doing when He gets here (cf. Matt. 16:27; Luke 21:34). Each day one way we can prepare for Christ's coming is by doing the things He wants us to do (12:42-47). Today each of us can take a moment to set the stage for His return, by reaching out in a simple way to a child, a coworker or neighbor. Here are three quick ideas: Give a book that has encouraged you to someone, send a thank-you note that's long overdue, make your favorite dessert and bring it to work.

Myth-crushing reality #3 is possibly the toughest. "Live understanding the realities of relationships." Mike and the Mechanics sing it this way: "Every generation blames the one before and all of their frustrations come beating on your door . . . we all talk a different language talking in defense".

Part one of this myth-crusher is that "broken family relationships are part of reality for the Christian." In our imperfect world, relationships are sometimes strained (vv. 52-53). The second part is "problem-solving in relationships brings freedom" (v. 58). Appropriate efforts at working through differences, even those guided by professionals if necessary, can keep you free from the traps of self-pity and unforgiveness. It's hard work that's worth the time and effort, but we must remember that sometimes we just have to experience the brokenness and live with it.

The Christian life is not the stuff of legends and myths. I've learned it is a myth-crushing relationship with a Saviour who calls us to live in the tough realities of our lives, " . . . but there is no joy in Mudville—mighty Casey has struck out." Living a mythological faith will leave you flat, living the myth-crushing reality of Christ will give you the strength you need today and every day.

For Additional Reading: Isaiah 45:15-19; Matthew 16:13-20
Michael Simone is the Pastor of Adult and Family Ministries at Virginia Beach Community Chapel in Virginia Beach, Virginia. From Virginia Beach, six single adults contribute the following devotional thoughts.

DAY TWO ■ Luke 12:13-53

Understanding the realities of relationships is a hard thing to do, but it is the only way to have true friendships. I've learned a lot about forgiveness in relationships. Everything is not 50-50. Communication and honesty are difficult to produce.

I had a friend in high school and we were really close. She started dating a particular guy and turned away from our friendship because of it. I was really hurt and disappointed, but most of all bitter! We didn't talk for several months and during that time I asked the Lord to take away my bitterness and give me a spirit of forgiveness. The Lord taught me a lot about forgiving and not keeping feelings inside. He also made me realize that you can't depend on other people for security and happiness. If you do, you'll set yourself up for disappointment.

The Lord is the only person I can always depend on. We're all prone to make mistakes in relationships. Since then I've learned from experience in God's reality, that an intimate relationship with the Lord is the key to successful personal relationships. I think I'll make it!

For Additional Reading: Micah 7:1-7; Luke 11:5-10
Kelley, Age 20
College Student

DAY THREE ■ Luke 12:13-53

I once heard a retreat message that changed my life. The speaker was the pastor of a small church in Argentina. He described a series of events that transformed that church. He had preached a sermon on the second part of the "Greatest Commandment" in Matthew 22:34-40 and Mark 12:28-34, "Love your neighbor as yourself." Afterward, he was deeply troubled that though everyone seemed to understand his teaching, very few people in his congregation seemed to be living out that command in their lives. So the next week when he got up to preach, he started to give the exact same sermon again. When one of the people in the congregation politely pointed out to him that he had already given that message, he responded by asking what good it would do to move on to some other, probably less important, matter in the Word if they hadn't even begun to apply this critical matter in their lives first. He then restated the command, "Love your neighbor as yourself," and then he simply sat down and looked at them as though he was waiting for a response. Several times during the next few minutes, he stood up, repeated the command and then sat back down. Eventually, people began to get up and walk around and talk to each other and invite others to their homes and to open up and look for practical ways to love one another. That church was never the same.

What I learned was this: there are so many things in the Gospels that we already know how to do—we just choose not to do them. That brings us to Luke 12 and Matthew 6 where Jesus commands us "Do not worry about your life, what you will eat; or about your body, what you will wear. But seek first His kingdom and His righteousness." If you're anything like me, you don't need sermons on how to do that. We already know how; we just need to do it!

For Additional Reading: Leviticus 19:15-18; Matthew 22:34-40
Rob, Age 28
Navy Pilot

DAY FOUR ■ Luke 12:13-53

I had to go to traffic court the other day for a summons. It was a ticket for having no brake lights. But I fixed them and I wanted to see if I could get the fine lowered. The minor cases were last so I had to sit through all the other cases. Many of them were first time DUIs. One young lady who had never been arrested before spent her first night in jail and now stood before the judge to be sentenced. This poor girl was probably in a daze feeling enormous amounts of guilt and fear for the future.

As I sat and watched all this hoping the judge would be easy on her and feeling glad I was not in her place I could not help thinking of the spiritual analogy here. I was standing before God, the Judge, and the prosecutor was listing my crimes: Inconsiderate to those in need, selfish, hatred toward others, lusting after women and material things. The list went on and on and I stood in a state of total guilt and shame much worse than a drunk driver. Expecting the worst from the Judge who knew I was guilty, I braced for my punishment. Suddenly, unexpectedly He dismissed the case. Citing friendship with the family and that His Son had already taken care of those crimes, He cleared my record. What a feeling of freedom! To know that you deserved the worst punishment but were set completely free! "Whom the Son set free is free indeed!"

By the way the young lady was given a suspended sentence and my ticket was dismissed.

For Additional Reading: Psalm 7:6-11, 17; Matthew 7:1-6
Vinny, Age 34
Actor

DAY FIVE ■ Luke 12:13-53

In J.R.R. Tolkien's epic, *Lord of the Rings*, the Ring of Power gave the wearer special abilities. However, the consequences of wearing the ring were subtle. The more the owner wore the ring, the more he believed he needed it; the more greedy he

became about possessing it, and the more preoccupied and com-
pulsive he became of it and its power.

So it was with my credit card. At first I kiddingly explained
the parallel to my friends, but soon it became painfully evident
to me that there was more truth than jest in the comparison. I
had played into the world's lies—"Indeed more. More will make
me happier . . . Why wait . . . CHARGE!"

Through the discipline of a loving Father, the verses in Luke
12 have transformed from words of conviction into words of
assurance. God speaks of the complete care that He provides for
us and reminds us that life is not measured by the "things" we
possess. The ache inside which yearns for "more" can be filled
by Jesus Christ as we respond to Him with honesty and
obedience.

"For your Father has been pleased to give you the kingdom"
(Luke 12:32).

For Additional Reading: Proverbs 11:23-30; Ephesians 5:15-21
Pattie, Age 34
Speech Therapist

DAY SIX ■ Luke 12:13-53

As I walked along the oceanfront, my feet sank deeply in the
soft sand. The waves were pounding furiously, making wild
swirling motions when they broke on the beach. My heart cried
out for peace, for security, and the safety I had once known in a
relationship; yet life's reality spoke of pain, loss, and uncertainty
as evident as the sinking sand and uncontrolled surf.

Standing still, my balance was soon lost to the shifting ocean
floor. "Dear Lord," I pleaded. All the "whys" in the world
wouldn't change my circumstances. As I began to walk, sharing
my hurt with the One who I knew would understand, I looked
down the shoreline, seeing a different perspective than when I
watched the water frantically racing around my ankles. In the
distance, as far as I could see, there appeared beautiful patterns
on the beach rather than the fury of destructive tides.

"O you of little faith" (Luke 12:28). "Who of you by worrying can add a single hour to his life? Since you cannot do this very little thing, why do you worry about the rest?" (vv. 25-26) My Father has spoken clearly through this parable of the surf. He will bring meaning into these considerations we call life on earth. God's perspective of what seems to be confusing broken-ness to us, is beauty as He shapes us with loving hands. "But seek His kingdom, and these things will be given to you as well" (v. 31).

For Additional Reading: Jeremiah 18:1-11; 2 Timothy 2:20-21
Joan, Age 45
Educator, Writer

DAY SEVEN ■ Luke 12:13-53

Jesus cares about every facet of my life. He says, "Love not the things of the world but love the people." That's God's way. God loves me but He doesn't always love the things that I do. My happiness does not depend on what I possess but whom I possess in my heart and whom I profess before men. God called the man in Luke 12:20 a fool because:

● He forgot God
● He was self-centered (I, me, mine)
● His surplus was his security
● He planned for time, not for eternity—he thought he had plenty of time
● He was not rich toward God.

The fool's attitude is to, "Work as if you are going to live forever, live as if you were going to die tomorrow."

Semper Paratus—"Always be prepared." That is the motto of the Coast Guard. And, as the Coast Guard, God admonishes us to be ready when Jesus returns for His own. Only God knows when. How am I using the time God has allowed me? What did God mean when He said to redeem the time? (see Eph. 5:16) I must make the most of my opportunities to share God's plan of salvation with family, friends, and neighbors. "Now that you know these things, you will be blessed if you do them" (John 13:17).

For Additional Reading: Ecclesiastes 3:9-14; Colossians 4:2-6
Elizabeth, Age 86
Retired Teacher

WEEK TWENTY-SIX
■ ■ ■ ■

ARE YOU WILLING?
BE HEALED!

TEXT FOR THE WEEK: **JOHN 5:1-18**

KEY VERSE: JOHN 5:8   "Then Jesus said to him, 'Get up!
Pick up your mat and walk.' "

DAY ONE ■ Commentary on John 5:1-18

Did our Lord meet the need of everyone He met? Sadly, He did not. He could have, and very much wanted to, but in many instances there was a barrier to His healing touch. In order for Jesus to make a difference, there first has to be a willingness in our hearts to respond to the power He freely offers. The Apostle John shares a remarkable and beautiful story that illustrates this truth so clearly. Read John 5:1-18 carefully.

The Question of the Story—Do you want to get well? (v. 6) Imagine how the man could have reacted to this question. Jesus did not ask if he wanted to "feel" better. He offered complete and total healing. I know some people who seem to enjoy wallowing in their pain. It's a fair question. You can get used to being dependent after being paralyzed for 38 years! It is significant that our Lord asks a question of this person rather than just simply saying, "Be healed!"

The Command of the Story—"Get up! Pick up your mat and walk" (v. 8). The obvious human response to this might have been, "I can't get up. Don't You see I'm paralyzed?" Yet the man exercises incredible faith and rises. Notice there are actually three commands from Jesus: "Get up," "Pick up," and "Walk." The man appropriates power from Jesus and acts on it. Whenever we say we can't, we won't. The power is nevertheless there to do great things.

The Warning of the Story—"See, you are well again. Stop sinning or something worse may happen to you" (v. 14). There is something far worse than being paralyzed for 38 years. That would be going back into bondage after being set free. Not everyone was happy about this miracle. The religious legalists pointed out that in carrying his bed, the man was breaking the Sabbath Law. The teaching here is simply that beneficiaries of Christ's grace need to faithfully follow a life of obedience and discipleship.

The Hope of the Story—"Jesus said, 'My Father is always at His work to this very day, and I, too, am working' " (v. 17). The good news in this story is that God is still in the miracle business. Sometimes Christians have a hard time seeing evidence of the Holy Spirit's work around us. Yet, Jesus never gives up on us, no matter what!

So the same question is asked today, "Do you want to be whole?" "Will you trust Me?" "Will you let Me fill you with My power?" "Will you?"

For Additional Reading: Psalm 147:1-11; Matthew 9:1-8
Bill Flanagan is the Minister with Single Adults at St. Andrew's Presbyterian Church in Newport Beach, California. Six single adults from Bill's ministry write the following personal applications.

DAY TWO ■ John 5:1-18

"Thirty-eight years! How unproductive, and what a waste of someone's life," I thought. "All these people waiting for years for something to happen!"

Then I recalled that for better than a decade of my adult life I felt that I had put God on a shelf. I still believed, but some things had to happen before I could rise again to be a man of faith, seeking God's will and calling. I eventually came to the realization that I had really been putting *myself* on the shelf.

We can mislead ourselves into waiting for marriage, a better job, or health to "happen" to us. *Then* we'll be whole and happy

and can move on with our lives. Situations don't rescue us—
only God does when we respond to Him.

The option to get up and walk and be His man or woman is
always there for us, regardless of our situation. Jesus calls you
and me to a life of purpose and completeness *as single people.*
Let's not wait.

For Additional Reading: Isaiah 53:4-12; Luke 5:17-26
John, Age 47
Psychologist

DAY THREE ■ John 5:1-18

Do you want to get well?"
What do You mean? I'm doing great! Couldn't be happier. Things are going well and I have everything I could want: a
good job, nice car, lots of friends, a nice home. I'm respected
and people enjoy being around me. There's nothing I'd want to
change.

"Do you want to get well?"

Why do You ask that? There's nothing wrong with me! I'm a
success, not some cripple whose home was the side of a "healing
pool." I've worked hard to get ahead in life, and though I'm not
at the top, I'm enjoying the view from my current position.

"Do you want to get well?"

Sometimes I can do a pretty good job of fooling myself that I
have things all together and that there's nothing wrong with me.
To be honest, I don't like recognizing there are needs in my life
I can't control and admitting that I have to be dependent on
God. But there are, and I do. One of the things I most appreciate about God is His patient love for me. No matter how un-
faithful or stubborn I am, no matter how blind I can be to the
needs in my life, God doesn't take no for an answer and leave
me. Instead, He patiently waits for those moments when my
defenses break down—the times when I see the emptiness in my
life and feel the hurt and recognize I don't have it all together
and that I very much need His healing hand in my life and. . . .

"Do you want to get well?"
Yes, Lord, I do.

For Additional Reading: Exodus 15:22-27; James 5:13-16
John, Age 30
Singles Associate

DAY FOUR ■ John 5:1-18

When Jesus asks the man if he wants to be made whole, the man answers that he does, but circumstances have prevented him from being able to be healed.

Sometimes I live my life as though my circumstances dictate whether I can be healed, or that the circumstances themselves prevent my being healed. I expect to be made whole by the right job, the right mate, or by leading the right kind of life. I once thought that being complete, being healed was something I was to attempt on my own, maybe with His help, but still I was responsible for it. But I've discovered that I can't heal myself, and neither can anyone or anything else in this world.

Only Jesus can make me whole. And I only need accept His invitation to do so. He doesn't require that I be without sin before He chooses to make me whole. And when I yield to Christ, He heals me, then asks for my love and obedience. I live my life according to God's commandments because I have been made whole by Him—not in order to be healed.

For Additional Reading: Psalm 79:8-13; Luke 5:12-16
Ellen, Age 31
Systems Analyst

DAY FIVE ■ John 5:1-18

Out of the hundreds of people gathered at the pool, one man was chosen. Why was *he* the one chosen? What was his background? Did he have a wife and children? Had he divorced his wife? Had he never married? Had he any friends? What had he done to make Jesus say, "Do not sin as you did before?" So many questions to be answered, but are the answers really important? Wasn't the man just one lost soul hungering after "wholeness"? Jesus had picked him out of the crowd. He loved him as a father hearing his son's cries of pain.

This story shows us we must be ready to recognize Jesus' power to forgive and heal. Anywhere, anytime, our Saviour may pick us out of a crowd and make us an example of His power. He never gives up on us. We must also trust Him.

For Additional Reading: 2 Kings 5:1-16; Luke 19:1-10
Dorothy, Retired
Secretary

DAY SIX ■ John 5:1-18

Recently I read a health article that discussed how doctors classify patients who do and do not follow their advice. We are either compliant or noncompliant. Most of the rest of the article was directed to the excuses we use for not following doctors' instructions.

I knew immediately that I am "compliant" as far as my doctor is concerned. If I ask his advice I give it a try.

This set me to thinking about the excuses I use with Jesus. Often in the rush of everyday life my excuse is nothing more than time. I need to rely more on His Word. God the Father and His Son Jesus are *always* working on my behalf (v. 17). I need to be as compliant with Him as with my own doctor.

For Additional Reading: Hosea 14:4-9; Luke 5:17-26
Nancy, Age 56
Teacher

DAY SEVEN ■ John 5:1-18

One who was there had been an invalid for thirty-eight years" (v. 5). This passage reminds me of the virtue of patience and faith. For over one third of a century this man had been so physically crippled he could not walk. He had to be carried on a mat and helped into the pool. Yet he hoped for a miraculous cure and received it.

"See, you are well again. Stop sinning or something worse may happen to you" (v. 14). Jesus reminds us that even though He knows we are not above sin, He expects us to make every effort to avoid it. The repentant sinner who tries to lead a good life is forgiven, other sinners may have "something worse happening to them." A message from a loving God, but also one from a just God. Once again Jesus lets us know that we are not to go on in sin, but in love and goodness.

For Additional Reading: Psalm 41:1-12; 1 John 3:4-10
Robert, Age 57
Retired, Writer

WEEK TWENTY-SEVEN
■ ■ ■ ■

A COURSE IN GARDENING

TEXT FOR THE WEEK: **JOHN 15:1-27**

KEY VERSE: JOHN 15:4   "Remain in Me, and I will remain in
                              you. No branch can bear fruit by it-
                              self; it must remain in the vine. Nei-
                              ther can you bear fruit unless you re-
                              main in Me."

DAY ONE ■ Commentary on John 15:1-8

As Jesus taught His disciples the words of John 15, we must keep in mind that He was on His way to Gethsemane. It would be in the garden place that He would pray to the Father and willfully commit His life to the cross for our sins. The counsel that He gives here is of deepest concern and greatest importance. So, these final hours of teaching His disciples had to be some of the tenderest moments for our Lord Jesus and those who knew Him best.

In this chapter of John's Gospel we see three very great lessons from the Chief Gardener. There is a lesson on "Affection" (vv. 9-17) and a lesson on "Adversity" (vv. 18-27). However, this devotional will focus on the first lesson, "Abiding" (vv. 1-8).

For the child of God there can be no greater lesson than learning to abide in Christ. The results of our ministry will be determined by this condition. The closer we abide with the Lord the more fruitful we will be and the more contented we will be in His service.

The Lord Jesus says in verse 1, "I am the true Vine and My Father is the Gardener." This reveals the source of all blessings. God is the Gardener and Christ is the true Vine. In our world, there are many other things that claim to be vines. Every false religion and movement in the world tries to be a vine, but only

Christ is the true Vine. Jesus is the true source for our life.

In relation to this, we are the branches on (or in) the vine. That happens when we invite Christ into our lives as Saviour and Lord. In verse 2 we discover that God will not put up with an unproductive branch for long. We will be given our chance and then if we do not produce, He will cut us off. The productive branches are pruned so that they will be more productive. At times, this pruning process can be very painful, but we know that it is for our growth and productivity.

Now we are clean and ready to grow (v. 3). This cleansing process must be referring to the group. In 13:10, Jesus said, "And you are clean, though not every one of you." This is an awesome condition for our groups as we come together as friends and believers in Christ. Might we all be involved in the cleansing process as we stand before our Lord, accountable to each other.

Christ's advice is to all of us. In 15:4-5 we hear that we cannot survive on our own. A branch severed from a tree is obviously not going to bear fruit or grow. And neither will we if we are not dependent and abiding (remaining) in Christ. To not be severed is to remain. We must stay, remain, abide! Our "success" is in Him and Him alone.

The abiding relationship in Christ results in a wonderful promise and hope. The promise covers everything and anything. The promise is answer to prayer. It is a promise of having all that we need from the true Vine. The branch that abides in the Vine will receive a portion of all that is in the Vine. The life, nutrients, and nature of the Vine flow into the branches. It is then that our Father in heaven is glorified.

So, lets abide together with Christ. And we will bring fruit into this world, receive answers to prayers, and bring great glory to God.

For Additional Reading: Psalm 33:1-5; Hebrews 1:8-12
Billy Miller is the Education and Outreach Pastor at Metro Heights Baptist Church in Stockbridge, Georgia. The following are six applications from John 15.

DAY TWO ■ John 15:1-8

Our devotional today deals with love. It all begins with God's love for us. Also, love is the greatest motive for living the Christian life. In John 15 we can discover many precious things about God's love for us and how we are to love each other.

Again, God loves us (v. 9). This is so simple, yet so profound. Jesus loves us in the same way that His Father in heaven loves Him. Because Jesus was loved by God, He in turn loves us.

And we are to continue this love pattern. So our verse in life can read, "As the Father loves Jesus, and as Jesus loves me, I now love you in the same way."

Now, if we are going to keep this cycle of God's love flowing to others, we need to obey God's Word, the Bible (v. 10). If we do not, then we miss out on discovering God's love for us. The result is the absence of real love coming from us to others.

But, if we do obey God's Word, abide in Him, and share God's love, His joy will be ours (v. 11). That is the joy that we are looking for during the tough days of loneliness or heartache. It is God's love and joy that lifts us up when we have fallen on our faces and we need to look into the face of our Lord. It is His love and joy that keeps us going and His love and joy flowing through us will keep others going as well.

For Additional Reading: Psalm 31:23-24;
1 Thessalonians 1:6-12

DAY THREE ■ John 15:1-8

Loving each other is not just a nice idea from God. It is not just a simple suggestion to be blessed in the Christian life. It is not an option. But, it is a requirement by God (v. 12).

Yes, God wants us to love each other the same way that He loves us. Now that seems overwhelming. But it need not be if we understand how He loves us.

Verse 13 is one of the first indicators of how Jesus Christ loves us. He gave His life for us. That seems like so much. It is.

But that is how God showed His love for us and by giving of ourselves to others we do what God wants us to do.

How can you give? What can you give? When can you give? These are the questions that our Lord is asking. You see, we do not need to wonder, "What is the return?" We have already been paid in full, up front by Jesus from the cross. Now out of Christ's love for us, we are to love those who are difficult to love. We are to love, with Christ's love, those who have hurt us and made our lives very difficult.

God bless you as you love with tough love, today. Make a new friend today. Love him or her with Jesus' love, the giving way.

For Additional Reading: Malachi 1:1-5; Romans 5:6-8

DAY FOUR ■ John 15:1-8

Of all of the people in the world that God could have chosen to be His children, He chose you! That is almost incomprehensible. And what is even more unbelievable is that He wants us to bear fruit for Him. This is God's wonderful purpose for us as members of His family. This is His ultimate goal for us.

So often we all wonder what is our purpose in life. Here it is. God wants us to be fruitbearers. He wants us to carry to others the fruit of His Spirit. He wants us to be the growers and suppliers to those who are hungry and in need of nourishment. What a thrill. What a joy. What a marvelous purpose.

Bearing fruit is one of the most bonding factors that two believers could ever experience. There are so many who need you to supply some good news or good fruit for them. Bearing God's fruit of righteousness has all of the built-in emotions of childbearing. One Christian bearing fruit to or for another, is a dynamic that brings new life that should last for all eternity. It is the ultimate picture of caring for each other. It is often the ultimate picture of one sacrificially giving to another. So plant, water, and let God bring the increase.

For Additional Reading: Hosea 14:1-3; Matthew 3:8-10

DAY FIVE ■ John 15:1-8

On the way to Gethsemane, Jesus continues to teach His disciples the important things that they need to know. He now teaches them about adversity. He knows that His disciples will be hated by the world. Jesus teaches them how to best face the adversity that will be theirs. He prepares them for the rough journey ahead.

Jesus comforts the disciples in the middle of a major crisis (He is leaving them) by reminding them that the abuse that they will take is not their fault. Jesus takes full responsibility for the tough days that will take place. His encouragement is:

- Jesus is their fellow Companion.
- Jesus is one with them through these tough days.
- They are not of this world.
- They can share with Christ in their suffering.
- They will suffer because God is at work in them and they belong to Him.

These are powerfully positive statements to hang on to when others create painful situations for us. These truths from Jesus will sustain us through times of persecution from others when we would just love to give up. But don't! Hang in there by hanging on to Jesus.

For Additional Reading: Lamentations 1:12-22; 1 John 2:15-17

DAY SIX ■ John 15:1-8

In John 15 we have discovered that Jesus wants to have an abiding relationship with us. He is committed to our growth and nourishment. He wants to answer our prayers. He desires for us to bear fruit. These are wonderful thoughts. Yet, they come with the world of reality.

That reality is couched by a world filled with sin. Our world is filled with hatred because of a lack of knowledge of God (v. 21). Also, because the world is convicted of their sin and separation from God, they have turned in hatred for God and everyone who knows and loves God. We could respond, "It isn't fair to be hated for righteousness." But the world of sin is not fair.

So our response to the world's hate for us needs to come from Jesus. We do not need a sinful world to validate our worth. We do not need men separated from God trying to determine whether we have value or not. We are the King's kids! We are more valuable than anything. We are worth the price of Christ's life. So let's not feel condemned by hate, but loved by Christ.

For Additional Reading: Psalm 6:1-5; 1 John 4:19-21

DAY SEVEN ■ John 15:1-8

Jesus is planning to leave His disciples, but not alone. He will not be around to walk through the villages and towns anymore, but they will not walk alone. He will not be there to work the miracles that they had previously witnessed, but they will not be powerless. He will not be there to speak to them with words of wisdom, but they will not be without truth.

The Holy Spirit is coming, Jesus assured the disciples. You will not be alone. And that is true for each of us today. God's Spirit enters our lives at salvation, when we invite Jesus into our lives to be our Saviour and Lord. Life changes. We become brand new. A difference is seen.

The Holy Spirit is called our Comforter. He does just that. When a day ends with disaster, the Holy Spirit is there to comfort. He takes away our hatred for the struggles of life and reminds us of His fruit, which begins with love. When direction is needed or a decision must be made, He is there to guide and provide. When we are in need of help and hope, He is there with a reply from His Word and a supply from His storehouse.

We are not alone. We have a Comforter, every day. We have a Counselor, at no extra charge. We have a Teacher who does not fail us for mistakes and wrong answers. We have the Holy Spirit of God abiding in us.

For Additional Reading: Isaiah 44:1-5; John 6:63-65

WEEK TWENTY-EIGHT

■ ■ ■ ■

ENCOURAGEMENT OUT OF UNITY

TEXT FOR THE WEEK: ACTS 4:32-37

KEY VERSE: ACTS 4:32   "All the believers were one in heart
                                                          and mind."

DAY ONE ■ Commentary on Acts 4:32-37

I had just gotten back into jogging (or should I say exaggerated walking) following a two-year layoff. I entered a five kilometer race right away. I figured that would provide me with the incentive I needed to get back on track. However, at the half-way point (one and one half miles), I realized why I had not been jogging the past two years. I was in pain! Every muscle in my body was begging to stop. My lungs were gasping for relief, and I was sure everyone could see my heart pounding through my T-shirt. I knew then that I would never finish the race. So I did it. I stopped.

It was at that point I heard him. I ignored him at first because I didn't think he was talking to me. But then he pulled up alongside me and started walking with me. I had no idea who he was. Short, stubby, and bald, he was an unlikely candidate to pose as a runner. He asked again, "What are you stopping for?" And before I could answer, he suggested a strategy for finishing the race. He proposed that we run the remainder of the race together, each one encouraging the other. He was very persistent and wouldn't take no for an answer. So we worked ourselves up to a fast walk and then eventually a respectable jogging pace. We ran the remainder of the race side-by-side, mutually encouraging one another.

As we crossed the finish line together, a tremendous sense of gratitude overwhelmed me. For this modern-day Barnabas, whose life intersected mine at the halfway point of a 5K race, had offered me the encouragement I needed to pick up the pace and finish the race that I had started. Without his encouragement I would have given up. I would have quit.

The verses of Scripture for today's devotional indicate there must have been a number of Barnabases (both male and female) in the early church. One writer has labeled those referred to in Acts 4:32-37 as the "Barnabas Bunch." They were a community of encouragers. They supported one another, the wealthier members making provision for the poorer. And as a result, we read that "there were no needy persons among them."

As we take this Scripture and allow it to speak to us today, I believe it will challenge us to look more closely at those who are "needy"—the "needy" being those who are living in the slums emotionally and relationally as well as the economically impoverished. For some of the most "needy" individuals in our singles groups are those who feel they're running life's race alone. They need a Barnabas to run up alongside of them and say, "Don't give up, I'll join you in the race. Together we'll make it." Who in your life needs a visit from Barnabas? And could you be that instrument of encouragement to one who is ready to drop out of the race? I think so! So go to it "Son" or "Daughter of Encouragement."

For Additional Reading: Isaiah 1:16-17; Acts 2:42-47
Rick Eastman is the Singles Minister at Bethany First Church of the Nazarene in Bethany, Oklahoma. Three single men and three single women from Bethany First Church write the daily applications.

DAY TWO ■ Acts 4:32-37

I found Acts 4:32 to be true in the church I am now attending. For it was during a transition period in my life that I began searching for a church home.

Upon an invitation from a friend, I visited a church which was quite large. I was unsure as to how comfortable I would be in such a large church. However, I soon discovered a group of believers there who really cared about each other.

Through their encouragement and support, I came to know God in a more personal way. I know now that He is always there with me and will help me whenever I am in need. He used this "Barnabas Bunch" to show me that I really did matter to others and to God, and it caused me to feel good about myself.

It was through their encouragement that I found a place, not only in a singles group, but in the family of God. Ephesians 2:19 really sums up the result of what happened to me when a caring group of people reached out and touched my lonely heart. My own paraphrase of this verse simply says, "You are no longer a stranger, but a friend."

For Additional Reading: Psalm 133:1-3; Romans 12:9-16
Darrel, Age 42
Accounting Supervisor

DAY THREE ■ Acts 4:32-37

How do we define "a person in need"? Most of the time we would say it is someone who doesn't have all the monetary essentials of life like food or clothing. But sometimes we forget the child who needs to be loved for who he is and not what he looks like or accomplishes. We forget the lonely, elderly person who needs a word of encouragement or a hug. We forget our coworkers who need to be told they're doing a good job. We forget the strangers who just need a kind word and a smile. The Lord tells us to give to those in need and yet sometimes we fail to give the thing that costs the least—ourselves. So, as you're going through your day, look around you. There are needy people everywhere who need what you have to give.

For Additional Reading: Psalm 10:12-17;
1 Thessalonians 4:7-12
Tyler, Age 27
Graphic Designer

DAY FOUR ■ Acts 4:32-37

She was part of the team. We had begun work together along with our other colleagues initiating a new adolescent chemical treatment center. Her role was that of primary counselor. Mary Ann, at the age of 40, was divorced with two daughters. But now, at 50, she was meeting the greatest challenge of her life.

I remember walking into her office, sitting at the chair beside her desk, for what I thought would be one of our enjoyable afternoon chats. It was then she proceeded to tell me of her newly discovered malignancy. Little did we know that in the months to follow she would become our "Barnabas in Affliction" (see Acts 4:36). Paul's explanation of administering encouragement in our affliction in 2 Corinthians 12:7-10 was lived out in her life.

Mary Ann allowed her family, friends, patients, and fellow employees to walk this journey with her and her Christ. The journey included hope, despair, joy, and tears. But above all else, there was the powerful presence of God as she confronted her pain, brokenness, and limitation.

A few days before her death she was talking to her pastor and stated: "The thief almost stole my joy and peace today, but I reminded him . . . God said he couldn't." The melody of her life continues to live on in the lives of those who knew her . . . she was our Barnabas in Affliction.

For Additional Reading: Isaiah 61:1-3; 1 Thessalonians 2:6-9, 17-20
Dan, Age 40
Pastoral Care Coordinator
Chemical Dependency Center

DAY FIVE ■ Acts 4:32-37

Trust Me." These words often have swirled through my mind as I have had to reevaluate priorities, face situations never before faced, and realign a budget that simply refused realignment!

Suddenly, a single mother of a college freshman and a high school sophomore, I often felt our mother/daughter roles were switched. Daily pressures and unexpected emergencies would overwhelm me. However, my daughters would keep me going, with their simple trust in God.

Looking back, I can see God putting a Barnabas in our lives at the right times. When the transmission went out on our only car, an old friend "happened" along and took charge of the towing and the cost of repairs. The summer the central air compressor decided to "die," a Christian businessman prayed and replaced it below cost.

Daily, I'm learning to put total trust in the Lord. I'm thankful He never leaves us alone.

For Additional Reading: Nahum 1:2-7; 1 Corinthians 12:4-7, 12-27
Jadean, Age 47
University Secretary

DAY SIX ■ Acts 4:32-37

I know what it's like to feel you're running life's race alone. There probably isn't a more lonely feeling in the world. I remember feeling that way about one year after my college graduation. It was the most emotionally and spiritually dry time of my life.

During this time, a "Barnabas" came into my life. She spent time with me, saw beneath the surface, and cared enough to find out who I was, and what I was all about. Only then was she able to become the encourager that I needed. This was not a quick process.

Encouragement takes time, and it requires a commitment to follow through to the end. Discouraging someone takes far less effort. All it takes is an insensitive or insincere word, or ignoring a need. It's easy! My friend could have patted me on the back and said, "Just hang in there. You'll be OK." Thankfully, she chose to be a "Barnabas." She didn't take the easy way out.

Look around you today. Ask God to show you how you can be a solid, committed friend to someone struggling with discouragement.

For Additional Reading: Exodus 17:10-13; Romans 12:3-8
Lisa, Age 26
Downtown Revitalization Director

DAY SEVEN ■ Acts 4:32-37

In today's society, materialism is constantly tempting us to believe that there is happiness and satisfaction in having "things." In reading Acts 4:32-37, I wonder if it was easy for this group of early believers to give all they had, or did they struggle with the temptation to hold on to their "things"? (We see in chap. 5 that some did indeed struggle to give it all.)

In my own life, the challenge of giving is not always a financial one. Giving friendship, encouragement, and especially giving my time is sometimes a struggle. It is difficult to give to others when I have so much to worry about in my own life; but just as God blessed the "Barnabas Bunch" ("much grace was upon them all, there were no needy persons among them," 4:33-34), He is faithful to meet my needs also. The challenge of giving is to take your eyes off of yourself and allow God to meet your needs (Matt. 6:28-34). He is faithful!

For Additional Reading: Isaiah 63:7-9; Luke 6:37-38
Michael, Age 23
Graphic Designer

WEEK TWENTY-NINE
■ ■ ■ ■

PRAYER WORKS. KEEP PRAYING

TEXT FOR THE WEEK: **ACTS 12:1-17**

KEY VERSE: ACTS 12:5   "So Peter was kept in prison, but the
church was earnestly praying to God
for him."

DAY ONE ■ Commentary on Acts 12:1-17

In Acts 12, Peter was in deep trouble. King Herod put him in prison to await trail.

And the people of God, the church, began to earnestly pray for Peter.

The night before the trial, Peter was sleeping between two soldiers, bound in chains, with two sentries at the door. An angel of the Lord suddenly appeared, the chains fell off, the iron gate opened, and Peter silently escaped, moving past the guards into the streets of the city.

The people of God, not knowing what had happened, continued to pray.

Peter went to the house where they were praying and knocked on the door. Rhoda recognized his voice. Some thought it was his angel. Still others were astonished to see him. Peter then silenced them and described how the Lord had brought him out of prison.

Isn't it a wonderful thought to know that God really does answer prayer?

What sort of trouble are you in today? What kind of prison do you find yourself in right now? What chains are shackling you from the freedom to do what God wants you to do? What gates have to be opened to allow you to move in the direction God wants you to go?

I recently led a singles mission trip to Trinidad. We needed to get into a school for a special goodwill project. I prayed. We prayed. He opened those doors, and we went in. We needed opportunities to evangelize. I prayed. We prayed. He provided those opportunities on planes, in hospitals, and on the streets. Several people were freed from the prison of sin, as they personally accepted the Lord Jesus Christ.

Keep on praying. It really works! You may not see it right now, but God is working at this very moment. Working to answer your prayer, for His glory, and for your best interest within His will.

Be faithful, be clean, be obedient. And by the way, don't be afraid to look for the answers to those prayers, or be surprised when you see that He really does answer them.

Prayer works. It really works! We serve a very great and good and powerful and loving God who is eager and willing and able to answer our prayers. Will you come to Him and trust Him to work in your life today?

For Additional Reading: Job 22:21-28; John 16:22-24
Larry D. Coufal is the Director of Singles 30+ Ministries at The Chapel in Akron, Ohio. Six singles from The Chapel write the following.

DAY TWO ■ Acts 12:1-17

As a woman struggling through the anguish of divorce, barrenness, aloneness, physical exhaustion, emotional fatigue, home responsibilities, and struggles with my job, God has heard my prayers. He knows the needs and desires of our hearts. When we open our hearts to the Lord and pray without ceasing to know His will, He hears and answers our prayers.

My prayer life consists of the "CATS" approach. First is Confession: as a sinner I need to confess my sin, ask for forgiveness, and to forgive. Next is Adoration: to praise and glorify our sovereign, loving Lord and Saviour. Then Thanksgiving: for all the gifts our Lord gives us, such as faith, hope, love, people, possessions, time, and the miracle of blessings. And finally Supplication: where we seem to be most of the time, God intervening for our needs and (His) desires for our lives.

For Additional Reading: Psalm 100:1-5; John 14:11-14
Joanne, Age 43
Certified Registered Nurse, Anesthetist

DAY THREE ■ Acts 12:1-17

As a professional salesman, it was necessary that I knew and was convinced in my mind and heart of the truth and benefits of any product or service I was involved with. The Lord convinced me on one momentous day 27 years ago that He was *real* and that I needed Him. I prayed the sinner's prayer and became born again.

Life since that time has not been a bed of roses for me. There have been good times and bad, difficult and heartrending times, but prayer works and keeps me moving forward. Prayer in my life has kept me from destroying myself when my marriage failed, when my family split, when most of my possessions were taken away and when I had nothing left but clothes, furniture, and a 10-year-old car. Since that time, He has brought a godly woman into my life. He has done so much more, both great and small. God answers prayer.

For Additional Reading: Psalm 50:14-15; Mark 11:22-25
Ward, Age 67
Real Estate Broker

DAY FOUR ■ Acts 12:1-17

I went through a time when I did not feel needed anymore. Fortunately, I started reading books on prayer in my times alone. That is when God showed me not only what an impact prayer can make in my life, but in the lives of others. The world is full of hurting people with needs that the Lord wants me to pray for. I can pray that His perfect will be done in their lives, that He gives them the Spirit of Truth, that He protects them from the evil one, and much more.

I have given up the helpless feeling that "there's nothing I can do," and replaced it with the peace of knowing that my prayers are in the hands of my Almighty God. Intercessory prayer makes me feel needed again in a special way. I thank Him for the privilege of being able to pray and for His grace to faithfully continue.

For Additional Reading: 1 Samuel 12:18-25; Ephesians 6:18-20
Diana, Age 43
Chiropractic Assistant

DAY FIVE ■ Acts 12:1-17

I have searched for an understanding of how this invisible, unpredictable, powerful process called prayer works, but find only the reality that it does work.

I would prefer that prayer worked like a vending machine—push the button and receive. Certain prayers have been answered that quickly. Sometimes, though, the results have become visible only after a process similar to the cycles of a washing machine. Other times, the prayer process works like my heating and humidifying system. I turn it on with a request and the sensing device triggers the power at just the time it is needed.

The most mysterious answers to prayer are those unexpected blessings that seem to come with no effort on my part; like a life-support system that saves a helpless child in an emergency room.

The mystery remains. Prayer is not a machine to be controlled by me, but to be participated in by me with my Lord.

For Additional Reading: Psalm 65:1-7; 1 Peter 3:8-12
Sally, Age 46
Elementary Education Teacher

DAY SIX ■ Acts 12:1-17

Galatians 6:9 says to "not become weary in doing good." I had always thought it meant to keep on doing good, to obey the Lord, and not allow yourself to be discouraged. I still believe it means all of these things, but in recent months I have begun to believe it also applies to prayer.

We have concerns in our lives that we constantly bring to the Lord because they are heavy on our hearts. David talked about "pouring out his heart" to God. But sometimes it gets "wearisome" pouring out the same things. That's where the latter part of this verse comes in; it says, "We will reap a harvest if we do not give up."

It's hard to wait, but God's Word tells us that if we are asking according to *His* will, He hears us and we have what we are requesting. Be not weary in praying, because there will be reaping.

For Additional Reading: Job 42:10-17; Acts 4:24-30
Jan, Age 43
Senior Records Clerk

DAY SEVEN ■ Acts 12:1-17

While reading James 5:16, the word "fervent" caught my attention. I wondered what praying fervently really meant. One definition defines it as showing great emotion or warmth; glowing.

Meditating on this verse of Scripture and my personal prayer life, I came to the conclusion that one way we can view prayer is like a warm blanket on a cold, wintry night. Nothing feels quite like it (except maybe waterbeds for those of you who own one).

Going to the Lord in fervent prayer, thinking His thoughts, through His Spirit, and being in the center of His will brings a warmth during the storms of life, or during the daily routine of life, covering us with a sense of His presence and love. Prayer is the answer.

As you come to our loving, Heavenly Father, think of prayer as His covering over you to protect, energize, renew, and restore. The warmth of your time with the Lord will carry you through the day or night.

Make it a priority in your life to get "glowing" with the Lord. It works!

For Additional Reading: Jeremiah 33:1-6; 1 Timothy 2:1-8
Betty, Age 40
Director of Meetings and Promotions

WEEK THIRTY

■ ■ ■ ■

STRUGGLING? STRENGTH AVAILABLE

TEXT FOR THE WEEK: **ROMANS 5:1-11**

KEY VERSE: ROMANS 5:3   "Not only so, but we also rejoice in
                                 our sufferings, because we know that
                                 suffering produces perseverance."

DAY ONE ■ Commentary on Romans 5:3-5

Amazing! Writing to a church that lives under the threat of daily persecution, Paul tells us that we are to rejoice in our sufferings. Why? Because it is through our suffering that we develop perseverance, character, and hope. Why is it that Paul seemingly dares us to boast about our afflictions?

First, we must look back to verses 1-2. It is God who took the initiative "through our Lord Jesus Christ" to accept us into a relationship with Him. In this new relationship, we are completely reconciled to God and, because our spirits are no longer in rebellion against His, we can now enjoy an inner sense of peace.

Second, we now have access to God. By virtue of His initiative of love, we can approach Him without needing a human intercessor, and each of us can have a personal relationship with God. That's "the grace in which we stand."

Third, our hope does not just lie in the present, with all its troubles, but in a future time when Christ returns and we will appear with Him in glory (Col. 3:4).

Paul goes on to tell us to not only boast about our new relationship with God, but to also boast in our times of suffering and affliction. Because it is in those times that we develop endurance, patience, and perseverance. A strong perseverance that inevitably results in a person of godly character; tried, prov-

198

en, and approved. A character which is clearly marked by an attitude of hope; a committed expectation of our own glory in Christ which never shames or humiliates us before others. Therefore, our trials should not be viewed as a time when God is punishing us, but a time when He is building within us the strength and character that brings honor to Him.

And so, Paul says it is because of God's initiative that we have peace with Him, stand in His favor, and possess an attitude of hope that is so strong that it permits us to literally boast about our trials. He has poured out and continues to pour out His magnificent love into our hearts through the Holy Spirit. That is what enables us to live lives of hope and to stand fast in times of trouble. We can hold our heads high no matter what is going on around us because we are surrounded by and filled with God's love, knowing a "peace which passes all understanding" and a deep, abiding hope.

What suffering have you experienced and what did God teach you through it?

For Additional Reading: Jeremiah 31:16-20; Matthew 24:9-13 **Woodleigh H. Volland** is the Singles Minister at St. Stephen's Episcopal Church in Sewickley, Pennsylvania. The following six applications are written by single adults from St. Stephen's.

DAY TWO ■ Romans 5:3-5

My first high school teaching job sent me home in a heap of tears daily. This was not what I had expected because I knew God had put me there. Circumstances had made it obvious that I was to accept the position. Why would He do this to me? Had I misunderstood Him?

My dignity was systematically being destroyed by students who would not accept me, anything I stood for, or any effort I made. Spending five hours on a lesson plan, getting a guest speaker, or developing field trips only produced more snide remarks and surly attitudes. Nasty things whispered behind my back would cut me like a knife.

Each day I would pray out loud as I drove to work that I could make it through one more day. I would picture angels standing in each corner of the room, granting me wisdom to deal with angry students from abusive, broken homes who were using me as their scapegoat. "God! Help me to not take this personally," I would cry out and keep on going.

It started to come clear. The very problems and trials that puzzled me were actually good for me (v. 3). I learned to lean on God every step of the way, even to pray for the students who hated me most. It was the only way to survive. That's how I came to learn. God does not always keep us from difficulty but He will always keep us through it.

For Additional Reading: Job 5:1-16; Matthew 5:43-48
Susan, Age 25
College Recruiter

DAY THREE ■ Romans 5:3-5

The first time I remember reading this passage, I was in the midst of a divorce. Now left to raise three children alone, losing the one person I believed would always be there, I had to decide how I would respond to my situation. What did I want my life to be like? What character in me did I want to become evident? Who was I, apart from this man?

I read and reread Romans 5:3-5. As I clung to this passage for hope, I found the promises that through these times of suffering we develop a new strength, not our own, but one that comes from acknowledging that God is in charge. We develop perseverance.

Years later I look back at that time and passage and see the truth that is written. My life has taken a different course, one I would not have chosen, one that never would have occurred without that time of loss. People tell me I am a different person now. I know it is true. God strengthened me during a time of loss, taught me to depend on Him and has given me the gift to be able to reach out and guide others in like situations to a new hope and strength as well.

I have had other times of suffering since then, but when suffering comes so does new growth; with it an increased reliance on God. When trouble comes, I continue to feel the physical and emotional pain, but I can also rejoice in the knowledge that no matter what happens, I have the strength of the Holy Spirit, which comes from God's gracious love, to carry me through.

For Additional Reading: Isaiah 49:5-7; 1 Peter 2:19-25
Sandi, Age 39
Manager of Oncology Nursing

DAY FOUR ■ Romans 5:3-5

The year 1988/89 was the longest of my life. At 28 years old, I had settled down into my chosen profession of education, was involved in a relationship that was the best I had ever had and would never think of asking for more. The Lord began to move ever so slowly at first but eventually led me to start my own business. The Lord was changing my life in many ways and the support I had from Mary, my girlfriend, was great. We began to talk of marriage and our future together. She was in law school, out of state, and the relationship was stronger than ever. What more could a young Christian guy ask for? A great Christian woman who loved him with all of her heart, a new growing business that was going nowhere but up. Surely God was pleased.

I had given more of myself than I ever had. But, He wanted more and started by prying my fingers away from Mary. She left me for a fellow student, and I was devastated. My only thought was, "Dear God, surely You have made a mistake!" He didn't. In the last year my great and loving Saviour has taught me more about His love and goodness for me than I ever thought possible. I have so much peace knowing that He loves me and is only going to give me the very best for my life. My parent's can't, Mary couldn't, and my business will never be able to give me the "peace which passes all understanding."

The last year of my life has been very difficult. But with Jesus' love, I would go through it all over again. Because having access to God through Christ is not a warm fuzzy feeling but the secure knowledge that He will never leave me or forsake me. My family may all let me down and my business may fall flat, but my hope no longer lies in those things; my hope is in Christ Jesus. He has a plan with a great future for me full of hope and peace. My job is to seek Him with all my heart; He takes care of all the rest.

For Additional Reading: Deuteronomy 4:29-31; 1 Corinthians 4:8-13
Brad, Age 30
Financial Investment Counselor

DAY FIVE ■ Romans 5:3-5

My most intense period of suffering occurred when my nine-month-old daughter was in the midst of several deadly complications following open-heart surgery. Nothing seemed to be going right and I knew that she might die. I was terribly angry at God, but continued to feverishly pray for her to live. One particularly bad morning, as I awaited the doctors verdict on more possible surgery, I felt directed toward the chapel in the hospital. Suddenly, my entire body loosened up, a flood of tears flowed down my face, and I began to pray new prayers. These were prayers for God's grace. At that moment, I gave my child's life back to the Lord. I let go of all my anxiety and hurting anger. He filled me with His peace and an absolute trust that He would take care of everything in His time. I knew without a doubt that the Lord would carry me through in her life or her death. I had never known or felt that incredible trust and pa-tience in the Lord. My daughter did indeed live and every day she is a wonderful reminder of God's loving gift to me through our sufferings.

For Additional Reading: Psalm 107:1-16; 1 Timothy 1:12-17
Chris, Age 36
Registered Nurse

DAY SIX ■ Romans 5:3-5

I was well aware that I had more compassion for people than my friend, who had never known tragedy. She was an only child, who had both parents all of her life.

When I was 12, my father died, leaving my mother alone with myself and three younger brothers. My mother had to work the afternoon shift, so we didn't receive a lot of parenting. However, I did notice that my mother was kind to unfortunate people and tried to help other widows. Her example in our tragedy gave me the ability to have compassion for others and to be sensitive to their needs.

Both my brother and I would like to work with orphans, and this desired work would not have come about without going through our own loss. Though we wouldn't have chosen to lose our father, God has brought good out of the experience, and given us the desire to work with orphans.

For Additional Reading: Ruth 2:8-12; Hebrews 12:1-3
Donna, Age 36
Employee Relations

DAY SEVEN ■ Romans 5:3-5

We have an incredible God who loves us so much that He can take our seasons of trial and use them to shape and mature us into the godly men and women that He desires us to be. This process requires two responses from us.

First, we must *allow* God the freedom to work as He chooses, and not limit His work in our lives by purposefully manipulating the circumstances to achieve the results we want. Our ways are not His ways, and He already knows the outcome — we just have to wait a little longer before it's revealed to us. We must learn to claim the promise of Proverbs 3:5-6, to trust Him with all our hearts.

Second, we need to *look expectantly* for the results of God's work in our lives as He molds us into the image of Jesus Christ.

Each trial *will* produce patience, endurance, godly character, and hope in Him—what a great promise from a loving Father! Ask the Master Sculptor to reveal to you the rough, unfinished areas of your life, and He'll chisel, smooth, and polish them into strengths that are beautiful in His sight. Trust in the promise of Philippians 1:6 that He will finish the work started in our lives.

For Additional Reading: Psalm 8:1-9; James 1:9-18
Cathy, Age 32
Underwriting Consultant

WEEK THIRTY-ONE

■ ■ ■ ■

A LOT OF PAIN, A LOT OF HOPE

TEXT FOR THE WEEK: **ROMANS 8:18-25**

KEY VERSES: ROMANS 8:22-24

"We know that the whole creation has been groaning as in the pains of childbirth right up to the present time. Not only so, but we ourselves, who have the firstfruits of the Spirit, groan inwardly as we wait eagerly for our adoption as sons, the redemption of our bodies. For in this hope we were saved."

DAY ONE ■ Commentary on Romans 8:18-25

My life is filled with expectations. I am more aware of this every day. Quite often these expectations are not met, leaving me disappointed and confused. However, this appears to be reality for human existence in this life. Life is difficult at times. It is a struggle; there are many disappointments. The painful reality is that the impulses of my life for happiness and bliss will go unsatisfied.

Winston Churchill, standing in the wreckage of war-torn Europe, told the House of Commons on the 13th day of May, 1940, "I have nothing to offer but blood, toil, tears and sweat." From the beginning of creation life has been a struggle, a battle against a world strongly reluctant to yield its benefits. Discouragement and disillusionment prevail and man's wearisome struggle seems endless. Similar words are used by the Apostle Paul in the key verses for today. Words such as "groaning," "pains," and "groan inwardly" describe life as we know it. We groan; we ache; we do experience disappointment and confusion.

Dr. Larry Crabb writes, "None of us is fully enjoying what we long for. People let us down. We let people down. The simple fact we must face is this: *Something is wrong with everything.* No matter how closely we walk with the Lord, we cannot escape the impact of a disappointing and sometimes evil world. A core sadness that will not go away is evidence not of spiritual immaturity, but of honest living in a sad world" (*Inside Out*, NavPress, p. 74).

Are there answers for us in the midst of our pain? The thought that comes to my mind is, "I hope so." That's it! Hope is the answer God's Word presents. Romans 8:24 reads, "For in this hope we were saved." The verse continues to focus on hope as the author uses the word four more times. Hope is without doubt the answer verses 22-25 give us while we groan in this mortal body.

What is hope? Hope is not easily or precisely defined. That is what makes hope so profound. Hope has great certainty for something better. It has the strength to persevere today. Hope is anticipation; hope is patient assurance. Hope is a wonderful truth that God's Word presents. "We rejoice in the hope" (Rom. 5:2).

Let hope come alive as you trust in the Lord Jesus Christ. His strength can be yours. His comfort is real. He is your hope. "Christ in you, the hope of glory" (Col. 1:27). Hope will sustain you as you wait patiently for the promise of life eternal found in Christ Jesus alone.

For Additional Reading: Psalm 62:5-8; 1 Peter 3:13-17
Barry Braun is the Singles Pastor at the Church of the Open Door, Minneapolis, Minnesota. The following six applications were contributed by single adults from Barry's ministry in Minneapolis.

DAY TWO ■ Romans 8:18-25

Before becoming a Christian, I was in a state of total hopelessness, despair, and depression, to the point of suicide. Once I received Christ, for the first time I experienced hope. Romans 8:28 and Jeremiah 29:11-14 became alive to me. I prayed with all faith and hope that God would use the disasters in my life to bring me joy. It became a painful journey, but I knew God was with me guiding every step—healing me, purifying me, and drawing me into deeper intimacy with Him. He taught me not to rely on my feelings, circumstances, or the bleakness of the situation I was in but to look beyond what appeared to be defeat. He wanted me to believe that there was and is victory ahead because of His promises.

Every disaster I have faced has been turned into unspeakable joy, because I placed my hope in what God is able to do and not the circumstances around me. Against all hope I believed. I refused to waver in unbelief regarding the promises of God. This has strengthened my faith and has brought glory to God because I knew He had the power to work through my circumstances just as Paul, in Romans 4:18-21, said Abraham believed.

For Additional Reading: Psalm 72:12-14, 18-19; Romans 15:10-13
Rosie, Age 41
Registered Nurse-Surgery

DAY THREE ■ Romans 8:18-25

The deterioration of my spirit came to an end when Christ came to live in me and brought His Holy Spirit as a permanent Resident. I want to cultivate my awareness of that reality and see evidence of beautiful, mature "fruit" as my days unfold.

But the facts tell me that as my life proceeds I'm getting older, work is getting harder, and I just can't get it all done no matter how hard I try. Even though I'm forced to pay attention to my body and its needs, someday its demands will be silenced by death. Then my freedom from the bonds of decay will be complete. Such a deal!

Between now and then I know that the Holy Spirit's fruit-producing presence is the answer.

The next trip will be better! Romans 8 says so and that's *hope!*

For Additional Reading: Psalm 42:8-11; Galatians 5:13-16
Marion, Age 44
Hair Design Artist

DAY FOUR ■ Romans 8:18-25

Surrender. Resignation. The abandonment of self. The evacuation of the flesh. These are the reactions and immediate applications from Romans 8:18-25 for me. I am mindful of Paul's Second Letter to the Corinthians. In chapter 5, he continues on his teachings about the temporal nature of our existence in this life, contrasted with true reality found in our spiritual lives. His thoughts begin in chapter 4:16, but are crystalized in 5:6-7. "Therefore we are always confident and know that as long as we are at home in the body we are away from the Lord. We live by faith, not by sight."

Our human frailty and condition finds us expecting, sometimes longing after, the things of this world. Though God knows that they cannot satisfy His spiritual children, He allows us to learn about this ourselves, through experience. The wonderful thing is: Our life with God and from God grows as we increasingly look to Him to truly satisfy. We increasingly "taste and see the goodness of the Lord." Indeed, we come to hope more and more in God alone and, as God's Word promises, that hope does not disappoint.

For Additional Reading: Psalm 90:13-17;
2 Corinthians 4:16-18
Ron, Age 29
Computer Sales

DAY FIVE ■ Romans 8:18-25

One of the most wonderful ingredients in my life has been that of relationships. Yet, to be truthful to what I know from experience, my own and others who share, relationships can be filled with disappointments and pain.

As I struggle within my own relationships and hear from others who do the same, I am reminded that we are living in the "pains" and "groanings" of a sin-filled world. As good as relationships *can* be, *reality is* that relationships are imperfect, and people hurt people.

In the midst of my world I find great hope in my relationship with the living Christ. He came into this world and He experienced the cruelty and pain of our sin-filled world (Isa. 53:3-4). He is the One who can sympathize with our weaknesses (Heb. 4:15). He calls us in these situations of hurt and disappointment in relationships to draw near to Him for help, comfort, perspective, and life change in the midst of difficulty.

For Additional Reading: Psalm 3:1-8; 1 Peter 1:3-9
Barb, Age 34
Associate Minister to Single Adults

DAY SIX ■ Romans 8:18-25

As a teacher, I am constantly searching for better ways to motivate and train my students. However, implementation of new methods is often frustrated by resources that for a variety of reasons are beyond my ability to bring together. And so the "groanings" begin to rumble.

I noticed that even our most expensive "toys" contain the seeds of eventual dissatisfaction and boredom. Repeatedly, we find ourselves discarding the old and seeking the new and improved.

Surprisingly, the desire for something more is also experienced by believers in the realm of spiritual blessings. Presently, we are enjoying a multitude of benefits from the Spirit's work within us. And yet, even these gifts from God cause us to long for all the additional blessings He has promised.

But thanks be to God, in our resurrection bodies all of our righteous expectations will be fully and permanently realized.

Together we will forever be thoroughly satisfied and complete in every way as "co-heirs" with Christ sharing in all His glory (Rom. 8:17).

For Additional Reading: Isaiah 25:6-9; 1 Corinthians 15:50-57
Oliver, Age 42
Elementary Teacher

DAY SEVEN ■ Romans 8:18-25

I hope for many things in this life. I hope to be married, to have the "normal" American family of 2.5 children, to be financially independent, and to live a suburban life. I hope for these things, but is God obligated to give me the kind of lifestyle I've always desired? I think not. Yet I hope. . . .

Hope in the New Testament does not deal with such earthly and material things. It also does not deal with the uncertain issues of our lives. The outcome of hope in the Scriptures is certain. We hope for the future righteousness (Gal. 5:5), for eternal life (Titus 1:2), for salvation (Rom. 8:24), for Christ (Col. 1:27). These things are ours by faith. They are not uncertain material desires, but spiritual realities as sure as God Himself.

So, as we go through life single, we must remind ourselves that God has not failed us. Rather, may our disappointments and unfulfilled expectations cause us to look to God Himself, our true Hope.

For Additional Reading: Proverbs 13:12-20; 1 Peter 5:8-11
Paul, Age 27
Seminary Intern

WEEK THIRTY-TWO

■ ■ ■ ■

BY GRACE AND MORE GRACE

TEXT FOR THE WEEK: **1 CORINTHIANS 15:1-11**

KEY VERSE: 1 CORINTHIANS 15:10   "But by the grace of God I am what I am, and His grace to me was not without effect. No, I worked harder than all of them — yet not I, but the grace of God that was with me."

DAY ONE ■ Commentary on 1 Corinthians 15:10

"Bᵤₜ by the grace of God I am what I am." This powerful statement reveals the miracle of grace worked out in the life of the Apostle Paul. When I consider the grace bestowed on my life and others' lives, I'm deeply moved and left with a profound feeling of assurance that God's people are guided by a wisdom greater than our own. We are creatures of a good God, who leads us in an unpredictable way.

Paul freely ascribes all that he has done in Christian work *to the grace of God.* That alone transformed him from a religious persecutor into a zealous preacher. Paul did many things hostile to the name of Jesus Christ. He imprisoned many Christians, cast his vote against them while they were being put to death, punished them in the synagogues, and even tried to force them to blaspheme (Acts 26:9-18). Paul followed the Law religiously, but his unbridled zeal corrupted him, and his personal pride gave him a false sense of security (Phil. 3:4-9).

I'm reminded here of my college years where I found great pride working as a "bouncer" at the most popular bar in town. I was also recognized as an exceptional athlete and student, and admired for being independent and allegedly secure. Though I possessed these gifts and talents, I was corrupted by the world and deceived by pride.

When we look back on our old depraved state and reflect on how as Christians we've gone from one grace to another, from one victory to another, we are obliged to say, "By the grace of God I am what I am." Grace is the doctrine of our dependence on God. It is the free favor of God shown in the regenerating, sanctifying, illuminating, and comforting influence of His Spirit. All whose hearts are changed and souls redeemed are great debtors to grace (Eph. 2:8-10).

Paul mentions to the Ephesians how he "worked harder than all of them" but immediately adds, "yet not I," so he won't be interpreted as taking credit for these great labors. He clearly ascribes them to the same grace of God by which he was made a Christian.

We must always keep in mind that we are only channels of grace; we are not even pools or reservoirs—we must continually draw off His supply of divine gifts. We need an abiding union with the fountain of life (John 15:1-11), or we will soon run dry; only as fresh streams of grace flow into us are we kept from becoming dry beds of sand. His might is our strength, His resources are our never-failing supply, and His grace is our source for pure and noble living.

For Additional Reading: Numbers 6:22-27; Colossians 1:24-29
Michael G. Moriarty is the Singles and College Pastor at Immanuel Bible Church in Springfield, Virginia. Six single adults from Immanuel Bible Church write the following.

DAY TWO ■ 1 Corinthians 15:10

When Paul said, "But by the grace of God I am what I am," he was not just referring to the kind of person that he was. He also meant that his whole life, including everything he would ever do or become, was because of God's grace. Paul knew that God put every person on this earth for a reason and that a purpose existed for everything that happened in his life.

Sometimes with all of the tragedies and hardships that can come along, we forget that every aspect of our lives is a part of

God's plan. When my brother was killed in a motorcycle accident in 1986, I could not understand why God would allow such a young person to die. Because of that experience, however, I have been able to mature faster and understand more about God's grace and plan for my life. Our light and momentary troubles are achieving for us an eternal glory that far outweighs them all.

For Additional Reading: Psalm 33:8-11; Ephesians 1:7-10
Kendra, Age 19
College Student

DAY THREE ■ 1 Corinthians 15:10

Realizing that the grace that made me a Christian is the same grace that allows God to use me for Himself shows that my successes are not my own doing. They are God's instruments for bringing praise to Himself.

In school, I sang in a small Christian college-sponsored group that toured the country during weekends and summers. Though we worked hard rehearsing and performing, we had surprisingly little trouble giving God all the credit for our programs. No doubt singing in churches for Christians helped us focus on the real reason we were singing—to glorify God.

Giving Him the glory without a live Christian audience is much harder now because my job rewards me with a byline (a writer's pat-on-the-back). I must learn to be proud only of how God has used my work to glorify Himself.

For Additional Reading: Psalm 44:1-8; Galatians 6:11-18
Karen, Age 25
Magazine Editor

DAY FOUR ■ 1 Corinthians 15:10

The only thing I agree with philosopher Friedrich Nietzsche about is that "what doesn't kill you makes you stronger."

Though that does not seem very comforting, it provides the character and fortitude I need to give Satan and company a real bad time. I realize that it's only by the grace of God that I have the power to overcome.

In the pain and frustration of our trials, God continues to love us, and He has our very best interests at heart. I was reminded of this in court when I was cited falsely as the cause of an automobile accident. The last thing on my mind then was Matthew 6:27, "Who of you by worrying can add a single hour to his life?"

I won the trial, but, you know, I could have lost. From it I learned that nothing in a believer's life is by chance or happenstance; everything works together for a believer's good (Rom. 8:28). Stand on these Scriptures, and remember that nothing can separate us from God's love through Christ Jesus (vv. 38-39).

For Additional Reading: Psalm 60:11-12; 1 John 5:1-5
Eric, Age 23
Electronics Technician in the Military

DAY FIVE ■ 1 Corinthians 15:10

By God's grace, I was able to make it through a divorce a year and a half ago. During those trying times, He showed me how to lean on Him, not to become bitter, and to learn who He really is.

God's love for me was beyond belief in how He provided for me family and friends throughout the church. As He showed me His love and support, I was able to trust His leading me where He wanted me to go. I felt no bitterness because He showed me how to love through adversity and the intent of others to destroy me. He showed me who He really is by His love, His support, and His children.

He even brought some good from my experience. As I went through those trying times, two women at work watched my life and came to know the Lord as their personal Saviour.

For Additional Reading: 1 Chronicles 16:34-36; 2 Peter 3:14-18
Betty, Age 48
Military Personnel Technician

DAY SIX ■ 1 Corinthians 15:10

I have a favorite poster in my room that reads "I may not be perfectly wise, perfectly witty or perfectly wonderful, but I am always perfectly me." God has made each of us unique. Some of us are more richly endowed with talents and gifts than others, but God created each of us for a reason and loves each one equally well. He expects from us only as much as we are capable of giving (Matt. 25:14-30).

A great temptation of mine has been to make mental comparisons of myself with others in order to see if I compare with them talent-wise. I find that I often sell myself short. This is a pointless and frustrating exercise (Gal. 6:4).

As the poster says, God wants us to be who we are; that is all—no more, no less. By God's grace, I am what I am. Only He can change me, only He can sustain me.

For Additional Reading: Genesis 1:27-31; Matthew 25:14-30
Gerry, Age 28
Children's Counselor

DAY SEVEN ■ 1 Corinthians 15:10

The intensity of reading the popular novel *The Hunt for Red October* should never compare with our quest for our quiet, hidden prayer closet where the victorious life "in Christ" is won or lost (Matt. 6:6). We must pursue that place where God's grace is found. We clearly acknowledge that we are saved by grace and by that grace "we are what we are" (Eph. 2:8-9; 1 Cor. 15:10), yet we allow the world to hold us captive to its priorities.

Oswald Chambers shows the need for persistent escape to

prayer in his daily devotional, *My Utmost for His Highest:* "The battle is lost or won in the secret places of the will before God, never first in the external world. . . . Nothing has any power over the man who has fought out the battle before God and won there" (December 27). Our daily prayer illumines our understanding of grace and God's perfect will for us.

For Additional Reading: Psalm 55:16-19; Titus 3:1-8
Ray, Age 42
Retired Military Officer, Seminary Graduate Student

WEEK THIRTY-THREE
■ ■ ■ ■

RECEIVE COMFORT – GIVE COMFORT

TEXT FOR THE WEEK: **2 CORINTHIANS 1:1-11**

KEY VERSES: 2 CORINTHIANS 1:3-4   "Praise be to the God and Father of our Lord Jesus Christ, the Father of compassion and the God of all comfort, who comforts us in all our troubles, so that we can comfort those in any trouble with the comfort we ourselves have received from God."

DAY ONE ■ Commentary on 2 Corinthians 1:3-4

Last year I decided to take my girls and drive home for the holidays. We found ourselves driving a hundred miles on solid ice as a bitter winter storm blew into the Texas panhandle. With each passing mile my anxiety began to fill all the spaces where my courage was leaking out. But in the backseat was a wonderful contrast. My girls played games, laughed, and napped in perfect security. Daddy was driving . . . and they were still young enough to believe that daddies never make mistakes and can always keep them safe. And so they found comfort in the storm while I drove tensely on.

In this text Paul uses the word *comfort* nine times in just five verses. In Greek the word is *parakaleo* and means "one who stands alongside." It refers to a best friend, a wise counselor, or a mighty protector. Jesus used the same word in John 16:7 to describe the Holy Spirit whom He called the *paraklete*. The word carries with it a sense of peace and security.

Paul makes three assertions here that we need to know. First, he tells us that *comfort* has a spiritual dimension that flows from the reservoir of God's compassion for His children. Second, *comfort* is found when life becomes so oppressive that we are driven to God through our own despair. Third, times when we need His comfort actually equip us for Christian ministry to others.

When we find ourselves hopeless and desperate, God finds many ways to stand beside us—a promise from His Word, the Spirit silently ministering to our hearts, encouragement from a friend, or a sunrise reminding us of our Father's sufficiency. Peace and security come when we finally let our *Heavenly* Father drive our lives trusting in Him, like children in the backseat on icy roads. When it comes, we have that moment of comfort as a gift forever to share with others the comfort their lives need. That is ministry.

When trouble comes we all feel the despair and hopelessness Paul experienced (vv. 8-11) But when we call on God to stand beside us, comfort comes . . . comfort to share with others in the days ahead. That is God's way. Our own comfort is completed when we pass on the comfort we received to others. Reflect on your hurt, loss, and disappointments. Have you gone to God for comfort? What have you received? And now who needs you to share that with them?

For Additional Reading: Isaiah 51:12-16; 2 Corinthians 2:5-11
Tom Vermillion is the Minister to Singles at the Church of Christ in Midland, Texas. The following six authors are from the ministry in Midland with Tom Vermillion.

DAY TWO ■ 2 Corinthians 1:3-4

On February 5, 1988, I found myself lying in a hospital bed waiting to be rolled to the operating room. I was already aware that the surgery I was about to undergo would have an enormous impact on the rest of my life. Having a few more minutes to meditate and pray in pre-op, I was determined that I wanted the Lord to somehow use me through this experience. Yes, I was afraid, and at times felt very alone but I always believed God was in control. Though my mind could only try to answer the whys, my heart was consoled because I knew that God would reveal His plan for this in His own time.

Second Corinthians 1:3-7 has a deeper meaning for me now. Just as God comforts us through His Word and unfailing love, so we too should demonstrate the mind of Christ by bearing one another's burdens with compassion and humility.

It has been almost two years now since the surgery. In retrospect, I see how God has answered my prayers and used me in so many ways to comfort others in similar situations. Through my painful experience, I now can respond to the sufferings of others with a kind of compassion and mercy that can come in no other way.

For Additional Reading: Psalm 119:76-77; Luke 6:32-36
Anita, Age 34
Artist

DAY THREE ■ 2 Corinthians 1:3-4

In March 1989, my son, who was living with his father, was visiting my daughter and me. Our visit was filled with love and laughter. But on our way to the airport, "the enemy" climbed into the car with us. We found ourselves fighting about everything and arrived hurt and frustrated. Because the plane was delayed, we had a few minutes in the airport restaurant to apologize but left with the good feelings drained away.

When I got home, I prayed. After each thought of despair, I cried, "But I praise You anyway, Lord!" Soon an unexplainable peace came over me. My problems were not solved, angry words spoken were not taken back, but I knew everything was in His almighty hands. Psalm 17:8 promises that God will hide me in the shadow of His wings. In times of turmoil or peace, I claim that promise and that comfort for my family. It is in despair that we search for the promises of God and when we have found them we feel His arm around us. "But this happened that we might not rely on ourselves but on God, who raises the dead" (2 Cor. 1:9).

For **Additional Reading:** Psalm 31:8-22; John 5:19-23
Phyllis, Age 35
Executive Secretary

DAY FOUR ■ 2 Corinthians 1:3-4

Why me? How many times have you asked yourself that simple question? So many people seem to be searching for answers today. Unfortunately, many look in all the wrong places. Newspaper headlines and television broadcasts proclaim daily our society's efforts to find our own answers. How reassuring to know that God already has real answers to today's real problems. Paul said, "But this happened that we might not rely on ourselves but on God, who raises the dead."

Several years ago, I learned how true Paul's words are. I found myself on the receiving end of a divorce. I quickly realized I could neither rely on myself nor the woman I loved and had trusted for 17 years. I did discover I could trust God, who Paul said "comforts us in all our troubles." By God's daily grace and compassion I survived that ordeal. When we bare our souls to Him in prayer, accept our part in our failures, and commit ourselves to a closer walk than ever before He comes with comfort. Surely, the Master and Creator of the universe can solve our problems and put order in our chaos if we will look to and rely on Him.

For **Additional Reading:** Nehemiah 9:19-24; Ephesians 4:29-32
Bruce, Age 39
Geologist

DAY FIVE ■ 2 Corinthians 1:3-4

When I reflect on the times in my life when everything was falling apart, they were the very same times when I felt I should take charge of the situation. "Get it together!" "Shake it off!" and "You can do it!" were the mainstays of my private conversations. But at the end of each episode always came the never-ending tears, nagging regret, and grief.

During times like these, I'm sure there will always be friends to console, but true comfort — that sense of well-being no matter what — comes only from the Lord. I can face each day, good or bad, knowing that the Lord has given me an assurance I can't get anywhere else. He continually covers me with compassion and comforts me in ways no other can. All I need is to turn to Him. There is my security.

I find too that my trials and suffering are not senseless. I can offer others all the patience, compassion, and understanding that He offers me. And through this, I find in some small way, my comfort continues as I share in their comfort.

For Additional Reading: Isaiah 66:10-13; Hebrews 13:15-21
Sheila, Age 35
Resource Teacher

DAY SIX ■ 2 Corinthians 1:3-4

Job declared that "man born of woman is of few days and full of trouble" (Job 14:1). No one understood this more than the Apostle Paul and yet he also understood that a God who can change water into wine can make any burden into a blessing. The latter part of 2 Corinthians 1:9 in this chapter says that "this happened that we might not rely on ourselves but on God."

Thinking back on my own life, my most painful experiences were the ones that truly taught me to put my eyes on my Saviour and no one else because there was no place left to turn. Now I can see those desperate times as a blessing because of the relationship I established with Him during my heartache. I realize this special relationship could never have reached the heights it has reached had I not suffered with Him, as verse 5 teaches.

It is because of our own suffering that God is able to mold us into the kind of Christians that can feel the pain and heartache of others, teaching us how to comfort them as Christ comforted us. It is only then that we can genuinely fulfill the law of Christ.

For Additional Reading: Joshua 22:3-4; 2 Timothy 1:8-12
Verna, Age 44
Hair Stylist

DAY SEVEN ■ 2 Corinthians 1:3-4

When the boss has chewed on you, and the bills are overdue and payday is 10 days away, and some friends went to a movie but didn't think to call you, and you're lonely, there are a lot of things that won't help: an idea, a philosophy, contemplation of the "cosmic other," or admiration of your possessions. All those things suddenly become cold and impersonal.

But there is a person who will help. The Holy Spirit comforts us with the unfailing truth of God: We are strangers and pilgrims seeking a homeland, groaning within ourselves, waiting for redemption. But Jesus is risen and indeed now prepares a place for us where He is.

Comfort comes in many ways from the Spirit. When you're troubled, look beyond yourself and focus on greater realities than your troubles—things from above—then pass it on.

For Additional Reading: Psalm 85:10-12; 1 Peter 2:10-17
Glenn, Age 40
Computer Programmer

WEEK THIRTY-FOUR

■ ■ ■ ■

THE THRILL OF VICTORY – A SWEET AROMA

TEXT FOR THE WEEK: 2 CORINTHIANS 2:12-17

KEY VERSES:
2 CORINTHIANS 2:14-15

"But thanks be to God, who always leads us to triumphant procession in Christ and through us spreads everywhere the fragrance of the knowledge of Him. For we are to God the aroma of Christ among those who are being saved and those who are perishing."

DAY ONE ■ Commentary on 2 Corinthians 2:12-17

Jesus promises to give us victorious lives. But more often it seems we're plagued by inadequacy. What should we look to in times of hardship, when we are haunted by our own weaknesses?

The Apostle Paul faced those moments many times. In 2 Corinthians he recalls an extremely stressful time in Troas. Though he experiences loneliness, frustration, and anxiety, he models vulnerability and a transparent honesty for his feelings and weaknesses. He goes on to describe the New Covenant's power, released into every believer who wishes to walk in its strength.

As the story unfolds, Paul reveals his mixed feelings as he waited for Titus. Even though an "open door" from the Lord had caused a multitude to respond to the Gospel, during those weeks he felt restless in spirit, anxious, and uneasy—recalling, "I had no peace of mind."

In a previous "painful letter" Paul had forcefully exhorted the Corinthians to moral conduct. Titus' failure to report quickly and fears that Corinth might be spiritually bankrupt left Paul worried and distressed. Unfocused in his work, he leaves a successful ministry in Troas for Macedonia and, hopefully, a reunion with Titus.

On the way, Paul is released from despair to joy. He realizes that the people God uses to display His power are those who, in their weakness, delight in trusting His adequacy. For this reason Paul cries out in grateful thanksgiving and describes the believer as always being led in triumphal procession.

The metaphor of a victorious Roman military procession with all of its pageantry, illustrates beautifully the life we have in Christ! These parades were led by the conquering Roman general. Surrounding him were temple priests, swinging their incense pots. Next came the shackled prisoners of war facing execution or life as Roman slaves. Finally came the captains leading their respective divisions.

Imagine the scene; citizens applauding and shouting their praises, the ceremony, and the aroma of incense. For most, the spicy scent was a sweet-smelling fragrance celebrating victory; but for the prisoners, it was the very odor of death!

What a fantastic picture for every believer—particularly the single person—because it's the "single" apostle who points to the togetherness of our triumph. Every believer is promised an honored position in God's victory procession. We become a fragrant manifestation of God's triumph in a broken world.

For Additional Reading: Psalm 45:1-8; Mark 11:1-10
Bill Rose is the Director of Gateway Singles Ministries in Concord, California. Six single adults from Gateway Singles Ministries respond in the following to 2 Corinthians 2.

DAY TWO ■ 2 Corinthians 2:12-17

Triumph through Christ. In our hectic, pressure-filled lives, we often lose sight of the fact that God is always with us. We feel inadequate, and unsure of our ability to be God's fragrance to those around us.

Two years ago my daughter fell and cut her leg open. The injury required stitches. When the doctor began, he asked me to hold her down as he injected a shot into the wound. She screamed out in pain, yelling "Mommy, make them stop!" Tears began to stream down my face as I held her down.

Later that evening, she hugged me and said, "Mommy, thanks for being there with me tonight. I couldn't have gotten through it without you." Once again, tears came to my eyes. "Stacy," I said, "I love you. You are my daughter. Where else would I have been tonight but with you? I'll always be here when you need me."

As soon as I finished saying those words, my whole being was filled with the presence of God. He spoke to me, saying, "Linda, I love you. You are My daughter. Where else would I be when you need Me except right here by your side?"

What a triumph to know that in those difficult times, as we are asked to be there for others, God's love and strength can shine through us.

For Additional Reading: Joshua 1:6-9; Matthew 18:18-20
Linda, Age 36
Computer Programmer

DAY THREE ■ 2 Corinthians 2:12-17

I have been a Christian for many years. At times, as in any important, growing relationship, there are periods of boredom, even frustration with the Christian life. But, praise God for His Word, and the importance He places on our need to be disciplined in studying daily, no matter how we feel.

During one dry period recently I read this section in 2 Corinthians. What an encouragement! God is faithful and triumphant. He is not limited by my weaknesses. God is moving forward in triumphal procession, and as a Christian I am in this procession with Him. As I am reminded of this proper perspective, I find hope and purpose in my life and in the relationship I have with God because of Christ's work.

I ended that particular Bible study time with renewed fresh-ness in my relationship with God. Christ is moving ahead trium-phantly, and He is causing my life to have the aroma of His character. Disciplines are never easy, but you realize their value as you experience the joy of triumph.

For Additional Reading: Psalm 21:1-7; Colossians 2:13-15
Carolyn, Age 33
Massage Therapist

DAY FOUR ■ 2 Corinthians 2:12-17

Yes, all of us have sinned and because of our sinfulness we fall short of the glory of God. These days it's easy to criticize and judge fellow Christians. However, Paul's submission to others as a servant is a tremendous reminder to seek humility, and humbly seek the Lord.

Paul had written an extremely important letter to Corinth instructing them how to deal with flagrant sin in the church. Yet Paul was also very concerned with how it would be received.

I love to see Christians caring that much for one another. We are instructed to esteem each other as better than our own selves and walk in forgiveness and love.

Today, public leaders in every sector are falling due to moral wrongdoings. Yet we are instructed to restore our brothers and sisters in a fall. God's discipline is always redemptive. This is a major challenge for the Christian church entering the 1990s as a "fragrant aroma of Christ."

For Additional Reading: Psalm 25:8-15; Romans 3:21-26
Suzi, Age 39
Businesswoman

DAY FIVE ■ 2 Corinthians 2:12-17

Does your heart belong to others?
In 2 Corinthians 2:12-14, Paul describes his anguish for

Titus' news from the Corinthian church; specifically their reply to a stern letter of warning and call for action he had written to correct a member who was sinning flagrantly in their midst.

Despite a flourishing ministry in Troas, Paul is heartsick to know the result of his letter. Had his dear friends in the Corinthian church obeyed, or abandoned his instruction?

Parents know the agony well. Some children, warned not to "touch the stove when it's warm, honey" will doggedly persist until they learn the hard way. Paul's heart is breaking to know whether Corinth has learned without being burned.

"There is nothing so whole as a broken heart" said Rabbi Nachmann. When our friendships are often "out of sight, out of mind," we must learn, like Paul, to love so much that it hurts.

For Additional Reading: Psalm 51:16-19; Matthew 13:11-17
Guy, Age 30
Teacher

DAY SIX ■ 2 Corinthians 2:12-17

The news came as a shock: an unexpected separation followed by abandonment, divorce, and a diagnosis of multiple sclerosis. I struggled with painful, tearing emotions; alone with a fragmented life, insufficient finances, and sole responsibility for three young children.

My Christian life was young and weak. All I did was receive. I barely held onto my faith. Though it sustained me, my feelings of uselessness remained. God had commissioned me for battle, and I was failing Him.

Eventually, acquaintances came to me, and their faith strengthened by observing mine. My mind staggered with the thought: how could this be when I had not talked to these people about my difficulties or my wavering faith?

The *fragrance!* Without my realizing it, Christ had used the agony of my life to touch many others. I didn't set out to make a difference: it happened by the fragrance of Christ in me, in spite of my wounded soul.

For Additional Reading: Judges 6:11-16; Ephesians 6:10-17
Lissa, Age 34
Writer

DAY SEVEN ■ 2 Corinthians 2:12-17

In Christ we are worthwhile and valuable people even when our social groups, certain life events, and our own inner response seemingly place us in the position of being second-class citizens.

When I was married, my husband and I gave our marriage, our time, our energy, and our resources to God to be used as a way of expressing our love for Him and for others. However, for reasons too complex to discuss here, after 15 years of marriage, my husband had an affair. When a divorce was imminent, a few men from our church stopped by to shame him into reconciliation. Ultimately, he was excluded from all church life. He continues to be disconnected from the church and separated from God.

After our divorce, I moved to a large city where I met a group of believers who actively participated in each others' lives. Compassion abounded. We were accountable without being judgmental; open and honest without being evasive. Since then I have experienced healing and discovered a whole new life. Let's make compassion and reconciliation our bywords for today.

For Additional Reading: Isaiah 49:14-15, 25-26; 2 Corinthians 5:16-21
Rosemary, Age 54
Marriage and Family Therapist

WEEK THIRTY-FIVE
■ ■ ■ ■

MAKE UP YOUR MIND

TEXT FOR THE WEEK: **2 CORINTHIANS 10:1-18**

KEY VERSE: 2 CORINTHIANS 10:5   "We demolish arguments and every pretension that sets itself up against the knowledge of God, and we take captive every thought to make it obedient to Christ."

DAY ONE ■ Commentary on 2 Corinthians 10:5

Second Corinthians 10:5 admonishes us to watch over our own thinking in such a way as to take our thoughts "captive" or as "prisoners of war" and to lead them into submission to Jesus. In other words we need to take all the big (and little) ideas we operate by day-to-day and compare them to the principles in God's Word and make any necessary changes. To accomplish this we need to:

● Honestly *determine* what thoughts and ideas influence our thinking.

● Compare these ideas and attitudes with God's Word.

● Make changes as necessary to stay obedient to our loving Lord.

For years I operated with the idea that I should take care of my own interests first, then from a position of security, reach out to others. This was especially true of my attitude toward money.

In His kindness and love for me the Lord brought some Christian friends in my life who gave of themselves and their finances without reservation to minister God's love to others. Their example and the resulting closeness in their walk with the Lord, challenged me significantly.

I began to realize that like the rich young ruler in Luke 18:18-23, I had my security in a bank and not my Lord. Though I wasn't wealthy it was still a difficult decision as I turned my savings account over to Him.

For several years following, my wife and I didn't have a savings account at all. As we continued to follow and really trust the Lord He not only always provided for us, but He also helped us learn the joy of sharing freely with others. As a result I grew closer to the Lord than I had ever been before. You see, the issue was not whether having a savings account is right or wrong, the issue was where I placed my trust. As I have learned to take my thoughts "captive" and compare them to God's truth it has dramatically changed my life and led me to more closely know and love the One who loves me most.

For Additional Reading: Jeremiah 31:33-34; Philippians 3:17-21

Rusty Coram is the Minister to Single Adults at Grove Avenue Baptist Church in Richmond, Virginia. Days Two—Six are written by single adults from Richmond, Virginia. Day Seven is by a single adult from St. Andrews Presbyterian Church in Newport Beach, California.

DAY TWO ■ 2 Corinthians 10:5

Second Corinthians 10:5 brings tremendous hope to my daily life as a single woman. I first became acquainted with this verse and its powerful truth at a singles' retreat. At that time I was experiencing the overwhelming despair of an intense depression. I had recently lost someone very important to me and the grief of that loss seemed unbearable. I tried praying and claiming verses, but I fell deeper and deeper into despair. I kept thinking, "Why doesn't God *do* something to help me?"

I shared my situation with one of the retreat leaders and she pointed me to 2 Corinthians 10:5. Slowly I began to see that through the Holy Spirit I could take those negative thoughts and bring them under captivity. I didn't have to remain under the control of my grief and Satan's use of it over me.

As singles, we daily battle the enemy. For some of us, a major concern is depression. But the hope of this verse is that with Jesus' help we can take the offensive against negative thoughts and feelings. We don't have to be at the mercy of satanic attack.

Speak out against the adversary, quote promises from the Word, and ask Jesus to help you bring every thought pattern under His lordship. Over time, you'll begin to realize a change — from turmoil to peace, and from fear to confidence. You'll also discover a deep and abiding love for our Lord, who is always faithful to His own.

For Additional Reading: Psalm 119:162-168; Romans 8:5-11
Paula, Age 33
Teacher

DAY THREE ■ 2 Corinthians 10:5

Last year I was struck down with infectious hepatitis. At that time, the job that I had carried no benefits for their employees. There I was without health insurance, sick leave, and with no income for what the doctor said could take as long as three to four months for me to completely heal. In a moment of desperation I asked, "God, is this the result of my being obedient to You in my tithes?" For a moment, I thought that if I had put that money aside in a savings account, then I would have at least had some money to carry me through for a while.

Paul tells us that we are to "take captive every thought to make it obedient to Christ" (2 Cor. 10:5). I decided to simply put my trust in a sovereign God whose eye was on the sparrow and to trust Him to look out for me. Within a matter of hours of that moment of desperation, God began to pour out His blessings. One by one, God started meeting all of my needs. While all of my physical needs were met, the need that He met the most was my spiritual need. I can say that in those three months I never wanted for anything.

By taking those thoughts captive and by depending on a

sovereign God, I learned a valuable lesson that I hope will stick with me for the rest of my life. Rather than trust in my meager finances, God taught me to trust in the One who had all the resources at His disposal. I can honestly say that at this difficult time in my life I experienced the peace that passes all understanding.

For Additional Reading: Psalm 119:50-56; 1 Timothy 6:17-19
Merrill, Age 36
Photographer

DAY FOUR ■ 2 Corinthians 10:5

Recently I realized that our thought patterns affect our prayer life. Many times the Lord uses circumstances to help us see where our thinking is off track and needs correction. For me, in the midst of a tragic circumstance, I learned that quite often my prayer life had been governed by some wrong thoughts.

I truly learned to "pray continually" (1 Thes. 5:17) during the year-long illness that my husband suffered before God called him home Christmas Eve three years ago. I learned too the difference between selfish and unselfish praying. At first, I prayed for my husband to live — just as long as he was breathing, I wanted to keep him on earth with me. As I continually watched him suffer, I finally learned to thank God for the time He had allowed me to have with my husband. I realized he'd only been loaned to me anyway, that he belonged to God. I asked God to not let him continue suffering but to take him home with Him. The very morning I prayed this prayer, relinquishing what I felt were my rights to my husband, God took him home that afternoon. While I experienced loneliness, emptiness, and all that widowhood brings, I had God's peace within me and a real sense that I had grown in my prayer life.

For Additional Reading: Isaiah 55:8-11; Hebrews 4:12-13
Gloria, Age 51
Church Secretary

DAY FIVE ■ 2 Corinthians 10:5

There was a time while I was taking a psychology course when God revealed a great truth to my young Christian mind. It was a major turning point in my walk with the Lord.

I had a teacher who, in my opinion, was very concerned about giving his students an accurate picture of the framework of psychology. His intentions were good. We learned about Freud, Jung, and others. With all this information we were absorbing, it seemed to me that these intellectual giants had all the answers about why humans did things and thought things. None of which had anything to do with the Lord.

I desperately went to the Lord to ask His help in understanding these things. Through His Word and the Holy Spirit God reminded me that He is almighty and I had to rely on His truth. He reminded me that He created all those experts but that they didn't necessarily have all the answers.

As I read magazines, books, and watch movies, there is a lot of misinformation given, whether it's intentional or unintentional. Through all of it I realize in order to "take every thought captive" for Christ this information must be filtered through the Word of God and determined whether it is true or not. If we are going to be capturing thoughts we need a trustworthy trap.

For Additional Reading: Proverbs 14:12-22; Philippians 2:1-11
Jay, Age 31
Printer

DAY SIX ■ 2 Corinthians 10:5

The negative thoughts which tempt each of us at times to retreat from life must be taken captive and supplanted with the promises of His Word if we are to survive difficult times and remain obedient to Him. It was during such a period recently in my own life that I saw how only through obedience to my commitments to service could I avoid making that retreat.

While healing from a broken relationship, a dear friend told me that "out of obedience comes joy." While struggling with the desire to withdraw from my commitments to the children's choir and other ministries in our church, I discovered His promise in Psalm 126:6. It gave me strength and courage to stay obedient to my commitments to Him even though it was at first an emotional battle, a sheer act of will to continue on in these activities.

"He who goes out weeping, carrying seed to sow, will return with songs of joy." He had given me "seed to sow" in the talents and gifts with which I had been blessed, and slowly, as time goes on, I have come to see that promise fulfilled.

If we are students in His Word, He will teach us the promises we need to take our thoughts captive, enabling us to move on in obedience in all situations, and regain our peace and joy.

For Additional Reading: Psalm 126:5-6; John 16:12-20
Glenna, Age 38
Bank Product Manager

DAY SEVEN ■ 2 Corinthians 10:5

Some years ago, I experienced what was the lowest point in my life, physically, mentally, and spiritually. I was quite alone, my mother had passed away a few days before, and my nearest relative was 4,000 miles away. I fell on my knees and prayed for something, anything, that would take away the numbness in my heart. I wanted to be "whole" again, in every way, but I didn't know how. Suddenly, I was conscious of a soft voice at my shoulder saying, "Pick yourself up—get on with your life—I am with you always—trust Me!" There was no one there.

Unlike the man at the Pool of Bethesda in John 5:1-15, I knew that it was Jesus. He had not forsaken me. Now, I was willing to let Him fill me with His power. I came alive again, as in a miracle, and knew that I would never again be alone.

For Additional Reading: Isaiah 54:10-13; John 16:30-33
Dorothy, Age 60+
Retired Secretary

WEEK THIRTY-SIX

■ ■ ■ ■

ILLUMINATION—MUCH MORE THAN LIGHT

TEXT FOR THE WEEK: **EPHESIANS 1:1-23**

KEY VERSE: EPHESIANS 1:17

"I keep asking that the God of our Lord Jesus Christ, the glorious Father, may give you the Spirit of wisdom and revelation, so that you may know Him better."

DAY ONE ■ Commentary on Ephesians 1:15-23

Do you find yourself fitting this description: You are a Christian, aware of the working of the Holy Spirit in your life and of the inheritance awaiting you in heaven, but you are not entirely happy with your current condition in the world?

Paul has a special prayer for you in Ephesians 1:15-23. Paul asks that the Spirit of wisdom and revelation make certain things obvious. The Ephesians needed wisdom and revealed truth because they were surrounded by pagan fears, superstitions, and immorality, even as we are today. We are surrounded by fears of the future, superstitions about our personal success, and immorality that extends from grade schools to grandparents.

When Paul prays for the Ephesian Christians, he does not pray for the "Pop" psychology of the day to help people cope, rather his primary concern is that they should *know God* through the Spirit of wisdom and revelation. When we know God we discover three very important gifts that God gives to us. The first gift is *hope*. We need hope in order to cope with today's pressures. Without hope the human spirit withers and dies. An ancient proverb said "Not to be born at all—that is the best fortune: the second best is to die as soon as one is born." The hope to which we have been called as Christians releases us from this type of fatalistic thinking.

The second gift of God that we discover is the riches of God's glorious *inheritance* in the saints. Our inheritance looks to our future, for as God's children, we are God's heirs. This inheritance of ours is not described in the clearest terms as we would prefer. The original word used for our word "glorious" is *doxa*, from which we get our word "doxology." It means "brightness, splendor, and radiance": something so bright that you and I cannot look right at it, but must turn our heads and shield our eyes. Paul wants us to be enlightened about our glorious inheritance so that we can be comforted while we are still in this world. Romans 8:18 says, "I consider that our present sufferings are not worth comparing with the glory that will be revealed." We need to get to know our inheritance by reading and memorizing the Scriptures, to set our eyes on a goal for the future, so that we can be comforted in our times of pain, suffering, and trial.

The third gift of God is His incomparably great *power*. It is because of this great power that we know that God's promises and gifts to us are true. We may despair because our hope and inheritance are so distant from the present. But when Paul tells us about God's power we see that the power is absolute. There is no beginning and there is no end to God's power. This power is not a power that God gives but rather is the power of God at work within us. It is God's incomparable *power* that energizes *hope* and activates our *inheritance*.

For Additional Reading: Psalm 18:20-32; 2 Corinthians 4:1-6
Paul Petersen is the chairman of the NSL Board and Minister to Singles at Highland Park Presbyterian Church in Dallas, Texas. Six single adults from Paul's ministry write the following devotionals.

DAY TWO ■ Ephesians 1:15-23

Have you ever felt like a victim of amnesia, cut off from your past and any sense of family and friends, lost in a strange mystery of who you are? I know I have and still do at times. Occasionally, we seek to fabricate a new family, carving out a niche to make us feel a part of it all, but with only fleeting success. And in our despair, we attempt to relieve the pain by various means of denying that we have a past. It seems we are constantly searching to find ourselves or trying to convince ourselves that there's nothing to find—living to escape from the moment.

"Thanks be to God," says Paul the apostle when he sees the Ephesians' faith. For it is our faith in Christ that reveals our true heritage, who we are in God's image. God is our Father and Jesus our Brother—knowing that, the chain of our amnesia is broken. May we each be moved by God's Holy Spirit to see the ties that bind us together and so be reacquainted with our Heavenly Father.

As we are reborn (John 3:3) and grow, we become aware of the riches of our inheritance, that we have long forgotten and denied. And too as we are renewed by the wonder of our newly opened eyes, we realize the power of the limitless resources of the Spirit of our family which empowers us to live as the children of God.

But the power at our disposal to live our life rediscovered is beyond natural description. It's the same power which raised Christ from the dead. The strength of *our* family cannot be diluted by any rule of law, nor by any political power; and, like American Express, it's nontransferable—we can't leave home without it. Our place in the family is a blood related inheritance.

For Additional Reading: 1 Chronicles 16:23-29; Romans 5:1-5
Jim, Age 37
Financial Management Consultant

DAY THREE ■ Ephesians 1:15-23

Today is a gift, God created, Jesus delivered, and the Holy Spirit is waiting to activate through hope. Paul prays that I will "light up my life" through the hope offered to me and that through this I will (experience) the wisdom and the power that I can inherit.

The choice is mine! To see no hope is to become closed and unavailable to God, family, and friends. When I am hopeless, I am powerless, I am useless, and I am unable to experience what God has prepared for me.

Or, I can let the eyes of my heart experience hope and become vulnerable to new life, choices, and change. When I have hope I have energized my faith with God's power.

Father, the choice is mine to open the eyes of my heart, to turn the key, and release the power that Christ has given me through the Holy Spirit. Then I will know the hope of Your calling.

For Additional Reading: Psalm 71:1-6; Colossians 1:3-8
Norma, Age 60
Student and Counselor

DAY FOUR ■ Ephesians 1:15-23

I study the passage like a puzzle, or a code I want to break. I read the words many times. The Apostle Paul speaks to me, I conclude, as well as to the endangered Christian community at Ephesus. "Pray constantly," Paul says. "Thank God." I consider the varied private and public circles and communities I live in. Each contains its own dangers and snares. ("Pray constantly.") And Christian joys! ("Thank God.")

The Apostle Paul unites the mind and the heart to be "flooded with light"; I know that I need and desire this Spirit of wisdom, this light. Daily I pray that I will live today in the presence and light of Jesus Christ, my unfailing Friend, Saviour, Lord.

For Additional Reading: Psalm 27:1-3; Revelation 21:22-27
Marilyn, over 50
Historian

DAY FIVE ■ Ephesians 1:15-23

Hopes, riches, and power. I suspect that these are the answers to all of our deepest yearnings. Most of us spend our lives grasping for one or more of them. Even we believers often find ourselves wondering, "How can I be a Christian and still feel such despair?" "How can I be a Christian and still want for more?" "How can I be a Christian and still feel so victimized?"

The blessings of hope, riches, and power are not standard features of salvation. I do not have them merely because I have said yes to Jesus. Indeed, there are many hopeless, impoverished, and powerless Christians around. I have been one.

It is Paul's message that the true joy and excitement of the Christian life is in growing in our knowledge of Jesus. It is by getting to know Him better, day by day, that I find I have sure hope for a future that is eternal, the kind of riches that only the Owner of the universe can give, and the power of God Himself.

For Additional Reading: Psalm 92:1-8; Romans 11:33-36
Walter, Age 30
Senior High School Teacher

DAY SIX ■ Ephesians 1:15-23

I beg you to live worthy of your high calling. Accept life with humility and patience, making allowances for each other because you love each other. Make it your aim to be at one in the Spirit, and you will inevitably be at peace" (Eph. 4:1-3, PH).

Living the above lifestyle is difficult. As an attorney I see people in disputes each day. The source of many disputes is based on how we treat each other in daily business. I've known many lawsuits to have been fought because of a small grudge over how one party treated the other.

As singles, we have a tendency toward intolerance, because we are self-sufficient in our ways. As we deal with the elderly and children in our communities, we will find a place to strengthen our ability to live in peace.

Our passage this week gives me three reasons why I can live a life of high calling. First, I know the God of our universe and He desires to reveal Himself to me. Second, I know the hope of our inheritance, which allows me to be long-suffering in this world. Last, I have the power of Christ—resurrection power—which equips me to love my enemies, as well as my brothers and sisters.

For Additional Reading: Psalm 96:1-6; Philippians 1:27-30
Bill, Age 28
Attorney

DAY SEVEN ■ Ephesians 1:15-23

Prayer is a powerful thing. Few faithful Christians would argue with this fact, and I myself see answered prayers every day: when God gives me the discipline to study and do well on a test, when He gives me the words and insight to comfort someone who is hurting and when He gives me the strength and courage to meet a challenge I am apprehensive about (just to name a few!). There's no doubt that God holds my hand and walks me through difficult situations that I pray about.

I wonder, "Are my prayers *big* enough?" Paul says, "I pray also that the eyes of your heart may be enlightened in order that you may know the hope to which He has called you, the riches of His glorious inheritance in the saints, and His incomparably great power for us who believe."

This is the prayer of the "big picture"—asking that we realize the hope God has for us and that we experience His power and glory by listening to God and doing what He calls us to do. If we pray this prayer, things will naturally fall into place.

Imagine what God will do in our lives if we pray this prayer daily for ourselves, our family, our Christian and non-Christian friends. What incredible miracles can occur? I can't wait to see!

For Additional Reading: Psalm 66:16-20; Acts 16:25-34
Ruth, Age 26
Graduate Student

WEEK THIRTY-SEVEN

■ ■ ■ ■

GOD'S GOOD WORK...
OUR GOOD WORKS

TEXT FOR THE WEEK: EPHESIANS 2:1-10

KEY VERSE: EPHESIANS 2:10   "For we are God's workmanship, cre-
                                ated in Christ Jesus to do good
                                works, which God prepared in ad-
                                vance for us to do."

DAY ONE ■ Commentary on Ephesians 2:10

Colors of lemon-peel yellow, ocean blue and sunlight orange leaped from the movie screen. Sounds of lawn mower roars and bumble bee buzzes caused electrifying chills to race up my spine. Suddenly, without warning, the intermission came, and the movie screen was transformed into a big boring blank screen serving no purpose.

Have you ever felt as though the theater of your life was like that big, boring, blank screen? Moreover, have the words "belonging" and "purpose" been foreign to your vocabulary lately? Frequently, I answer yes to those questions, and one of my most encouraging passages of Scripture is Ephesians 2:10.

This verse reminds me that I am God's workmanship. In fact, workmanship comes from the Greek word *poiema,* and from this we get the word poem. Have you ever read a poem? Once I had the opportunity to take a poetry class, and immediately I began to realize all the hard work, time, and careful word choice involved in writing poetry. Just think of it! We are God's workmanship, His poem. We are a unique, one of a kind creation. It is great to know that God does not make generic imitations or carbon copies. He creates masterpieces full of potential.

Furthermore, Ephesians 2:10 states that we have a purpose; and that purpose is to do good deeds. Just as poems are written

241

for leisure reading and careful study, we are designed to touch peoples' lives with God's love.

In fact, Luke 10:25-37 is a great example. Jesus tells the Parable of the Good Samaritan to illustrate the importance of mercy and compassion toward others. The parable even teaches that sometimes personal sacrifice is involved.

On the other hand, even those little, unnoticed deeds of love make a difference. Presently, God is helping me understand this truth at my job because I work with the public, and sometimes things get rough on busy days that are crowded with hostile, frowning faces. But God never fails to help me smile when I'm boiling with frustration, and He is always available to help me be extra patient.

So be encouraged. You are a unique individual, not just a face in the crowd. Moreover, you have purpose. What a destiny!

For Additional Reading: Isaiah 29:22-24; Ephesians 4:16
Richard A. May III is the Singles Lay Leader at the Cucamonga Christian Fellowship in Rialto, California. The following applications to Ephesians 2:10 are written by six single adults from Richard's ministry.

DAY TWO ■ Ephesians 2:10

It is indeed comforting to know that God has a plan, or purpose for my life. Even when I feel like a big boring blank screen, I have the assurance that He loves me no less than before. Instead of panicking and worrying that I've lost out or disappointed Him, I can dwell on His unconditional love.

As a student, I frequently question what my purpose is and what I'll do when I graduate. There are many directions I can take with a degree in psychology, but I haven't discovered which one is for me. Satan uses this by attacking me with despair and depression. During these times God often speaks to me through a children's song "I Am a Promise" and lets me know that He's already taken care of it.

Since God knew me while I was yet in my mother's womb, He

surely has a purpose for my life. "For I am confident of this very thing, that He who began a good work in [me] will perfect it until the day of Christ Jesus" (Phil. 1:6, NASB).

For Additional Reading: Isaiah 43:1-7; Ephesians 1:11-14
Tanya, Age 20
Student

DAY THREE ■ Ephesians 2:10

The definition of workmanship is the art or skill of a workman. Isn't it incredible to know we are God's workmanship, His art?

Like any art, you have to study it to determine what you like about it. In my life, I've had to study in order to discover that I am art, *God's* art. I've tried to change a lot of things in my life (i.e., looks, personality, style). I realized later that I was changing the colors in God's painting. That acknowledgment struck hard, and soon after that, one Sunday my pastor called forward all who really wanted to know God's will for their lives. I knelt down before God with tears in my eyes and asked God to forgive me for changing the colors of His painting, the structure of His art. I asked that His will be done in my life.

The more I study this art, God's art, me, I discover God's will, purpose, strength, and even His beauty. God's a pretty awesome artist!

For Additional Reading: Isaiah 26:7-13; Mark 14:3-9
Melanie, Age 27
Sales Manager

DAY FOUR ■ Ephesians 2:10

I am God's *special* creation! As a writer I understand the value and love that goes into creating characters; and most important, I understand that each one is created for a purpose. Characters are not just created to occupy space. Instead, they are created to move the plot of the story along and to tell the story through dialogue and action.

Sometimes I forget that God created me to move the plot along. He created me for a purpose. I do not just occupy space, I touch people's lives and show others the happiness and supreme joy in being a child of God by living for Him.

The Lord is truly great! I love Him so much! He proves to me every day that I am special and that I can make a difference through His grace. After all, that is what He called me to be and created me for.

For Additional Reading: Proverbs 19:20-24; 2 Corinthians 5:1-5
Sean, Age 20
Customer Service Representative

DAY FIVE ■ Ephesians 2:10

God's workmanship, created in Christ Jesus to do good works."

These are encouraging and exciting words especially in the midst of the New Age philosophy where individuals make their own successes in life, where God has no master plan or design.

When I read these words, I am reminded of God's direction in leading me back to school after being away from it for 10 years. All kinds of fear and anxiety swept over me. How could I relate and even compete with these younger people who were to be my classmates? There are even times I get so overwhelmed with my busy life that I feel like giving it all up.

It is in these times God says to me, "Be still" (Ps. 46:10), He will complete the work He has begun in me (Phil. 1:6) and, I am His work of art, His design that He is molding according to His purpose to do good things in this earth.

For Additional Reading: Isaiah 45:11-13; Luke 1:76-80
Susan, Age 37
Administrative Secretary and Student

DAY SIX ■ Ephesians 2:10

In the midst of trials it's hard to see the plans God has for me. The trials seem to blind me from God and the work He is doing in my life. He desires to run the projector on the blank screen of my life. But still, I'm there wanting to help.

He is constantly pouring out His unconditional love on me. How can it be that He loves me so unconditionally? I'm rebellious and I desire to do things my own way. He knows that I don't know how to receive His love, but promises to love me until I can. He draws me closer and closer to Himself, causing me to only want to please Him and do the things He is calling me to do and has planned for me.

So when you feel like running, stand back. Give Him control. Trust that He knows all and hold on to His unconditional love.

For Additional Reading: Psalm 13:1-6; Galatians 2:17-21
Carla, Age 26
Assistant Cashier Clerk

DAY SEVEN ■ Ephesians 2:10

I am always amazed at the beauty produced when God is allowed to work in us. The wonder here is that God's work not only achieves salvation in us, but brings us to the point of being used by Him to do good works.

Several years ago a young lady worked for me. Her life was in a chaotic spiral downward. She quit abruptly and I did not see her for over a year. When I saw her next, the change shone in her! Knowing the before and after allowed me to truly appreciate the wholeness of her transformation. Christ got hold of her life and the result was miraculous. How miraculous? Enough that by her testimony, now I believe in Christ as Saviour.

For Additional Reading: Psalm 125:1-5; Philemon 4-7
Barrett, Age 33
Independent Roofing Consultant

WEEK THIRTY-EIGHT

■ ■ ■ ■

RECONCILED TO GOD AND EACH OTHER

TEXT FOR THE WEEK: EPHESIANS 2:11-22

KEY VERSE: EPHESIANS 2:14

"For He Himself is our peace, who has made the two one and has destroyed the barrier, the dividing wall of hostility."

DAY ONE ■ Commentary on Ephesians 2:14-18

Forgiveness is a much talked about subject for most Christians. In our relationship with God we are forgiven because of Christ's death on the cross and reconciled with God. Reconciliation is guaranteed because of Christ's death on the cross when we ask for forgiveness. However, with people it is different. We can and need to forgive, but reconciliation with man has its limits.

Reconciliation is "to reestablish friendship between, to settle or resolve, as in a dispute"; "To settle differences: to be in harmony again between people." The Greek word for "reconciliation" means: "to change from one condition to another. To remove all enmity and leave no impediment to unity and peace."

When somebody wrongs us we are to forgive them (Eph. 4:32; Col. 3:13). Whether or not we are obedient to His Word will affect our relationship with God either in a positive or negative way. How many times do we forgive? Jesus tells us in Matthew 18:22 an infinite number of times. We are commanded to forgive and the decision to do so is ours.

This is what Paul refers to in Ephesians 2:11-22. He is writing to the church of Ephesus because the Jews in the early church were separating themselves from the Gentiles. Paul was calling for oneness — reconciliation. In verses 11-13 he reminds the Gentiles that it is through Christ we are reconciled to God. It was through God's grace that it was possible for the Gentiles to have a relationship with God.

Because of God's grace the barrier has been destroyed. The two have become one, the dividing wall of hostility has been destroyed. The purpose of Christ's sacrifice is to create peace between the two — to fulfill the Law by being the final sacrifice, to bring people to the point of reconciliation, relating by grace and mercy instead of the law and fairness. If we only relate to others with fairness and justice, we will rarely experience God's plan of reconciliation with others.

We must forgive, but all the more we must be brought to peace and love with each other — in God's way — in God's time.

For Additional Reading: Jeremiah 33:8-9; Mark 2:1-12.
Kelley Schroder is the Minister with Single Adults at Christian Fellowship Church in Vienna, Virginia. The following devotionals are written by singles from Vienna, Virginia.

DAY TWO ■ Ephesians 2:14-18

The Lord commands us to forgive an infinite number of times. But that's not always easy when someone you really loved has wronged you. When our pastor taught on forgiveness and reconciliation, I felt like God was speaking directly to me.

Brian (not his real name) and I were once best friends. Then we dated. It was a mixed-up relationship that had a lot of hurt involved. When we stopped seeing each other, we said that we would still be friends. Well, we were more abusive (verbally) to each other than we were friendly. So our relationship ended in anger and I never talked to him again until two years later when our paster taught on forgiveness. I had forgiven Brian long ago, but something inside me said I needed to be reconciled with him. A lot of things had been bothering me about our relationship when it ended so abruptly.

Since then I've called and seen him a few times. Though we

may never be best friends again, at least we are relating to each other in a "nonabusive manner."

For Additional Reading: Hosea 3:1-5; Matthew 18:21-35
Debbie, Age 23
Student and Medical Secretary

DAY THREE ■ Ephesians 2:14-18

For many years, I related to my father on the basis of "law and fairness" instead of with grace and mercy. My parents are divorced and I was accustomed to spending a weekend with my father about once a month. When I was able to drive, he stopped calling to arrange time together. Instead, he left it to me to come whenever I wanted to visit. I felt abandoned. Unconsciously, I began to punish my father. Gradually, I called and visited my father less and less. By the time I was 21, I talked to my father only three or four times a year. I loved my father and always meant to call, I just kept putting it off.

As my relationship with God began to grow, He showed me areas of my life which weren't consistent with His Word. Deuteronomy 5:16 says, "Honor your father and mother, as the Lord your God has commanded you." It was obvious to me that my relationship with my father was not what God intended. I sincerely tried to call my father regularly and to visit him. I didn't know my father any longer. I wanted a close relationship but I didn't know how to "break through" the wall holding me back. I needed God's help to release the hurt and anger I felt. With that, I could rebuild my relationship with my father.

Today, I'm beginning to know my father. God has taught me how to relate graciously instead of fairly. Jesus became our peace and He has, indeed "broken down the middle wall of division between us."

For Additional Reading: 2 Chronicles 6:18-25; Luke 23:32-34
Kristine, Age 23
Accounting Clerk

DAY FOUR ■ Ephesians 2:14-18

If you're driving your car and a tire goes flat, usually praying will not repair and inflate the tire. However, praying for the peace that has been promised will allow you to face the situation with a cool head and make the best of it.

Jesus Christ is Peace. It is one of His names for He is called the Prince of Peace. Ephesians 2:14 says Jesus is our peace. In 2 Thessalonians 3:16 Jesus is called the Lord of peace. This means He is in charge of peace. In John 14:27 He promised to leave us peace and He did. Paul in Philippians 4:6-7 tells us not to worry or be anxious about anything but pray about all things and God will guard our hearts and minds through Christ Jesus. We should not worry or fret about anything. We should pray asking God to give us the peace Jesus promised.

So, we have Jesus who is Peace promising us peace. Peace of mind and tranquility is what Jesus promised. Peace for God's children is a major theme in the Bible. Peace is something that we can count on Jesus giving us.

For Additional Reading: Psalm 37:8-11; Romans 12:17-21
Jon, Age 47
Student and Law Enforcement Officer

DAY FIVE ■ Ephesians 2:14-18

The turning point in my life was my reconciliation with God. For me it was a process, the first step of which was returning to church. Week after week, God spoke only to me in that congregation! Each sermon and lesson pertained to exactly what I needed to know and how to apply it.

I knew why "things" weren't right in my life. I also knew that I had every reason in this world to be angry and to have an unforgiving spirit—after all, the "things" that happened were "unforgivable." From our Singles' Sunday School lessons (once I got the courage to attend) I learned that I used anger as a shield to keep God and His healed helpers away from my heart.

A miracle! Once I listened to God's words on forgiveness and how He would have me forgive the person who harmed my family, I learned how anger controlled my life and how my unforgiving spirit kept me at arms length from the one Person who could help me put it together—Jesus Christ. Though I will never forget, I was able to forgive and remove the anger that ruled my life.

This began my process of being reconciled with God. As always, it is that first step. In order to take a step, you must make a decision to move. Do it today. I did and now I know that all my steps are headed in the right direction.

For Additional Reading: Exodus 34:4-9; 1 Corinthians 13:5-7
Deborah, Age 39
Manager/Compliance Services, Legal Department

DAY SIX ■ Ephesians 2:14-18

I will forgive him, but I will never forget what he did! Sound familiar? How often have we said and done that very thing? What if Jesus Christ said as He hung on the cross, "Father, forgive them for, *but don't forget,* what they have done"? Would that hinder our relationship with our Lord?

Does it hinder our relationship to the Lord when we take that attitude? (Matt. 5:23-24) Sometimes we cannot immediately forgive or be reconciled. It takes time for man to forgive. However, forgiveness and reconciliation must take place so that we can continue to mature in our Christian walk.

We are so blessed that God can and does forgive us and is immediately reconciled with us when we confess how we have grieved Him. Shouldn't we try to live the same way? Let us pray that God gives us the strength to forgive and be reconciled to those who hurt us.

For Additional Reading: Isaiah 44:21-23; John 20:19-23
Theresa, Age 36
Program Analyst

DAY SEVEN ■ Ephesians 2:14-18

I try to live every day by not sinning and not letting the sun go down on my anger (Eph. 4:26). Though I try to live this, I end up failing miserably.

It brings me great peace in knowing that when I have failed in relationships with people around me, or I have committed sins in my anger, I can be forgiven and reconciled to God through His Son Jesus Christ (Col. 1:20-22). All I have to do is simply ask for forgiveness.

I'm also reassured that for as many times as I do sin, I will always have Jesus who speaks my case to God in my defense (1 John 2:1). It's great knowing there is *no* limit as to how many times I can ask for this favor!

Living with Christ as my best Friend, it's a relief to know He will always forgive and forget my transgressions (Isa. 43:25).

For Additional Reading: Daniel 9:4-9; Hebrews 10:15-18
Joe, Age 28
Passenger Service Agent

WEEK THIRTY-NINE
■ ■ ■ ■

A PRAYER FOR STRENGTH AND LOVE

TEXT FOR THE WEEK: EPHESIANS 3:14-21

KEY VERSE: EPHESIANS 3:16   "I pray that out of His glorious riches He may strengthen you with power through His Spirit in your inner being."

DAY ONE ■ Commentary on Ephesians 3:16-19

Do you remember the story about the prince and the pauper? It told of two boys from vastly different backgrounds who were able to switch places because they looked so much alike. But regardless of their similarities, each found it quite difficult to act convincingly like the other. No matter how hard the poor child worked, he could not live up to the sophistication of a prince; and, try as he might, the prince was no pauper.

Our lives as Christians seem very similar to this story. God's Word tells us we're princes and princesses, but we often act like paupers. Paul wrote to the believers in Ephesus about this very issue. In fact, he spent the first half of his letter explaining what an honor it is to be a Christian; then, in 3:16-19, he prayed that three qualities would be developed which reflect this position.

First, Paul prayed that we would be strengthened with power in our inner being through the Holy Spirit. The word "strengthened" is the opposite of "discouraged" in verse 13 and Paul has already told us in 1:19-20 that the "power" available to us is equal to that which God exerted when He raised Christ from the dead.

Second, Paul prayed that we, being rooted (like a tree) and established (like a building on a sure foundation) in love, would have the power to perceive the immensity of God's love. It is this love which makes the fullness of Christianity available to us.

And third, Paul prayed that we might know God's love which surpasses knowledge. Notice the paradox. We're supposed to know something which is beyond being known! Now, the only way we know the unknowable is to experience it. Therefore, to remove the paradox, Paul described what our experience should be: we are to be filled with all the fullness of God! That is what it means to know God's love.

No wonder we get discouraged in the Christian life. For some reason we lay aside our royalty in a way that is no more comfortable for us than it was for the young prince in the story. We have power through the Holy Spirit to live like Jesus Christ, to comprehend God's unlimited love, and to experience that love. Christians, married or single, have incredible resources; we are princes and princesses. Now we simply need to begin living in light of the truth.

For Additional Reading: 1 Chronicles 29:10-13; Acts 1:6-8
Daryle Worley is the Single Adult Pastor at Moody Church in Chicago, Illinois. Six singles from Chicago write the following devotional applications.

DAY TWO ■ Ephesians 3:16-19

As the sea gulls glided peacefully over her head, my Christian friend attempted to persuade me that she no longer had any reason to stay alive. Why shouldn't she jump into Lake Michigan and drown herself? "Life is too difficult," she said. "I just can't make it in this world anymore. There are too many temptations and nobody really cares about me." That's ridiculous, I thought, at first. But then I remembered the times when I had been discouraged, giving myself a "pity party." Though I have never considered committing suicide, I could relate to her feelings.

Ephesians 3:16-19 reminds me that the Christian life is definitely worth living because of the abundant riches available to me and you through the power of the Holy Spirit. We can be strengthened with Christlike power to overcome the temptations of this world and we can drown ourselves in God's deep abiding love.

For Additional Reading: Psalm 20:6-9; Jude 20-25
Diana, Age 30
Receptionist

DAY THREE ■ Ephesians 3:16-19

The key to turning our being "discouraged" (v. 13) into being "strengthened" (v. 16) is found in four areas of our lives: fervent prayer, listening to the Holy Spirit, reading from God's Word, and seeking counsel from godly friends.

When we are so despondent that we don't feel like praying, telling God exactly how we *do* feel helps us know He hears our cry (Ps. 142:2). "I pour out my complaint before Him; before Him I tell my trouble."

With this telling, we need to listen to the Spirit within. We are strengthened through Him (Eph. 3:16). He is our Teacher, our Guide, our Intercessor. He convicts us of sin—of unbelief (John 16:8-15).

The Lord speaks most directly through His Word. Paul prayed that believers would comprehend God's love and what better way than reading His love letter, the Bible.

Throughout our struggle with discouragement and despondency we need the solace of friends, experiencing God's power "together with all the saints." Their prayers strengthen us, as Paul's did the church at Ephesus. And their insights help broaden our perspective.

For Additional Reading: Psalm 142:1-7;
1 Thessalonians 3:11-13
Ron, Age 38
Artist

DAY FOUR ■ Ephesians 3:16-19

Be not discouraged.
You have strength for this day
  and all things.
Strong in the Lord's mighty power.
Power through Your Holy Spirit, Lord.
Christ, be completely at home in my heart.
In my weakness be strong.
You empty me of despair, sweep out fear, unbelief.
You fill me with Your love.
Christ-filled.

Planted like the oak,
Foundationed on His love, today be glad, heart, perceive the
  fullness.
The King of kings loves you.
Be still and know.
His love filling—widest lengths, deepest deeps.
Too great, yet You grant power to grasp it.
Grasp Christ's love.
Empty out the lies, Lord.
Today expose misperceptions, confusion, and
Fill us with sight to see You.

You say, Come, walk this day with Me, draw near.
And know My love.
Live it.
Empty-handed, trusting, walking—in faith.
Know Christ's love unknowable
Like His peace transcending understanding.
Emptied so He may fill you with all the fullness of God.

For Additional Reading: Psalm 119:57-64; Colossians 2:9-12
Lisa, Age 24
Teacher

DAY FIVE ■ Ephesians 3:16-19

The greatest need and joy of the child of God is to fully abandon self to know and enjoy the incredible love of God. This realization is crucial to our daily walk with God. A correct understanding of our position in Christ should be the basis for life and ministry. Without this realization and the security it brings, the believer will inevitably develop a mind set of fear, apathy, or disobedience.

It is God's desire that we continually rely on His resources. He has given His Spirit to enable us to comprehend the power to which we are entitled. Christ Himself lives within us by His Spirit through faith. We have been given fellowship with other children of God. Our journey is not a solitary one. Paul writes that such understanding "surpasses knowledge"—for such love can only be known not with the mind, but with the heart.

For Additional Reading: Psalm 145:8-13; Ephesians 1:3-6
Ruth, Age 32
Teacher to Handicapped Children

DAY SIX ■ Ephesians 3:16-19

Before I became a Christian I wandered aimlessly. I kept thinking to myself, "What's the purpose in all this?" We all know how painful such questions are. Now as Christians we can plant our feet firmly and say, "I know what life is all about!" The purpose is "to know the love of Christ which surpasses knowledge." That's life! God isn't an abstract concept; He's real! He wants us to take part in the fullness of His glory—His amazing grace!

By making the step of faith in His promises, we can enjoy all of Him. Think of it! We "may be filled to the measure of all the fullness of God." There is a reason and a purpose for those who dwell in the will of God. Rejoice! We have found the end, but it's really just the beginning of an eternity of glorying in the presence of the Almighty God!

For Additional Reading: 2 Chronicles 7:1-4; Colossians 1:15-20
Andrew, Age 27
Sales Representative

DAY SEVEN ■ Ephesians 3:16-19

The choices seem diverse—opposite sides of the same coin. But the answers seem clear. Why, then, is it so hard to decide? Will today's coin fall on the side of compassion or confusion? A difficult choice must be made. Afterward I wonder, "Was it really the right way to go?"

It's a familiar struggle—the process by which we make decisions. But Jesus understands. How can I be so certain? The very essence of compassion itself is Jesus Christ my Lord. The Holy Spirit's power and presence is intimately involved in sorting through doubts and confusion. It is the Holy Spirit that enables me to fit the pieces of the puzzle together. He alone can address the doubts and fears that arise in any situation. Paralyzed by doubts and fears or prompted by the Spirit—the choice is ours. Which will it be?

For Additional Reading: Deuteronomy 20:1-4; Mark 5:24-36
Roger, Age 34
Accounting Administrator

WEEK FORTY

■ ■ ■ ■

BODY BUILDING

TEXT FOR THE WEEK: **EPHESIANS 4:1-16**

KEY VERSE: EPHESIANS 4:12   "To prepare God's people for works
of service, so that the body of Christ
may be built up."

DAY ONE ■ Commentary on Ephesians 4:11-16

Picture a small Christian fellowship group. Suddenly, 3,000 converts are added to their circle in one day, and they do not even have an organizational chart! Will they make it?

Well, that first-century church continued to grow, because Jesus had done exactly what He wanted to do. He left followers who knew Him and desired to follow Him. At Pentecost, the Holy Spirit brought in the necessary structure that would free the young church to multiply naturally. Ephesians 4:11-16 gives us three keys that will help us understand how this body of Christ, the church, functions:

You are gifted to play a unique role in the body of Christ. Ephesians 4:11 mentions 5 specific spiritual gifts which are part of at lest 20 identified in the New Testament. Every Christian has been energized with at least 1 of those gifts to fulfill their role in body life. The early church grew so dramatically because each person knew they were empowered by the Holy Spirit to play a vital, gifted role. Get the picture?

We grow up together or we do not grow. Note verses 12-13. Those with equipping gifts enable others to serve for what purpose? So that individuals might grow or be fulfilled? No, first and foremost it is so that the *whole* body of Christ gets built up! It is so that "we all" reach unity in the faith and become mature (v. 3). We grow up together!

God decided that the context of our personal, spiritual growth is in community and nowhere else. Verse 16: "From [Christ] the whole body, joined and held together by every supporting ligament, grows and builds itself up in love, as each part does its work." If you are not actively involved in a local church or fellowship, then you are out of context!

Speaking the truth in love is essential for body life. Rumors and gossip tear apart any Christian fellowship, but we still love to hear second-hand what others think about us or others. The tender fabric which holds the body of Christ together depends on honest, direct, and loving communication—not indirect, behind the back "sharing." Build your fellowship by speaking directly and gently, even when one has stumbled (Gal. 6:1).

Thank You, Lord, for uniquely gifting me to fit in the body, so that I might even encourage others to grow! And Lord, please help me to speak the truth in love directly, not indirectly.

For Additional Reading: Psalm 68:28-35; Romans 1:8-17
Paul Ford is the Director of Discipleship at Heights Cumberland Presbyterian Church in Albuquerque, New Mexico. Six adult singles write the following personal applications.

DAY TWO ■ Ephesians 4:11-16

Being gifted is a term often used to describe people with exceptional abilities, whether it be in sports, school, or just in their work-a-day world. We Christians sometimes forget that, as it says in Ephesians 4:7 and 1 Peter 4:10-11, each member of the body, upon receiving Christ, is given certain spiritual gifts by the Holy Spirit. Those gifts will enable each Christian to fit into the body of Christ. This is an important part of each believer's growth because this allows us to find God's special niche which He has planned for us.

In my gift discovery, I have found the best way of investigation is through prayer, study, and trial. First, pray for God's eyes to be yours, to find what your gifts might be. Then, find out what it means to be gifted by studying the gifts. Third, if you feel you are gifted, try it out in specific ministry areas. By taking these steps, you are on your way to new heights of growth, and you are playing your part in building the body of Christ.

For Additional Reading: Proverbs 21:20-26; 1 Timothy 4:11-16
Dave, Age 26
Engineer

DAY THREE ■ Ephesians 4:11-16

Once a week I meet to talk and pray with four other women who have decided to take seriously the call of Jesus on their lives. We committed to spend daily time reading the Bible and praying. We fall short of what we set out to do, but we strive to be real about it.

As a result, I'm learning that humility begins in confession. When I'm struggling, doubting, or backsliding, I need to be honest. I'm not always. When I'm not, nobody probably knows for sure. Consequently I disqualify myself from experiencing God's plan and impair the full function of Christ's body.

It's a challenge; it's a risk. It's also God's design for us, the living body of Christ. It's maturing together. It's growing in understanding of the fullness of our Lord Jesus' love for us. Come on—let's get the body in shape.

For Additional Reading: Psalm 92:12-15; 1 Peter 2:1-3
Susie, Age 21
Student

DAY FOUR ■ Ephesians 4:11-16

It always seems amazing to me that God's Word applies to so many contexts outside the church and in everyday life. Consider Ephesians 4:15, "Speaking the truth in love" and its arch-enemy, gossip.

As a university sorority president, I often saw the cruel and quickly destructive power of illicit talk, generated by misinformation and fueled by a failure to seek the truth. One must admit, many times merely hypothesizing is a lot easier than seeking the truth yourself.

Yet, it is the person with the courage to take the step of prevention and stop the wildfire of gossip that ultimately gains the most respect. It is that person who will be trusted; building the body in ways never achieved before. As written in Proverbs 16:13, "Kings take pleasure in honest lips; they value a man who speaks the truth." And love is known through truth and trust.

For Additional Reading: Proverbs 12:13-19; James 3:1-12
Kristy, Age 21
Student

DAY FIVE ■ Ephesians 4:11-16

When the Lord gave us the gift of fellowship with other believers, He meant for us to use it! It's so amazing to think about the incredible network of support that we as Christians have. Covenant groups, study circles, singles fellowship; all of these are supports found within most churches and sanctioned by God!

So what happens when a Christian tries to stand on his own, without encouragement and support from the body?

While I was in high school, I did a considerable amount of drifting from my home church. I was hounded by a feeling of neglect. I'd sit in a service or class and wonder why it wasn't "doing anything for me." Only when I returned to my church and became involved in community projects and a small group of my own did I feel that the church was feeding me and helping me to grow. I was amazed that it had taken me all of my 17 years to truly know the joy of helping and learning from others!

My God used the people around me to show me that I too needed the fellowship and encouragement of other believers. He proved to me that while each person plays an essential role in the development of the church, no one can play that part alone.

I praise the Lord for the gift of friends!

For Additional Reading: Psalm 122:1-9; 1 John 1:1-4
Kristin, Age 17
Student

DAY SIX ■ Ephesians 4:11-16

Having recently learned of the suicide of my father, who was 54, a popular song rang through my mind, "United we stand, divided we fall," and I began to wonder what made my life so different, what guarantee did I have that I wasn't going to act so selfishly? I got scared.

I was part of an intercessory prayer group that met at the University of New Mexico early in the morning before classes. Each Wednesday, I would begin my routine: get up, bathe, pick up my friend Kristen, and go to prayer group. I began to realize, here in my very presence, were people with whom I had shared my sorrows and celebrated my joys. I had faith, a faith in Christ who provided me with a family of believers, and we were together through thick and thin. I was a part of "the whole body joined and held together," one part needing the other—not just to survive, but to thrive and grow. I had meaning and purpose.

I know my father was a lonely man, and he would not turn to his family in his weakness or in his time of need. He tried to stand alone. He stands no more.

For Additional Reading: Isaiah 56:4-8; Matthew 21:12-17
David, Age 28
Student

DAY SEVEN ■ Ephesians 4:11-16

My dad brought home a sapling during the windy part of the spring season. This was the time of year to transplant trees, watch nature grow, and hold onto our hats because the wind was ready to move and blow away anything without foundation.

The young sapling's root system was certainly lacking in this area. As any wily gardener would know, my dad was prepared with cables which would support and stabilize the small tree. Survival of the strong winds and straight upward growth were assured by these attachments.

The support that I offer forms a similar attachment. As a teacher, I offer words of encouragement to a slow-learning child. My consolation gives comfort to a heartbroken friend. I provide guidance to misdirected youth. These actions form the connection of love. I feel closer to the person as we begin to share feelings. I feel attached to the person as we share God's love.

The affections that I show toward people starts the process of stability. The encouragement, the caring, and the loving links me to them. My support promotes the building of their foundation. The preparation to grow straight begins. I help them to mature and to survive the winds that try to take them away from the body of Christ.

For Additional Reading: Job 4:17-21; Luke 6:47-49
Frank, Age 26
Applications Technician

WEEK FORTY-ONE

■ ■ ■ ■

GOD'S ARMOR – DAILY ATTIRE

TEXT FOR THE WEEK: **EPHESIANS 6:10-20**

KEY VERSE: EPHESIANS 6:13   "Therefore put on the full armor of
God, so that when the day of evil
comes, you may be able to stand your
ground, and after you have done everything, to stand."

DAY ONE ■ Commentary on Ephesians 6:13-18

As I sit here reviewing the major events of the last year, the importance of the "armor of God" in my life rings loud and clear. As a minister and as a man, the year has been filled with some expected and many unexpected circumstances. Each one was allowed to come into my life because of God's desire to shape me, to turn me once again to my total dependence on Him.

We daily need the armor of God to walk through the challenges of life, not as victims, not as expendable pawns in some cosmic game, but as conquerors, as triumphant members of God's family and army.

We need the armor properly and consistently in place to be successful. Sloppy or sporadic preparation only makes us prime targets for the enemy.

As unfair as it may seem, disaster may strike at any time. If the last few years have shown us anything, they have shown us that greater people than you and I have fallen. It only takes a few moments, a few bad decisions, to destroy years, even decades of consistent godly living. Putting on the armor *daily* helps to protect us from the unguarded word, the unguarded heart, the unguarded thought, the unguarded look.

One of the greatest steps toward godly liberty for me has been finally recognizing that I am not the originator of every thought that flits through my mind, especially the unacceptable thoughts, the dark things. I now know that my responsibility lies with how I deal with such thoughts, whether I cherish them and nurture them, or dismiss them aggressively with God's help. God knows what I am exposed to in this culture and He has given me authority to "take captive every thought" (2 Cor. 10:5). But I can only do that when the armor is in place.

In the same way, God knows that I will be assaulted by potentially destructive images, thoughts, and misunderstandings daily. Without God's armor in place guarding my passion, heart, mobility, and thoughts, the assaults will be effective. To protect against specific attacks, God has given us faith and His Word coupled with prayer.

This week as we share what the armor of God means to us, be encouraged to check your armor, not out of guilt or condemnation, but out of a healthy awareness of our unscrupulous enemy and a deep-rooted desire to become everything that God wants you to become. There is no bondage in the freedom we have as God's children, His ambassadors, His soldiers.

For Additional Reading: 1 Samuel 17:45-47;
2 Corinthians 6:3-11
Rod Chandler is a member of the N.S.L. Executive Board and an Administrative Director at Trinity Church in Lubbock, Texas. The following devotionals were written by single adults from Trinity Church.

DAY TWO ■ Ephesians 6:13-18

The past six years I have had a continuous lesson on "letting go." I had to learn to let go of a husband who no longer loved me, of my home, of my friends and in-laws, of my life as I knew it. Then, there came the time to let go of my only child and best friend as he moved to Chicago to go to college.

His interests and aptitudes led him into a career of counseling, particularly teenagers with drug and alcohol problems. He discovered that satanic power was becoming a powerful force in their lives.

I received a call from my son one evening, and he began to share his fears with me. Then he said, "Mom, just pray for me." I was frightened for my son's life and remembered Ephesians telling about our battle with the powers of darkness. What did it mean to wear the "full armor of God"? I could do nothing for my son except pray. His fight was not against people, but against the rulers and authorities and powers in this dark world. I knew that I had to trust God's great power and promises completely and truly let go.

I just came back from a visit with my son. As we were sharing, my son said, "Mom, thanks for your prayers. I have a peace in my heart that could only come from prayer. And I feel safe."

The greatest honor that I have is to be able to pray for my son and know, really know, that God answers my prayers.

For Additional Reading: 2 Chronicles 20:15-17; 1 John 4:1-4
Julie, Age 43
New Accounts Representative

DAY THREE ■ Ephesians 6:13-18

I remember as a child watching the snow fall outside and waiting for Mom to bundle me up to go out and play. For some reason, I never wanted to wear everything Mom said I had to wear. One time I didn't want to wear gloves. The next time I would want to leave off my cap. But Mother knew what I needed, what was best, and never allowed me to go out without each and every article of clothing.

In Ephesians 6:13, the Apostle Paul encourages us to "put on the full armor of God, so that when the day of evil comes, you may be able to stand your ground." Continuing in verses 14 through 18, he urges each of us to cover himself for protection and strength for the battle.

Each day may be a snowy one. But just as my hands stayed warm and dry with the gloves Mom said to wear, my life can be positive and protected regardless of circumstances *if* I choose daily to have God's armor in place.

For Additional Reading: Psalm 5:11-12; John 17:13-19
Jay, Age 27
Bank Employee

DAY FOUR ■ Ephesians 6:13-18

Ephesians 6:13 reminds me of my responsibility to do my part in preparing myself for the problems that I will be facing in the future. In order to prepare myself, I must study God's Word, pray, and develop a close relationship with Him. I must realize that God desires to be my closest and dearest Friend. I want to be able to talk with Him any time of the day. I know I can.

When situations arise, whether good or bad, I can instantly be in contact with God to praise Him, request help or guidance. Then He can instantly give me the help I need.

The last part of the verse is sometimes the hardest. When answers do not come immediately, then I have to choose to continue to trust God, knowing He is working out the situation in the proper way and in the proper time.

For Additional Reading: Psalm 24:1-6; Romans 14:1-4
Shirley, Age 40
Schoolteacher

DAY FIVE ■ Ephesians 6:13-18

A man once told me that the more knowledge I had of something, the more confidence I would have. This is true in almost every aspect of life.

The same can be said of knowing God and His Word. But the result of knowing God's Word is grasping the abundance of His grace. This knowledge and confidence helps me know how to apply the authority I have through Jesus Christ.

Knowing God's grace is important when it comes to the "full armor" of God. Armor is an implement, a utensil or tool used for warfare, sometimes defensively and other times, offensively. Unless you are near a battle, you don't need armor. We are on a battlefield in this life.

God desires that I know all that I can of His Word (my sword) so that I can take the liberty He has given to me and "stand firm" on my own. He takes great delight when He sees us, His own children, take faith in His Word and act on it. And "after you have done everything, to stand."

For Additional Reading: Psalm 57:7-11; 1 Corinthians 15:58
Gregory, Age 37
Art Teacher

DAY SIX ■ Ephesians 6:13-18

As I read this passage, the first thought that comes to mind is the necessity of being thorough when I put on the armor of God. I am to put on the *whole* armor of God.

Last week I did not wear a glove when I played racquetball. The blister I received reminded me that I had not been thorough in preparing for the game. I had not done what I should have done.

Thoroughness is an aspect of God's character. He never does a job halfway. Jesus' work on the cross thoroughly paid the debt for our sins and provided a way for us to have abundant life. The Bible tells about the schemes and tools of the enemy. Our enemy is a roaring lion who is seeking whom he may devour. God desires us to be thorough in putting on His armor, so that we may stand against the evil we see in these days. Therefore, put on the whole armor of God, consistently and thoroughly.

For Additional Reading: Zechariah 3:1-7; Luke 10:18-20
Berry, Age 27
Single Intern

DAY SEVEN ■ Ephesians 6:13-18

Praying always with all prayer and supplication in the Spirit, and watching thereunto with all perseverance and supplication for all the saints" (KJV). Sometimes this Scripture can seem overwhelming, but the Lord has taught me and is still teaching me what it is to "pray always" and "be watchful."

Have you ever faced a bad situation or avoided a car accident and found out later someone was praying for you at that moment? That is prayer in God's time. I believe "praying always" is to pray *in God's time.* To be in communion with Him and not be surprised by anything. Each day as I have learned to read the Word more faithfully and be in His presence, it becomes easier to remain there. When I am in His presence, or walking in the Spirit, I am able to hear God's voice more clearly and know what and when to pray. It is *His* guidance and strength that gives me "perseverance" and helps me to "be watchful." It is no longer a struggle, but a natural flow.

For Additional Reading: Daniel 6:10-23; Matthew 26:36-46
Diane, Age 29
Church Secretary

WEEK FORTY-TWO
■ ■ ■ ■

A GREAT START, A GODLY FINISH

TEXT FOR THE WEEK: **PHILIPPIANS 1:1-30**

KEY VERSE: PHILIPPIANS 1:6   "He who began a good work in you will carry it on to completion until the day of Christ Jesus."

DAY ONE ■ Commentary on Philippians 1:3-11

I'm a great starter, but a lousy finisher. My life seems littered with half-finished projects, uncompleted tasks, and partially fulfilled dreams. Impulsive by nature, I can get excited about something new, feeling the rush of exhilaration over the next challenge. Too often when I reach the stages that require persistence and follow-through, it is easier to become discouraged and move on to something else rather than see a project through to the end.

Paul's encouragement to the church at Philippi reminded me that God began something very powerful in them when they committed themselves to following Christ. No longer are they left to live out the ups and downs of life according to their meager abilities. Christ was at work in them and would bring them through to the glorious end.

Our confidence lies not in our abilities, natural talents, personal efforts, or individual cleverness. Left to live according to our own means will always leave us short of the goal. Rather, we see God at work in us, empowering us to handle the worst of circumstances, as well as the best that life can give with conviction and compassion. Christ's power in us means that we have the ability to live beyond our means. We can be victorious not because we are great, but because a great Lord dwells in us and empowers us to take the next steps of faith.

Discovering God's will in particular situations can be a difficult task for us as believers. It isn't so hard to decide between good and bad choices. (They are fairly obvious.) It can be difficult to choose between good things. Choosing the best is the challenge that Paul gives in verse 10. Sometimes in our efforts to please God and people in our life, we feel paralyzed by the pressure to make the right choice. We need the assurance of grace to remind us that even when we make wrong choices in our lives, and do dumb things, God's love for us is not diminished. His commitment to us is strong enough to withstand our failures and mistakes.

I received a card the other day with the simple message, "There is nothing you can do to make God love you any more than He does right now. There is also nothing you can do to make God love you any less than He does right now."

We all need to be reminded that following Jesus is a journey in which we grow and change, sometimes get side-tracked and occasionally fall down. But our Lord is there to give strength and comfort when we need it as He completes the good work that He has begun in us.

For Additional Reading: 1 Chronicles 28:19-21; 2 Timothy 4:6-8

John Westfall is the pastor of Adult Ministries at University Park Presbyterian Church, Seattle Washington. The following devotionals were prepared by single adults from University Park Presbyterian Church.

DAY TWO ■ Philippians 1:3-11

When I was a young girl in school the message was clear: get good grades; be perfect. To my dismay, however, I was not the best student and I often felt like a failure. This idea of perfectionism not only influenced my academic endeavors, but my Christian life as well. I became obsessed with doing everything right, convinced that God was judging me solely on how closely I resembled Christ, how perfectly I imitated Him.

As hard as I tried I could not be perfect. As I began to understand Paul's message to the Philippians, I realized that if I was committed to God then He would be faithful to continually work in and through me, despite my indiscretions. As it says in Zechariah 4:6, " 'Not by might nor by power, but by My Spirit,' says the Lord Almighty."

For Additional Reading: Zechariah 4:5-9; John 4:34-38
Dori, Age 30
Cytogeneticist (Prenatal Diagnosis)

DAY THREE ■ Philippians 1:3-11

For years I have had Philippians 1:6 underlined in my Bible, knowing that it was special. Suddenly, though, when asked to write my thoughts on it, I couldn't think of what "good thing" God had begun in me. I sing in the church choir, but am not an outstanding soloist. Like others, I've taken my turn at teaching Sunday School but know that is only a role, certainly not my gift. I was married for many years, but that crumbled in a painful divorce. That couldn't be the "good work" either, because of its failure. God blessed me with two wonderful sons. They are now young men leading their own lives and stepping into the adult world. My major duties as a full-time mother are slipping behind me. What is the "good work" He began in me?

As I pondered the verse, the thought came to me, all these things had been experiences of life the Lord allowed to come to me. The good work began in me the day I gave my life to Christ. No longer did I need to fear or question God. The answer has been here all along. The "good work" He began in me was when He gave me His love. I don't need to try to be special to get Him to notice me, nor do I have to be especially talented and gifted. God will never reject me. He loves me. He loved me when I was just a child reaching out to Him and He will continue loving me through all eternity. I can be confident of the very "good gift"!

For Additional Reading: Psalm 19:1; Acts 20:22-24
Marianne, Age 45
Secretary to Adult Ministries

DAY FOUR ■ Philippians 1:3-11

I sometimes struggle with the fact that God has promised in Philippians 1:6 to perfect the good work in me, and yet as I look both at my life, and at the larger world around me, I see the consequences of sin. How can God's work be complete in a world of starving children, political injustice, AIDS, and other tragedies? Shouldn't the completion of God's good work be mutually exclusive with these things? Yet, we do have the confidence of knowing from this Scripture that the work which He began and is completing is a good work.

Understanding that the completion of God's good work does not remove the consequences of my own, or the world's sin is not always easy. I do know that God loves me; that God is good, and that His work in me will reflect these attributes. Though I have had victory over many of the sinful desires and actions in my life, some of the broken relationships and lost opportunities have not been undone. But even as the consequences of the past are still evident, I know that they are not the controlling part of my life. There is evidence of God's continuing presence and action each day. This is the confidence we can have.

For Additional Reading: Numbers 8:5-11; Titus 1:7-16
Jerry, Age 37
Attorney

DAY FIVE ■ Philippians 1:3-11

My relationship with my father is special. Recently I had time to reflect on his effect on my life. This time, he was having emergency surgery in Rhode Island while I was staying on Orcas Island, Washington. While I waited for news of his surgery, I read Philippians 1:3-11. I wondered what God's Word could say to me during a time of separation from someone I loved.

God's Word told me of a love relationship separated by distance and prison walls. This relationship between Paul and the Philippian church was characterized by joy, thankfulness, encouragement, and concern for one another's welfare. Paul received joy in sharing Christ's grace with these people. Paul was thankful for the existence of their relationship. He also encouraged these friends to continue the good work Christ started in them. Furthermore, he prayed for Christ's love to yield knowledge and insight in their lives to help them focus on what is "best and may be pure and blameless."

Consequently, my relationship with my father is a love relationship separated by distance and hospital walls. He receives joy in seeing my faith in Christ grow. He is thankful for our relationship. He encourages me to depend on Christ as he sees the effect of Christ in my life. He also prays for me to make wise decisions about my life.

I am thankful for my relationship with my earthly father and my Heavenly Father. I am thankful for the good work that Christ is doing in my life and my father's life as he recovers from heart surgery in a hospital room in Rhode Island.

For Additional Reading: Psalm 102:24-28; Acts 14:21-28
Betsey, Age 31
Geriatric Nurse Practitioner

DAY SIX ■ Philippians 1:3-11

Instant answers in an instant society. We all want instant answers: instant coffee, instant printing, instant communication, and instant gratification. My whole walk with Christ has been a struggle (usually a losing one) over decisions about instant gratification or long-term joy and happiness. The temptation arises everywhere. The instant mentality has plagued my life in areas from cheating in school, to manipulating relationships for personal gain, to lying about my feelings in order to avoid the long painful situations. Whether it is compromising for sexual pleasure or stealing a roommate's milk in the refrigerator we all desire instant answers.

We want these quick answers in our spiritual life also. We want to be made perfect now. It is God who is in the business of perfecting us. Long-suffering is a spiritual gift from God. And here Paul assures us that while purity may not come as quickly as we wish, it does come. Because we are in God's grace He will never cease the work of perfecting us. As we continue to gain "real knowledge" of God we will be filled with the fruit of righteousness that comes through Jesus Christ.

If we continue to put our energies into knowing God "He who began a good work in [us] will carry it on to completion."

For Additional Reading: Psalm 106:13-15; 44-48; 2 Corinthians 8:10-15
J.D., Age 25
Urban Ministry Intern & Seminary Student

DAY SEVEN ■ Philippians 1:3-11

O Lord, I have had to climb out of the pit of despair and loneliness when my husband and both my parents died, all within 17 months. I have struggled to find myself—feeling shattered and abandoned—now only a "one" and no longer "number one" in anyone else's life.

You began a process in my heart years ago when I asked Christ to become Lord of my life, and You gave me the Holy Spirit's power to work out Your will for me, but this all seemed to stop. I felt dried up inside like a sun-baked and cracked riverbed. Slowly, as I have surrendered to You, hope has begun to trickle, then build into a stream of renewed faith.

You never gave up on me, did You? Thank You for strengthening my faith when I almost lost it. I stand remade before You.

For Additional Reading: Joel 3:14-18; Hebrews 3:6-15
Shirley, Age 63
Bible Study Leader

WEEK FORTY-THREE

■ ■ ■ ■

KNOWING CHRIST — RENEWAL AND CONFIDENCE

TEXT FOR THE WEEK: PHILIPPIANS 3:1-11

KEY VERSE: PHILIPPIANS 3:10   "I want to know Christ and the power of His resurrection and the fellow-
ship of sharing in His sufferings, becoming like Him in His death."

DAY ONE ■ Commentary on Philippians 3:10

Philippians 3:10 expresses the central concern of the Apostle Paul: to know Christ. Indeed this must be the central concern of all believers in Christ. What does it mean to "know Christ"? G. Hawthorne states that knowing Christ refers to a "personal encounter with Christ that inaugurates a special intimacy with Christ that is life-changing and ongoing" (*Philippians*, Word Biblical Commentary, Vol. 43, Waco, Texas: Word, 1983, p. 143). Knowing Christ is much more than knowing *about* Christ. It is relational and personal knowledge.

Paul goes on to say that knowing Christ means participation in "the power of His resurrection," as well as "the fellowship of His sufferings." The Christian life involves both of these realities. All believers are in the process of being resurrected daily. Christ transforms and redeems areas of our lives that have been scarred and tainted by sin and failure. It is His power at work in us that brings hope, change, and the freedom to be whole.

Every Christian also experiences suffering. Paul knew that knowing Christ involved "being united with Him in the likeness of His death" (Rom. 6:5, NASB). In order for resurrection to occur, there must first be death. Death is always painful, whether it means putting away old habits, forgiving grudges, confessing inward impurity, or to actually suffer and die physically. Living in Christ is not easy!

The good news, however, is that the Christian never suffers alone! Note Paul's words, "The fellowship of sharing in His sufferings." We suffer in fellowship with Him! The even greater news is that suffering is a preamble to resurrection! (See Rom. 6:5.) Philippians 3:10 is keenly relevant to single persons. Single adults, simply by virtue of their singleness, have a unique opportunity to focus on knowing Christ. Many of the hardships of single living such as the breakup of a marriage, parenting singlehandedly, loneliness, and fear of the future can drive one to depend solely on the resurrection power of God. The devastating divorce becomes a stepping stone toward renewed self-esteem, greater wisdom, and a deeper dependence on God. The stress of being a single parent can unleash confidence and un-tapped potential as one discovers that with God "all is possible." Loneliness and fear of the future can lead to deeper trust and intimacy with God. Pray this week that God will help you to know Christ in His resurrection power and in His sufferings!

For Additional Reading: Isaiah 53:1-5; Romans 6:5-14
Tom H. McEnroe is the Assistant Pastor at San Gabriel Union Church in San Gabriel, California. Six adult singles from San Gabriel write the following.

DAY TWO ■ Philippians 3:10

Philippians 3:10 has special significance for me since I have gone through a disruptive divorce, had the opportunity to be a single dad and, unfortunately, experienced the stigma of being single in a marriage-oriented church environment. There is suffering in divorce, in single parenting, and in being misunderstood and even ostracized by non-singles. Yet suffering can be used to solidify one's faith and to develop character (1 Peter 1:7; James 1:2-4). For me this has meant maintaining a proper perspective knowing that, by God's grace, the outcome of these experiences would be to His glory (Rom. 8:18). And in the long run they have: I've been made aware of the unique challenges and opportunities that singleness brings, I've been blessed with a beautiful daughter who is now maturing into young womanhood, and I've been given the privilege of ministry in the church I attend.

By adopting the humility of Christ in His death and sharing in His suffering, I have experienced the power of His resurrection. Like Paul, I can emphatically declare that all personal ambitions and attainments pale in comparison with the greater satisfaction and fulfillment that comes from knowing Christ.

For Additional Reading: Jeremiah 15:15-21; Romans 8:12-18
Bob, Age 45
Bookstore Manager

DAY THREE ■ Philippians 3:10

I have found that God often reveals His resurrection power in circumstances in life, particularly when we are suffering, and often through others. There were three incidents in my recent past through which Christ revealed Himself to me, causing me "to know [Him], and the power of His resurrection" (Phil. 3:10).

Awhile ago at work I helped a woman solve a problem with a routine computer punch-in. Her comment was, "I was up all night praying about this!" It then dawned on me that God directed this woman to me in answer to her prayer!

The second incident found me lying in the hospital with a crushed hip. The first person to step in the room was a Christian x-ray technician who ministered compassionately to me. Resurrection power was at work again!

Finally, having a part in leading a close friend to faith in Christ showed me that God could use me powerfully! I believe in the resurrection power of Christ!

For Additional Reading: Joshua 24:16-18; Colossians 1:21-23
Paul, Age 32
IRS Auditor

DAY FOUR ■ Philippians 3:10

I want to know Christ and the power of His resurrection," not just in passing, not just as a Person on the pages of history, not just abstractly, but personally.

I had heard about Him all of my life. My mother had read me Bible stories as a child. I was taken to Sunday School and church as my parents were Christians but, as yet, I did not know Him. His death and resurrection were only "something you believed" because you were told that was what made you a Christian. Nothing was said about knowing Him personally. Nothing about His being a part of one's very fiber, thoughts, or life. Finally, as an adult, I enrolled in a church program which was to train me to share Christ with others. Through the training I realized I was the one that needed to know Christ! I then decided to trust Christ as my personal Saviour for the first time. What a difference it is to know Him personally!

For Additional Reading: Exodus 6:6-8; John 1:29-34
Rae, Age 59
Office Worker

DAY FIVE ■ Philippians 3:10

After a number of years in a good marriage, my husband decided he wanted us to go our separate ways. I was left with a son four years old and a daughter two years old. I now know firsthand the fellowship of His sufferings and have seen His wonderful resurrection power in my trials and hardship.

Paul tells us "to be united with Him in His death" (Rom. 6:5). I've made a commitment to live a new life, dying and rising with Jesus, not looking back, but pressing "on to take hold of that for which Christ Jesus took hold of me" (Phil. 3:12).

For Additional Reading: Job 36:15-26; 1 Peter 4:1-6
Connie, Age 31
Bookkeeper

DAY SIX ■ Philippians 3:10

It is truly remarkable for me to be able to say, "I know God." How can anyone really know God? And yet, this is a day-by-day experience of every true believer, as the Apostle Paul makes clear in his Letter to the Philippians.

As a single parent I have endured some extremely painful and lonely times but, as I recall them, I can see clearly the Lord's "right arm" in each instance. It is in these weak, helpless, hopeless ordeals that I become strong. When the waters get too rough I surrender my will to God and it is His "resurrection power" that holds my head above these rough swells.

Each time I'm resurrected with God I have shared, to some degree, in "His suffering." It is in this way that He uses each one of life's trials to conform me to His death, so that I may truly live a life acceptable to Him. Praise God for His "indescribable gift!" (2 Cor. 9:15)

For Additional Reading: Joshua 4:23-24; John 17:1-12
Sheila, Age 42
Legal Secretary

DAY SEVEN ■ Philippians 3:10

Being single and 39 with no "prospects for marriage," I decided to pray for the gift of singleness. I'm not sure singleness *is* one of the spiritual gifts, but it sounded better than the loneliness and emptiness I was feeling!

But my Heavenly Father had His own plan for me, and immediately put a man in my life. He's completely wonderful and knows me better than I know myself. I've decided to spend the rest of my life with Him, striving to love, honor, and obey Him, in sickness and health, poverty and plenty, until death unites us in our Father's house.

Of course this "man" is Jesus and I have found that knowing Him has filled the void created by the impending "birthday at 40 with no prospects." Knowing Jesus has not come without a cost. Many selfish desires and excuses had to be confessed and renounced. Through this God has become my source of identity as a single person, so that I can approach the future with confidence.

For Additional Reading: Psalm 146:1-6; Philippians 1:19-26
Tisa, Age 39
Educator

WEEK FORTY-FOUR

■ ■ ■ ■

FELLOW PRISONERS, REJOICE AND RELAX

TEXT FOR THE WEEK: PHILIPPIANS 3:12–4:9

KEY VERSES: PHILIPPIANS 4:5-7

"Let your gentleness be evident to all. The Lord is near. Do not be anxious about anything, but in everything, by prayer and petition, with thanksgiving, present your requests to God. And the peace of God, which transcends all understanding, will guard your hearts and your minds in Christ Jesus."

DAY ONE ■ Commentary on Philippians 4:5-7

The Apostle Paul wrote this counsel from his prison cell to believers on the outside who were living under the threat of persecution. Thus the reminder about the importance of a gentle attitude toward others (v. 5). A recognizable mark of the followers of the living Lord, yesterday or today, is thoughtfulness and large amounts of forebearance and gracious goodwill when encountering closed minds, anger, or lack of understanding from neighbors or civil authorities.

Believers have always lived in this world where there's more than enough to bring anxiety and fear. Paul acknowledges (v. 6) that it is *not* a characteristic of people of faith to be free of worry, or have a distressing preoccupation with their personal welfare, or the safety of loved ones, or even of what might ultimately become of their witness in such a great big world.

But because Jesus' return is certain (v. 5), we are challenged to put anxiety behind us. We are actually instructed to "take it to the Lord in prayer." Notice the instructions (v. 6): Don't worry about anything, but, instead, in all your prayers ask God for what you need. This means identifying to ourselves and God what fears gnaw away at us and how we desire deliverance. It includes praying for the wisdom and discernment we need for making decisions and confronting issues responsibly. It certainly also includes getting off our chests (confessing) our lapses of faith and trust in God's good will for us and our loved ones, and our tendency to brood about the future and our place in it.

We may tell it all, and ask for what we need, but notice again the instruction (v. 6), not without a thankful heart. Be thankful for past mercies. Be thankful that the Spirit of Christ comes to help us pray, actually praying with us in accord with God's will (Rom. 8:26-27). Be thankful that there is nothing in all creation that will ever be able to separate us from the love of God which is ours through Christ Jesus our Lord (v. 39).

So someone in prison with plenty to worry about has written, reminding us that we don't have to be stymied by the uncertainties of tomorrow. Listen to his words. Follow his counsel: be active in prayer. And then relax! Yes, relax! Your life and concerns are in Christ's hands. And it has been the experience of men and women for thousands of years that even as they prayed, they were aware of an assurance, an inner confidence, that God's peace, the peace far beyond human understanding, was safely guarding their hearts and minds (Phil. 4:7) from giving in or giving up to anxiety's grip. Instead, with the power and love of Christ, they found themselves putting their energies into doing all they could about all they had been praying about. Try it yourself! Let God deal both with you and those worries that won't go away in serious prayer, and grant you the confidence of faith as you commit yourself today, to living and loving people after the manner in which Christ loves you.

For Additional Reading: Psalm 95:1-5; 1 Timothy 4:1-10
William Van Loan is the Associate Pastor at Arcadia Presbyterian Church in Arcadia, California. The following devotional applications come from six adult singles involved in the ministry at Arcadia.

DAY TWO ■ Philippians 4:5-7

Paul was physically imprisoned by others because of his deep faith in God and boldly telling everyone the Good News of eternal life through Jesus Christ. Even in prison his faith never wavered and he continued to tell those nearest him about Christ's love for them.

As I reflected on this Scripture, I thought about how often we imprison ourselves with worry and fear when we are in difficult circumstances.

At age 53, divorced and with meager financial resources, I was forced to make a major career change. I was frightened and I kept asking, "Why, Lord?" The answer didn't come quickly. God was teaching me patience along with two other lessons that came to me in the most unexpected places.

The first was through a speaker at a local church. He made reference to Paul's singleness and the fact that it enabled him to put his spiritual interests first. A couple of days later as I was driving down the street it came to me in a flash, "MY singleness is a gift." As a single person I am free to do many things I would not be able to do if I were married. And at this point in my career, that is necessary.

The second came to me one day while I was waiting for emergency car repairs, the least expected time I would think of God speaking to me. As I waited for my car I was looking up toward the San Bernardino mountains and it was as if God came and literally stood next to me and said, "Martha, this and the other things that have happened to you in the past couple of years are to teach you that you are to have total trust in Me. No person or job can take My place."

Each answer brought me an overwhelming sense of release from my own imprisonment of fear and worry. It was as though I could see through a small window the unconditional love and care God has for me. He is able and willing to see us through all the difficult times in our lives if we are willing to let Him.

As I write this, my prayer is that you and I will be more willing to let God love us and release us from our own imprisonment whatever it might be, so that we, like Paul, can tell the Good News of Jesus Christ.

For Additional Reading: Psalm 9:11-18; Philippians 3:1
Martha, Age 54
Insurance Sales

DAY THREE ■ Philippians 4:5-7

In Philippians 4:5-7, Paul gives a real and lasting solution, prayer, if we'll only take advantage of it!

I know that prayer has pulled me through lots of rough spots along the way. I've had five different jobs in the last five years and two major career changes. It's been a real roller coaster ride. Believe me, I've been confused and frightened many times as I've searched for the right path. But, time and time again, I was able to turn those fears and anxieties over to the Lord and let them go.

One of my favorite passages is in Jesus' Sermon on the Mount when He encourages the great multitude not to worry about material things like food and clothing, but to look to the birds and lilies to see how completely God provides for all His creation.

"If that is how God clothes the grass of the field, which is here today and tomorrow is thrown into the fire, will He not much more clothe you, O you of little faith? So we do not worry" (Matt. 6:30-31).

We, who were made in His image, have the most comforting promise of all. No matter what is happening in our lives, we can take our problems to Jesus, the dearest Friend and Counselor imaginable. And He will take the weight of all those concerns off our shoulders and onto His own.

Thank You, Jesus, for always being there to listen!

For Additional Reading: Jonah 2:1-9; Luke 22:40-46
Jan, Age 39
Technical Editor

DAY FOUR ■ Philippians 4:5-7

As singles, many of us have a lot of anxiety in our lives. I experience anxiety as a painful uneasiness and an agitated state of mind as I worry about my problems and my situation. For me, anxiety often comes as I worry about relationships, problems at work, health problems, money problems, or my car breaking down. Sometimes I feel all alone and overwhelmed by my situation, and I can't get my problems off my mind.

This passage is an oasis for me in those times. I experience a breath of fresh air as I read these verses which tell me to shift my focus; to stop focusing on *me* and *my* problems, and to focus on Christ. As I begin focusing on God and praying with a thankful heart, this passage assures me that the peace of God will be mine. I can't explain the feeling but usually I'm more relaxed, more realistic, and able to think more clearly about solving my problems rather than just worrying about them. As I read these verses I like to read verse 4 with the passage, "Rejoice in the Lord always. I will say it again: Rejoice." That sounds like a command and sounds out of context as the verses go on to talk about dealing with problems and anxiety. But when I'm dealing with my problems this is a helpful reminder to be thankful for all that I have and I'm *learning* to believe that God really does use these tough times in my life as a part of His plan.

In my Bible I've highlighted all the times the words "Rejoice," "Joy," "Glory," and "Praise" are used in the Book of Philippians. Remembering Paul's situation in prison and and seeing all these uplifting words helps me keep from giving in to anxiety's grip. What a source of hope and assurance! God's Word is just the refreshment we need when we get so wrapped up with our own problems that we can't see any way out. It also helps me to have the support of good Christian friends who will be encouraging as we share one another's burdens (Gal. 6:2). God is so good and His peace so comforting that we really can experience so much joy when we shift our focus away from ourselves and instead, focus on God!

For Additional Reading: Psalm 66:5-12; Luke 1:46-51
Diane, Age 34
Personnel Administrator

DAY FIVE ■ Philippians 4:5-7

Peace of mind and heart are high on the list of priorities in my life. Everything around us in our everyday lives would seem to interfere with that quest.

In these verses we are admonished not to be anxious about anything, but by prayer and petition with thanksgiving, present our requests to God. This has probably been the hardest lesson I have ever had to learn in my life. To turn my life, my will, and my desires over to the will of God, to trust that He will take charge and work things out, and then to believe that He knows what is best for my life requires giving up my independence. I am continually reminded of Psalm 37.

Commit your way to the Lord.

Trust in the Lord.

Delight yourself in the Lord.

Rest in the Lord.

On a daily basis, as I attempt to practice these principles, I have come to know God's precious peace.

For Additional Reading: Psalm 37:37-40; Hebrews 12:14-15
Elaine, Age 51
Engineering Administrator

DAY SIX ■ Philippians 4:5-7

Don't worry, be happy." This advice from the Bobby McFerrin hit song always struck me as being singularly unhelpful. Simply ignoring the worry and assuming the determined gaiety of the dance band (like on the Titanic) can be both irresponsible and foolhardy.

Paul is not telling us to ignore our worries. It is certainly true that most of the things we worry about are totally beyond our control to do anything about, but an important fraction of those worries are things about which we can and should be prepared to take responsible action. Paul is telling us to take our worries to someone who can tell the difference between what things he would lay on our hearts to take responsibility for doing something about and what things can be safely left in His capable hands to do something about. Wow, am I ever thankful about that!

The trick seems to be to *really* commit the worry to Him. Don't *share* it with Him, *give* it to Him—thankfully. If I've really committed the worry to Him, I experience His promised peace—peace of heart and peace of mind. If there is something He is asking me to do, to make a confession to someone, to offer or seek forgiveness with someone, to simply see a doctor, the peace He offers is a powerful incentive. My spiritual union with Christ is at issue here. To hang on to my worry is to mistrust Him. To not take the responsible action He shows me, is to disobey Him. God's peace is offered freely, but it requires trust and it requires obedience. Thankfulness? That's a cinch!

For Additional Reading: Proverbs 16:1-9;
2 Thessalonians 1:3-12
Gary, Age 42
Sales Manager

DAY SEVEN ■ Philippians 4:5-7

We live in a stressful time. The future for any one of us is uncertain. There are increases in violent crimes, disease (like AIDS), threats of terrorism, and the pollution of the environment. Through it all, God brings us hope and peace in this word from the Apostle Paul.

We are told not to "worry about anything." God knows what is best for us (Rom. 8:28). Only our Heavenly Father knows what the future will bring for us. We all tend to have worries in some form or another. Usually we spend time worrying about things we have no control over. Instead of worrying, go to God in prayer and ask for what you need. God will see that you are prepared to face the challenges ahead of you.

Paul tells us to ask God for what we need with a thankful heart. There are so many blessings God gives us every day, but we take them for granted. The very fact that we are alive is a blessing from God. Rejoice and give thanks. Remember, there is nothing for us to fear or to worry about because the peace of God will keep our hearts and minds safe in union with Christ.

For Additional Reading: Psalm 120:1-7; Mark 9:42-50
Kurt, Age 33
Life Insurance Underwriter

WEEK FORTY-FIVE

■ ■ ■ ■

GOD'S STRENGTH TO
DO ANYTHING

TEXT FOR THE WEEK: **PHILIPPIANS 4:10-23**

KEY VERSE: PHILIPPIANS 4:13   "I can do everything through Him
who gives me strength."

DAY ONE ■ Commentary on Philippians 4:13

At the age of 28 I married a young minister and felt that God surely had provided the perfect partner I had always prayed for. That's when my life began to fall apart. My marriage culminated in divorce five and one half years later.

For the first time my faith was really tested. Could I really depend on Christ to give me the strength to deal with divorce? Ministers aren't supposed to have to personally deal with this issue. I was stripped of my easy answers to life and had to truly rely on the strength that could only be provided by Christ. When my husband walked out, I was left to explain to a struggling congregation in the final phase of a building program that their pastor had deserted both the church and his wife.

God gave me strength and provided for my emotional needs by sending other Christian singles into my life who understood my pain. God also provided for my physical and financial needs by sending clients to my interior design business which I had neglected in order to supervise the church building program. God provided spiritual strength through the ever present peace provided by the presence of the Holy Spirit guiding me and comforting me daily through His promises preserved in Scripture.

In Philippians 4:13 Paul reminds us that the strength of the Christian is not his own, but Jesus Christ working through him and providing for him.

So many times we as Christian singles try to cope with the

stresses of our hectic lives with our own power which leads to frustration and burnout. Instead we should be strengthened with the mighty power of His Spirit promised in Ephesians 3:16.

I can't say I haven't questioned why I was allowed to suffer the agony of a failed marriage. I have to admit I questioned God, "Why me?" The only answer that I could find was, "Why not me?" Christ gave me the strength to survive an emotionally abusive marriage and empowered me to continue to seek God's will for me in His ministry. God did not promise that as Christians we would never experience hurt, trouble, loss, pain, or heartache. He did promise consistently throughout Scripture that He would be there to give us the strength, the power, and the support to cope with whatever life had in store for us. First Corinthians 10:13 assures us that God is faithful and He will not let us be tempted beyond our strength. Through my divorce I have a new appreciation for the true essence of this passage and can say with real assurance with Paul, "I can do everything through Him who gives me strength."

Only in union with Christ is real strength achieved.

For Additional Reading: Deuteronomy 11:8-12; 1 Peter 4:7-11
P.K. Fields is a leader and Community Outreach Coordinator through Ward Evangelical Presbyterian Church in Detroit, Michigan. Five adult singles from Detroit and one from San Diego contributed this week's devotional applications.

DAY TWO ■ Philippians 4:13

It was at the age of 23 that I met that special person. That sweet dream of a beautiful loving spouse, children, and happiness. My dreams became reality until the third year of marriage when we discovered that we could not have children. Through this period of time I became caught up in the trials of my life. My wife and I agreed to adopt. Logically we reasoned and shared the same goal, but the timing of adoption became a subject of stress. We both became emotionally torn and eventually grew apart. Why couldn't we resolve this conflict? We lost our focus on Christ. Our marriage ended in divorce.

Since the divorce I have renewed my commitment to Christ and have shared His love. I have seen lives changed and souls saved. Yes, I have been pulled from my "comfort zone." But always the Lord has blessed me and worked miracles through me.

You can do all things with Christ's strength. Never lose faith or hope. Ask the Lord to show you His purpose for your life. Seek and you shall find. Trials in our lives test our faith. May your faith endure.

For Additional Reading: Daniel 10:4-19; Romans 4:18-25
Ken, Age 29
Sales Director

DAY THREE ■ Philippians 4:13

A verse that goes hand in hand with Philippians 4:13 is Hebrews 13:5 where God says that He will not fail us nor forsake us. He not only lives within us, but God will not run out on us when the going gets rough, even though sometimes we might feel like He has abandoned us.

In my life these verses have given me the courage to grow and stretch when I probably would have been too afraid to try something new, especially when it came to speaking before large groups of people. At one time in my life I thought speaking was something I could never do. As I look back I can see how the Lord provided smaller groups of people at first and then larger groups of people with which to share. Each time when I got apprehensive, the Lord reminded me that He was there with me and cared for me no matter what happened. Even if I really messed up He was there for me and could use the situation for His glory.

For Additional Reading: Psalm 2:7-12; Matthew 20:20-28
Ruth, Age 45
Biologist

DAY FOUR ■ Philippians 4:13

Philippians 4:13 was one of the first verses I memorized as a child. Coming from a strong Christian family, learning Scripture was as routine as eating three meals a day. Going to a Bible institute also helped me accumulate Bible knowledge. It never occurred to me not to do God's will.

After getting married, I worked full time on staff at a church for almost eight years. "I can do" steadily became the norm. It was easy to become a "Martha" by doing more and more serving and less and less being.

After my divorce, getting involved in a large singles ministry was another avenue to continue living out the phrase "I can do all things." A new vocation was found, getting rid of remnants of the past life and starting out fresh. Learning to keep doing in the midst of being a single parent with two small children started to take its toll. Needless to say, my body gave out before my brain acknowledged the dilemma.

It was then that the second half of the verse struck me, "through Christ who strengthens me." Other verses like "Wait for the Lord" (Ps. 27:14) and "Take My yoke upon you" (Matt. 11:29 reinforced the need to slow down and rest.

Before the "I can do all things" can even be effective we must draw from the power only Christ can provide. When we are weak in our own abilities, then we are strong in God's power (2 Cor. 12:9-10). Life is easier when the emphasis is placed in the right direction. I'm learning to exchange His strength for mine.

For Additional Reading: Judges 15:18-20; 16:28-30; 2 Corinthians 1:18-25
Lynn, Age 37
Real Estate Salesperson

DAY FIVE ■ Philippians 4:13

I can endure all things" and "I can do everything God asks me to do." Either way I'm reminded of the ongoingness of His challenge especially at the time my world was crumbling around me. I would have bet anything that my marriage would never end in divorce. We were everyone's ideal couple — very much in love, romantic, complementary in talent and personality, and leaders in the church. It was the second time for each of us but the first real marriage in our minds. Because of that, we knew ourselves better — our mistakes, what we wasted, and we were trying much harder.

What we didn't know about was alcoholism, family dysfunction, and co-dependency. As it encroached further into our lives we didn't recognize its subtle, beguiling power. Personality changes, shifting priorities, denial, cruelty, neglect, and finally abandonment. I was enduring, but I didn't like it. It was a hellish nightmare that I couldn't change.

Finally, I had to look at my own life and what God wanted of me with or without my husband. God was asking me to love Him above all else. He began showing me that I could go on living, that I could be whole and complete in Him through Christ. He showed me to not only endure but also to do everything He was asking of me.

For Additional Reading: Psalm 28:6-9; Hebrews 11:32-35
Sandra, Age 39
Counselor

DAY SIX ■ Philippians 4:13

The Lord has given us Philippians 4:13 to battle daily troubles. Losing out on a job that one wants; friends getting married, leaving us to wonder why the Lord doesn't bring that right person into our lives; a particular health problem that is no fault of our own; or maybe office politics that have become unjust, often cause daily frustration which asks the question, "Where are You, Lord?"

However, through the years I have come to realize and know the Lord is slowly at work in my life. To make a man or woman after His own purpose takes time. We all have rough edges that are slow to change. The Lord allows us to go through disappointments, but ultimately there is Christian growth as we remain faithful to Him.

Job once said to his wife, "Shall we accept good from God, and not trouble?" (Job 2:10) I have learned to accept trouble, but yet be strengthened by the Lord. I strive to be consistent in daily prayer, daily devotions, public worship, active in service in a Christ-centered church, and engage the support of Christian friends. I have learned to give thanks to the Lord for daily circumstances and for the opportunity to be His example. For me adversity doesn't get me down, for I know the Lord wants me to grow, conquer, and endure.

For Additional Reading: Job 2:7-10; 12:13-16;
2 Timothy 4:16-18
Tim, Age 35
Purchasing Manager

DAY SEVEN ■ Philippians 4:13

My reasoning was blurred—even senseless as I wrenched inside! When I looked at the prosperity of those who did not know or love God I became like a raging animal (Ps. 73:21-28). I come to You like a frothing beast. Lord, it really upsets me. It seems so unfair.

But, in spite of that, I still have come to You, my Lord with no place else to turn. You always take a firm grip on my desperate state. You always know just the right things to say. Your counsel and strength lift me up from dishonor and disgrace. Who else can I turn to who has the right answer? *You*, dear God, alone! There is no one else. Time and time again I have become weak and failed miserably. But, God, You have always been there for me. It's like a rock that can't be moved.

At any point in time, circumstances will change. The wicked are sadly destroyed in a minute. You have silenced their scoffing. And You knew all along just how their sad end would come. I'm sorry for not waiting patiently for Your timing. You've been there all along—my Lord, my strength, my refuge, my sanctuary. I can't wait to tell someone about You.

For Additional Reading: Psalm 59:9-17; 1 Thessalonians 3:1-13
Paul, Age 44
Sales Representative

WEEK FORTY-SIX
■ ■ ■ ■

JOY, PRAYER, & THANKS ALL THE TIME

TEXT FOR THE WEEK: 1 THESSALONIANS 5:12-28

KEY VERSES:
1 THESSALONIANS 5:16-18

"Be joyful always; pray continually;
give thanks in all circumstances, for
this is God's will for you in Christ
Jesus."

DAY ONE ■ Commentary on 1 Thessalonians 5:16-18

Paul, along with his companions, Silas and Timothy, founded the European church at Thessalonica on Paul's second missionary journey. Later on Paul wrote back to that church to encourage and compliment the people for their dedication to Christ Jesus and to one another. His words to the Thessalonians are as relevant and encouraging to us today as they were to the people then. Three short verses are particularly encouraging and instructive.

"Be joyful always; pray continually; give thanks in all circumstances; for this is God's will for you in Christ Jesus" (1 Thes. 5:16-18).

"Be joyful always" (v. 16). A well-known Christian motivational speaker, John Haggai, writes, "You are what you think. No one can live a joyous life if the mind is full of negative thoughts." Those of us in the counseling profession encourage our clients to "pull out" what is inside of them because "it will always express itself in some way." If down mentally we can get down physically. The wife of President William McKinley was bedridden for many years. The President waited on her continually, even leaving important meetings to tend to her. Yet after his assassination she got up and lived a normal life. It was

297

said she was a negative person who was jealous of her husband. Her jealousy was exhibited in her dependent behavior. Her dependent behavior was a way to punish her husband. What joy she missed.

On the other hand, an elderly lady from San Francisco knows the meaning of "being joyful always." When she was interviewed by a reporter after the earthquake, she was asked if she was afraid? "No," was her reply, "I just rejoiced in knowing I have a God who can shake the world." She looked at the positive side, not the negative; she could rejoice in life.

"Pray continually" (v. 17). Praying continually involves filling the mind with good thoughts. Quoting Scripture such as Philippians 4:13, "I can do everything through Him who gives me strength," fills our mind with good thoughts. To paraphrase, I can do things, I am OK because Christ Jesus is pouring His power in me.

When I attended the University of Kansas, it was common in the spring of the year for severe storms to erupt. Two friends of mine were sitting watching the clouds swirling when the tornado sirens sounded and a funnel cloud formed. The one friend asked the other to pray, pray, pray. Her response to the request, "I did my praying before the storm broke." Pray without ceasing.

"Give thanks in all circumstances" (v. 18). This was the third challenge Paul gave. Philippians 4:11 reminds us "to be content whatever the circumstances." Give thanks for all things.

A postal worker was assigned to read the letters addressed to Santa Claus at Christmastime. He read thousands of requests for different gifts before Christmas. However, after Christmas only one child sent Santa a thank-you. In everything give thanks! Too often our prayers and thoughts are focused on what we want. Too seldom do we give thanks for what we receive.

Be joyful always, pray continually, give thanks in all circumstances. The reason? Paul answers in the second part of verse 18, "for this is God's will for you in Christ Jesus."

Steve McDonald is a New York policeman. His story was told in the *Parade* Magazine of our local Sunday newspaper. Steve was shot in Central Park. Bullets so damaged his spinal cord that he was left a quadraplegic. However, he went back to work on the New York police force. In spite of pain and grief, Steve McDonald finds a way to get outside himself so he has a remarkable impact on others. Steve knows the importance of rejoicing always, praying without ceasing, giving thanks in everything.

As Paul encouraged the leaders of that first church at Thessalonica, single adult leaders can be encouraged today. The San Francisco lady, the two friends, the postal worker, and Steve McDonald all can speak and be a witness to Christian leaders. "For this is God's will for you in Christ Jesus" (v. 18).

For Additional Reading: Nehemiah 8:5-12; Galatians 5:22-26
Ann L. Kline is the Minister to Single Adults at Frazer Memorial U.M.C. in Montgomery, Alabama. The first four days of devotional applications are written by single adults from Ann's ministry in Montgomery. Days six and seven were contributed by singles from Rob Arp's ministry in Athens, Georgia.

DAY TWO ■ 1 Thessalonians 5:16-18

Be joyful always." In our single adult community in our church, we have 12 support groups that meet on Tuesday evening. As people deal with different pain in their lives, we try to help them move out of "pity city," and begin to rejoice in living. First Thessalonians is a reminder to rejoice, and then Paul goes on to tell us how to do that—"pray continually; give thanks in all circumstances."

For Additional Reading: Psalm 35:9-10, 27-28;
Romans 14:17-23
Evelyn, Age 49
School Guidance Counselor

DAY THREE ■ 1 Thessalonians 5:16-18

Pray continually." Four years ago four single men got together and established a prayer group. I was asked to join this group.

The group focused on needs within the singles ministry. We also prayed for those in the hospital, those who had lost loved ones in death, and different concerns of individuals. I learned how to pray and I learned the value of prayer for people's lives. I have learned the importance of "praying continually."

For Additional Reading: 1 Chronicles 16:7-13; Acts 4:31-35
Neil, Age 38
Forestry Researcher

DAY FOUR ■ 1 Thessalonians 5:16-18

Give thanks in all circumstances." As a never-married single, I went through a time when I was very negative in my thinking. All my friends were getting married and I wasn't, as I had not found the man for my life.

As the result of that dilemma, I became negative and did not have a thankful heart. I did not feel I had that much to be thankful for. I was so wrong. Through sharing with our Single Adult Minister I learned how the power of Jesus Christ could work strongly in my life when I became more positive and thankful for so much that I did have in my life. I learned to be content in my circumstances. I learned to "give thanks in all circumstances."

For Additional Reading: Psalm 136:1-26;
2 Corinthians 2:14-17
Alice, Age 35
Teacher

DAY FIVE ■ 1 Thessalonians 5:16-18

Rejoice, pray, give thanks. . . . Now lets put those three to work! It seemed like a good project for our single's class. An abandoned inner-city church building had been targeted for renewal. Right in the middle of a low-income neighborhood and housing project area, the purpose was to establish a much needed ministry of reconciliation to a community that had more than its share of teenage mothers, drug pushers, alcoholics, crime, poverty, and hopelessness. Our church provided the much-needed salary of a young black man to be the minister. His God-given talents were evident as he displayed love and understanding to the people in the area. But, because of the deteriorating condition of the church building itself, he was spending less time ministering to the people and more on taking care of the building.

Our single's class learned that the two bathrooms were in disrepair with two of the three toilets not functional. With the backing of our singles minister, and the class leaders, an appeal was made to our entire singles group. One of the newest members, who had just started coming to our class, offered to provide his building skills in planning and supervision. Enough money and materials were given by singles to completely renovate both bathrooms. A work force made up of single volunteer workers was assembled to do the work. After working three straight Saturdays, the job was finished. During the workdays, singles who could not attend made lunches and provided refreshments for the work team. Other singles prayed or encouraged those who worked. Another group discovered other church needs and provided their talents.

The experience of this project has an important message to us singles of the church. The most important is that it is not the responsibility of our singles ministers and church leaders to do all the work of the ministry. Instead, they are to prepare us to work together in the ministry. And we singles can make it a lot easier on our ministers and leaders if we are willing to obey God's Word and serve. The result is that the entire church is built up, singles included, and the names which classify us into groups will disappear as we all grow in the unity of faith and knowledge in Jesus Christ.

For Additional Reading: Haggai 1:7-14; 1 Corinthians 9:16-19
Neil, Age 38
Lay Singles Ministry Leader

DAY SIX ■ 1 Thessalonians 5:16-18

Be joyful always; pray continually; give thanks in all circumstances, for this is God's will for you in Christ Jesus" (1 Thes. 5:16-18). These words of hope and encouragement ring throughout time to today's believers in Christ because suffering is a part of the believer's life—married or single.

Sometimes my life appears to be balanced like the tick of a clock. Then, wham! Every spring is sprung. My child finds another "stage" to go through, bills outnumber junk mail, and my job becomes stressful. It seems like all of the circumstances point toward the last tock.

I've learned not to panic since I committed myself to three essential areas: (1) obedient prayer and Bible study; (2) involvement in my church's singles ministry; and, (3) accountability— to my pastors, leaders, and fellow believers.

God has shown Himself faithful to me in unique and awesome ways during seasons of suffering. I am joyfully excited about arriving at the other side of the lesson. I can give thanks to Him, because all circumstances point to spiritual growth and an awesome depth of knowing Jesus more intimately.

For Additional Reading: Deuteronomy 7:7-9; 2 John 2-8
Shirley, Age 45
Company Manager

DAY SEVEN ■ 1 Thessalonians 5:16-18

Sounds simple, doesn't it? Well, just try to do it on your own—I couldn't. I have learned over the past year that even things that seem simple are not possible without the Lord. Jesus is the vine and apart from Him I can do nothing.

It was only when I begin to build on the rock, the precious cornerstone, that the Lord revolutionized my walk with Him.

● Be joyful always: In adversity this is not always easy but it's always right and God will change me through obedience.

● Pray continually: I first had to cast out misconceptions that

I could only pray on bended knee at night. Today I talk with my Lord all day long—a thought, a whisper, a smile. I'm set free in His endless love for me.

• Give thanks in all circumstances: Two things I thank God for (1) that He loved me enough to send Jesus to die for my sins while I was yet a sinner and knew Him not and (2) that He *will* complete the good work He started in me (though I am yet a sinner—saved by grace), and since I know that all things work for good and to conform me into the image of Jesus—in all things I give thanks.

For Additional Reading: Psalm 30:8-12; Revelation 19:5-10
Renée, Age 34
Nurse

WEEK FORTY-SEVEN

■ ■ ■ ■

GET CONTROL BY RECEIVING GRACE

TEXT FOR THE WEEK: **2 TIMOTHY 2:1-26**

KEY VERSE: 2 TIMOTHY 2:1   "You then, my son, be strong in the
grace that is in Christ Jesus."

DAY ONE ■ Commentary on 2 Timothy 2:1

A Pocket Personal Planner can be hazardous to your spiritual
health. It holds out the promise of a neatly ordered and
controlled life, yet is powerless to bring order where it is most
needed—into my internal world. Whatever satisfaction I gain by
controlling the events of my life is only "planner paper deep" if
my internal world is out of control.

Apparently Timothy (probably a single man) struggled with
the same issue we face in our "Just do it!" culture: What does it
mean to "get control" of my life? Paul counsels Timothy that
real control is an internal affair.

"You, then, my son, be strong in the grace that is in Christ
Jesus."

As I look at Timothy's life, I see a gifted young man (1 Tim.
4:14; 2 Tim. 1:6) with a sincere faith (v. 5) who was probably
very busy "doing" ministry (1 Tim.), and yet he was feeling
spiritually powerless (2 Tim. 1:7). Timothy had the "externals"
of his life under control, but he was neglecting the "internals." I
do the same thing when I allow my calendar to become the
measure of my life—when I'm so busy juggling external priorities, I start dropping the internal ones.

Paul instructed—actually, commanded—Timothy to re-evalu-
ate his priorities. Paul's admonition is my "How To" guide if I

really want to "get control" of my life.

My highest priority must be to be strengthened with divine power. Real control begins with God's strength, not my own. Even so, it is *my* responsibility to be strengthened.

It is God's responsibility, however, to provide the *means* of that strengthening—by "the grace that is in Christ Jesus." "Grace," like the rain that keeps a runoff pond fresh and alive, revitalizes my spirit and keeps me alive to God.

But God does not pour His grace into a stagnant pool. Paul says that the source of strengthening, revitalizing grace is "in Christ Jesus." A vital relationship with Jesus Christ will keep me from becoming a stagnant pool. I will find the grace that makes me strong wherever I find Him: He is in the Word of God, so I read my Bible; He is beside me, so I pray to Him; He is in His body, the church, so I fellowship with His people.

Through these channels God's grace flows into my life, strengthening me internally. Satisfaction is no longer paper deep, but as deep as the eternal wellspring of God's grace. And when He is in control, life is in control.

For Additional Reading: Psalm 38:10-22; Romans 5:15-21
Clay K. Clarkson is the Single Adult Pastor at Grace Church in Los Alamitos, California. All six applications come from single adults at Grace Church.

DAY TWO ■ 2 Timothy 2:1

My greatest fear was to find myself alone and "stranded" in a dangerous place. God used just such a situation to strengthen me and show me His grace in Papua New Guinea.

I was traveling alone in the highlands area of what some considered the most dangerous province in the country. When my borrowed car broke down I wasn't afraid . . . I was terrified! There were no tow trucks, no phones, and I was unable to speak the language of the people who quickly gathered around. I was disabled by fear—I couldn't even pray.

But God knew what I needed. Within 15 minutes He provided a free, English-speaking mechanic who had the car up and running long before dark.

God's Word says that we are to be strong in the grace that is in Christ Jesus. I learned that strength means trusting God's power and unlimited resources.

For Additional Reading: Psalm 144:2, 11-15; 1 Corinthians 16:13-18
Joan, Age 31
Teacher

DAY THREE ■ 2 Timothy 2:1

Like many people, I have embraced the fitness craze. Most mornings find me in the gym, sweating over the latest body-building machine, straining to lift great amounts of weight. All this energy is expended in the pursuit of strength.

The Apostle Paul also was interested in strength. But, unlike the physical strength I labor to develop, he was interested in spiritual strength (1 Tim. 4:8). Paul saw the great struggles of life being fought not on the physical level, but on the spiritual (Eph. 6:12). That is why he admonishes Timothy to "be strong in the grace that is in Christ Jesus."

I continue to work out. I like the extra energy it infuses into my day. But I also incorporate a spiritual workout in my schedule. I exercise my spiritual "muscles" through the disciplines of prayer, study, and fellowship. And God, through His grace, uses these to build up my spiritual body.

For Additional Reading: Psalm 118:13-21; Hebrews 13:6-9
Paul, Age 32
Medical Student

DAY FOUR ■ 2 Timothy 2:1

You know, it is absolutely staggering to me how much time and effort I expend each day fabricating my own little "reality": where I am master of everything I do with incredible strength to overcome all obstacles to success. And what is the ultimate proof of my strength? Achievements. Like trophies in a display case, they show the rest of the world just how powerful and important I really am.

But it's interesting . . . every time I get my universe set up just the way I want it, God finds some little crack through which He can shine the divine flashlight of His grace. He shows me the darkness of my own "reality."

I'm not really sure I understand God's grace — perhaps nobody can. But I'm thankful that God continually provides me with the grace I need, teaching me that real strength can be found only in a relationship with Him, not in achievements.

For Additional Reading: Isaiah 12:1-6; 1 Corinthians 15:9-11
Scott, Age 29
Graphic Arts Student and Corporate Employer

DAY FIVE ■ 2 Timothy 2:1

I am in control when God is in control of my life. If I study the Bible and talk to God before I go to work, major problems that occur don't faze me. Compared to God's power and the eternal scheme of things, no problem at work is major.

When I don't study the Bible or talk to God before going to work, minor problems upset me. Circumstances control me.

I am strong after meeting with God. I am prepared to respond to spiritual questions or filthy talk at work. I am aware of opportunities to tell the Good News.

If my relationship with Jesus has been stagnant, I don't know how to respond to a coarse statement. I am too timid to talk about spiritual things because my mind has not meditated on such matters for several days.

For Additional Reading: Psalm 81:1-10; Romans 15:14-20
Clark, Age 34
Videographer

DAY SIX ■ 2 Timothy 2:1

Organization. For me, that is the key to keeping my life under control. With so many demands on my time—work, family, my child, church involvement, soccer practice and games, worship services, friends—each new demand must fight for a slot on my calendar.

In my orientation to schedules and deadlines, though, it is easy for me to lose perspective. I have to continually check my heart and my motives, because I know God is not impressed with my calendar if my focus is on it rather than on Him.

It takes a disciplined, conscious effort for me to get outside my calendar and to refocus my spiritual eyes on my Lord. I am always reminded that His power is made perfect in my weakness when I step out of control and become vulnerable in His presence.

When I am in His presence, I see life—and my calendar—from a new perspective. And I am stronger from my time with Him.

For Additional Reading: Zechariah 10:6-12; John 12:37-46
Anita, Age 35
Secretary

DAY SEVEN ■ 2 Timothy 2:1

My days often seem so busy that I don't have time even to think about God. After days like that, my dreams sometimes reflect my spiritual frustration.

I see myself in a place far away, a "sanctuary," shall we say, where the righteous are living. A place where people are blameless, have humble hearts, and honor those who fear the Lord. And I am sitting at the feet of God. I sense Him looking at me, smiling, and saying, "Thank you for sharing some intimate moments with Me. Thank you for listening when I speak. Most of all, thank you for taking time out of your busy schedule to find Me and get to know Me better."

When I awaken, I realize that I need to meet God in His Word, not in my dreams. But I also realize that if I miss those intimate times with the Lord, He must miss me too and that encourages me to meet Him daily.

For Additional Reading: Genesis 28:15-21; Matthew 24:44
Rhonda, Age 26
Student

WEEK FORTY-EIGHT

■ ■ ■ ■

POWER TO LIVE, AVAILABLE GRACE

TEXT FOR THE WEEK: TITUS 2:11–3:8

KEY VERSE: TITUS 2:11   "For the grace of God that brings sal-
                                    vation has appeared to all men."

DAY ONE ■ Commentary on Titus 2:11-14

These verses speak to us of two critical elements of the Christian life: God's grace—that unmerited favor extended by our loving Creator, and our response to this grace. Titus, the Apostle Paul's associate in mission, needed to hear a word of encouragement as he worked with the church on the ancient Island of Crete, and nearly 2,000 years later, we too often need to be reminded and reassured of some "basics."

As believers in the one true God who chose—in Christ—to reconcile the world to Himself, we are empowered to live in a new way. As Christians, we can choose to focus joyfully on Jesus even though we find ourselves in the midst of a "crooked and depraved generation" (Phil. 2:15).

On Crete, centuries of godless living had produced a people so well known for their excesses that in the pop literature of the day, the very name "Cretan" was synonymous with a host of evils. Cretans had a notorious international reputation for self-indulgent living. There, Titus was working with new Christians, helping them to establish the church of Jesus Christ. In an uncommonly hostile environment where specific guidelines were greatly needed, Paul gave specific instructions for Christian living in his brief, but extremely practical letter. Chapter 2 provides a sketch of sound doctrine, and chapter 3, a picture of right behaviors: in a heart-to-heart sharing of love, Paul reminds Titus,

At one time we too were foolish, disobedient, deceived and enslaved to all kinds of passions and pleasures. We lived in malice and envy, being hated and hating one another. But when the kindness and love of God our Saviour appeared, He saved us, not because of righteous things we had done, but because of His mercy. He saved us through the washing of rebirth and renewal by the Holy Spirit, whom He poured out on us generously through Jesus Christ our Saviour, so that, having been justified by His grace, we might become heirs having the hope of eternal life (Titus 3:3-7).

Our style of living—in every age—is to be a joyous response to God's loving provision. We are even given the power to resist whatever temptations and evils beset us. Enslavement to our personal experiences—the good, the bad, and the ugly—our family history, even our culture, is finished when we truly trust in Jesus. With daily spiritual feeding and nurture, we grow in confidence and efficacy. Surrender to God's will, fed by diligent study of God's Word, frequent prayer, and healthy fellowship with other believers, is the beginning of freedom in Christ. We are made joint heirs with Jesus. We are given the power to become the sons and daughters of God. We may live unmarried, "alone" in society, but we are the family of God in reality. This is the Good News of the Gospel: in Jesus Christ we are made new.

In almost every age and every place, Christians need the reminders and encouragement Paul wrote to Titus on Crete. We can live boldly for Christ now. Life—with all its ups and downs, its unbelievable travesties, and its disasters—has new meaning and new hope when faced in the power of the Holy Spirit, our Counselor, Comforter, Teacher, and Advocate.

For Additional Reading: Isaiah 59:15-21; 1 Timothy 6:11-16
Sharon Horne is a single adult ministerial student at Princeton Theological Seminary, Princeton, New Jersey. The following devotionals are written by six single theological students preparing for the ministry at Princeton Theological Seminary.

DAY TWO ■ Titus 2:11-14

Saving grace" is, as the song states, "amazing grace." During my life of six decades I've seen many examples of that amazing, saving grace, and especially in solo parenting, I cling to God's grace. Each of my three children is known by the abbreviation P.K. ("Preacher's Kid") and that is something distinctive to grow up with in this culture. Expectations from without and expectations from within abound. The dynamics of parenting are both the same and different when children grow up with a mother or father in full-time Christian ministry. A divorce thoroughly complicates the situation. The "ransom" and "cleansing" Paul writes about are examples of comfort in God's Word.

The saving grace has dawned on the world with salvation for all. Preachers and preachers' kids need that same one-on-one relationship with Jesus Christ that Paul describes in this Letter to Titus. Each and every soul must personally bow to the King and say, "Jesus is Lord." Then there is strength for victorious living by obedience today, and the hope of eternal joy to come in the second coming of Christ Jesus. "Waiting" with the patience of Jesus, and eagerly pursuing "good works" are what I see as benefits of God's saving grace.

For Additional Reading: Deuteronomy 10:12-22; Acts 2:14-21
Joe, Age 60 +
Seminary Student

DAY THREE ■ Titus 2:11-14

Colleges, universities, seminaries, and just about every other sort of educational institution have admission procedures which require that applicants write essays and personal statements. My applications to seminary were no different. One application asked for the following, "Trace your Christian pilgrimage thus far." Pilgrimage, what a strange word!

The more I began to contemplate this word, the less strange it became. As people trying to live in the light of Christ's appearance, we really are something like pilgrims. Life is different in the new world of Christianity. We have to work diligently in order to live as Christians. We must leave behind the old way of life. It is in the saving grace of God that we are able to live the new way. Through Christ we are made new.

But all too often, we seem to fall back to our former lifestyles, slipping in and out of our commitment to Christ. Every time we regress, backslide, or drop out of Christ's training program we are violating His call to live as pilgrims with a new view of life. Actually, we are violating the essential command given by Jesus, to love God with all that we are and have, and to love our neighbor just as we love ourself.

May we truly surrender to Jesus the Christ who will—by the power of the Holy Spirit—enable us to joyously live sober, upright, and godly lives as we await the second coming of Christ.

For Additional Reading: Ezekiel 11:17-21;
1 Thessalonians 5:1-11
Daris, Age 24
Seminary Student

DAY FOUR ■ Titus 2:11-14

By age alone, many of us are categorized as "Yuppies" and this identification can have powerful effects on our lives. We feel pressured to succeed according to worldly standards. We find ourselves competing for recognition and status. We begin to conform to a value system that emphasizes careers and possessions above all else.

But this passage reminds us that we have been liberated from the entrapments of the world. Through Jesus Christ we have been freed to do the good deeds God has prepared for us to do.

The most fascinating thing happens when we center ourselves on Christ. We gain a peace and confidence that no worldly yardsticks of success can give us. The world will tell us that you can't be "good" and be successful at the same time. That is a lie. Through Scripture, study, prayer, and fellowship with our friends in Christ, we can experience the continual presence of Christ, a presence that will lead us to the right decisions.

For Additional Reading: Psalm 90:1-12; James 3:13-16
Anne, Age 36
Seminary Student

DAY FIVE ■ Titus 2:11-14

The Christian life is not marked primarily by a tight code of rules of conduct, nor by a rigid definition of doctrinal tenets. It is primarily a hope that we, sinful creatures loved by God, are awakened to. We are taught by our Lord through the Apostle Paul to set our hope on that which lies beyond the material universe, beyond the hope for all that pertains to what the world offers as its treasures. Our inheritance does not have to be a position at work won by hard labor and political hobnobbing, nor the accoutrements of suburban life, nor even a good name in the church. Our inheritance comes when Jesus comes to claim His own "special people," and takes that people into the kingdom of His Father where there is peace, love, and no lack.

The way of the world is marked by a profound lack of regard for God and for our fellow-creatures. The comfort of some is gained through the deprivation of many. One's emotional needs are met through the enslavement of another. But Christ calls us to bear witness to a life which is not a closed system (my needs can only be met if you meet them to the neglect of your own). He calls us to abundant life. He ransomed us from the bondage of the world's mind-set, and opened our eyes to the inexhaustible resources that we have in the Holy Trinity.

The one rule of the Christian life may be found in Galatians 2:20: "The life I live in the body, I live by faith in the Son of God." What a hope to which we have been called—to share in the life of God and know intimate fellowship with the One in whom all things dwell. Thank You, Lord, for rescuing us from living under the lie of emptiness, and for filling our hearts with Your presence and love!

For Additional Reading: Psalm 31:1-5; Galatians 1:3-5
David, Age 25
Seminary Student

DAY SIX ■ Titus 2:11-14

Sometimes we are single or alone because we have not begun a relationship; sometimes we have just left a relationship that was broken. We may think that we were not understood by our partner, but even if it were true to some extent, we have the realization that part of the problem was in our communication with that former loved one. Somehow we didn't know how to maintain an intimate connection. We didn't know how to keep on loving and love with Christ's love. The only way to Christ-like loving is through humility. The glorious accomplishment of a sustained relationship comes with the tenderness and the gentleness of humility.

Light comes into a darkness and shines warmly, and yet we must remember that the darkness was already there. In that darkness, we must never be brutal. We hesitate. We check. We are tender and gentle.

After humility informs our interaction with darkness, we can hope to see a warmth and shining newness of relationship. This is our right position in the world as we understand and apply what the Holy Scriptures teach us to base our relationships on: respect, soberness, self-control, and godliness. This behavior gives us a sense of hope to build up our lives.

For Additional Reading: Isaiah 60:1-5, 19-22; John 8:12
Teodor, Age 38
Seminary Student

DAY SEVEN ■ Titus 2:11-14

Dear Jesus,
Could You tell me where I can find the letter of Paul to Titus? Though I am one who has studied theology for a long

time and love to talk about God, theology, and life, now I need to find this word: "to live self-controlled, upright and godly lives in this present age" (2:12).

For the past two months, I have seen a glimmer of what "godly lives in this present age" should look like. As Christ came to the world where Herod exercised his real human nature to guard his ruling position, we too live in a world where we feel the existence of "Herods"—vividly striving to reign, not only in society, but in our own hearts. The cunning, cruelty, and ruthlessness of Herod are too much with us. But Herod can never hinder the coming of Christ—not in His birth in a lowly stable, not in His life in our hearts.

Jesus, You have shown me how to live the Christian life: anchored in fellowship, allowing others to be themselves, showing compassion in times of sorrow, and moving when action is required to meet needs. You have taught me never to regard myself as better than others (Phil. 2:3). You have clearly said, the "first will be last and the last first" (Mark 10:31). You have given me words of life: to be rooted and established in love (Eph. 3:17).

Saviour, Your very existence instructs my daily schedule. You call me to prayer and meet me there. I sense Your unceasing smile that cuts through my innermost self-deception. Somehow, in hectic schedules with many competing demands, I find Your peace. I find joy in You.

How can it be? In the night, my heart murmurs amid flowing tears, "Is it not what Christ has done for us that matters?" And I know. Nothing that the world does is important. I must stay my eyes on You, Jesus. I feel renewed strength to be an imitator of You. "Herods" are still around in this troubled world, but You, Lord, give us the power to live victoriously today. Thank You, dear Jesus. Shalom.

For Additional Reading: 2 Chronicles 32:6-8; Matthew 2:1–3:3; 2 Peter 3:11-13
Won, Age 25
Seminary Student

WEEK FORTY-NINE
■ ■ ■ ■

JESUS CARES—REALLY CARES!

TEXT FOR THE WEEK: **HEBREWS 4:14–5:10**

KEY VERSES: HEBREWS 4:15-16   "For we do not have a high priest who is unable to sympathize with our weaknesses, but we have one who has been tempted in every way, just as we are—yet was without sin. Let us then approach the throne of grace with confidence, so that we may receive mercy and find grace to help us in our time of need."

DAY ONE ■ Commentary on Hebrews 4:15-16

One of the necessities that we all share, though most hesitate to admit, is the need for sympathy. Far too many people tell themselves the lie that they don't need anyone. The reality, however, is that our problems are easier to endure when we feel like there is someone, anyone, who cares.

As a small child I was often afflicted with severe earaches; usually in the middle of the night. I remember how my pain was always eased by my mother who would hold me for many long hours. I was comforted because she cared; she genuinely hurt because I hurt. My children require this same instinctive care.

Our text tells us that Jesus was *touched* with the *feeling* of our infirmities. To understand God's great love and mercy is to be confident of this point (Lam. 3:22-23). Our Saviour "felt" fear, loneliness, pain, sorrow, and death. He is not only the sympathetic Christ, He is also able to empathize with our every hurt. One of the great aspects of God's nature is the reality that He is personally involved in our life; it is foundational to His character. He is concerned with our smallest weakness (Matt. 6:26-

30). His heart breaks when we suffer. This is why we may come "boldly" before the throne of grace to find help in time of need.

Our life is kept and preserved by God's mercy. His grace is adequate and sustaining; there is no substitute for it (Ps. 59:16). When we live by this word of comfort and assurance we know that life has meaning and purpose. Jesus understands our hurts and brings them to God. He feels our weakness and then He shows us His strength (121:1-2). He knows where we are but He also knows what we may become.

Have you ever noticed how it is easier to remember to pray for someone who is going through a trial that we have gone through? This is because we have been touched with the feeling of that same infirmity. In the same manner, Jesus sympathizes with us and offers help. May our sympathy for others be also more than just feeling (1 John 3:18).

For Additional Reading: Psalm 11:4-7; Acts 26:21-23
Pat Roberts is the Assistant Pastor at the First Baptist Church of West Hollywood in Hollywood, Florida. Six single adults from First Baptist Church write the following personal applications.

DAY TWO ■ Hebrews 4:15-16

Remember the last time someone tried to comfort you with the words, "I know just how you feel." You may have smiled sweetly, but in your heart you screamed, "No! You don't know how I feel! No one understands!" One by one, all of my close family members have passed away, usually after long illnesses. In those periods of grief, I was flooded by such a whirl of thoughts and emotions that even I didn't know how I felt. Can anyone else then really understand?

Yes, there is One who knows me completely and who feels the pain I feel. God wants to share in every sorrow, every joy, every detail of my life. Friends and loved ones are a great source of encouragement, but my life depends on the One who "sticks closer than a brother" (Prov. 18:24), and "who comforts us in all our troubles" (2 Cor. 1:4).

For Additional Reading: Psalm 54:1-7; 2 Corinthians 7:1-4
Margaret, Age 39
Bookkeeper

DAY THREE ■ Hebrews 4:15-16

In the last few years I have come to appreciate the reward of bringing everything to God in prayer. Before, I didn't want to "bother" God with anything less than life's more important events so I stoically did things my way. Eventually, it occurred to me I was placing limits on God as if there were only so many things He could handle.

As a result of trusting God more (Prov. 3:5), my faith in God has grown as has my love. Now I pray often about everything from the seemingly simple to what appears serious or complicated.

Interestingly enough, the more I trust God with everything the more manageable and rewarding life is. It isn't the events of life that get us down or make us fearful, but it is our reaction to these events. I am convinced that those who honestly seek His guidance and protection have a new outlook on life, without fear (1 John 4:18), and often find opportunities where there were problems.

For Additional Reading: Psalm 119:1-7; Luke 7:44-50
Nicholas, Age 44
Mortgage Broker

DAY FOUR ■ Hebrews 4:15-16

One of the hardest things for me to accept in my life has been the divorce of my parents. My parents were divorced when I was two years old and as a result I never had any kind of relationship with my father. I was mad and angry at my earthly father and believe those feelings hindered my relationship with my Heavenly Father.

It wasn't until I chose to forgive my earthly father and realized that he did the best he could, that I feel I truly could begin to understand my Heavenly Father's love for me.

My Heavenly Father loves me just as I am (unconditionally) and I'm so glad He understands our weaknesses. I know I still have a lot of growing to do, but it is great to know that my Heavenly Father will walk with me all the way.

For Additional Reading: Micah 7:18-20; 2 Corinthians 11:27-31
Barbara, Age 29
Receipting Clerk

DAY FIVE ■ Hebrews 4:15-16

Do you ever wonder if God is really watching over you? Does He really know what I'm going through right now?

It is hard to imagine that God would just watch as we go through a difficult time in our life, yet whatever we are going through He already has. Isaiah 53:3-5, 7-9 tells us He was despised and rejected of men, a man of *sorrows.* He knows *grief.* He was *smitten* of God and *afflicted, wounded, bruised, chastised, oppressed.* He was cut off out of the land of the living; and He had done no violence, nor had a deceitful mouth.

Oh, how He knows and cares. He can identify with that sorrow or pain you feel. That is why we can come boldly before Him and ask for help. We should be going before God and telling Him we understand how He felt, and that we can identify with Him.

For Additional Reading: Isaiah 38:14-20; 2 Peter 2:4-9
David, Age 29
Janitor

DAY SIX ■ Hebrews 4:15-16

As I live from day to day, it is my prayer that I have the mentality and heart of Christ — that I would conduct myself according to His principles of living and giving to the needs of others—by loving and being unselfish with material goods. I want to make decisions as he would.

As a college graduate and a business owner at the age of 26, I find myself asking that question at the crossroads of some increasingly difficult and multi-consequential decisions. Just how would Jesus run a business today? How would He respond to the receipt of a subpoena, or to an accountant giving "financial advice" on how to avoid taxation—or being mistreated to where the "only remedy" is litigation? How would He deal with employee/employer relations and compensation? How would He handle and respond to competition, and the capitalistic profit motivation which permeates our society? The answers to these are seldom clear-cut, or easily defined.

It is at these times of frustrated decision-making that I cleave to the promises that are given in Hebrews 4:14-16. It is comforting to know that we do have a High Priest who *is* touched with our feelings and our infirmities. We do not need to be ashamed to come to the throne of grace to find help in our times of need. These promises are deep-felt to me, and as I grow older, God reveals the meaning of these promises to me in ways I never imagined. It is as if He places His arms around me and gives me a hug, and tells me that He understands, as Christ experienced frustration, fear, anger, sorrow, pain, and loneliness. He is concerned with the smallest detail of my life—to the largest. And that gives me the strength to face another day.

For Additional Reading: Joshua 21:43-45; 2 Corinthians 1:18-24
Ken, Age 26
Business Owner

DAY SEVEN ■ Hebrews 4:15-16

Many times the question has come to me, in our fast-paced life—have we really lost the true meaning of worship? Today in our church services do we really worship the Lord? Or have we become programmed? I have realized in the years of my youth and young adulthood that throughout all the activities of the church, we often forget to truly worship the Lord. Though the services consist of singing, fellowshiping, and preaching, it seems as though we have fallen into a habitual routine. Is there a time in the "routine" that we gather as God's sheep and reflect on Him and His glory and power; quietly feeling the true presence of God, and not slipping into the same old Sunday morning "routine"? Quietly, we as the sheep in our stillness should prepare our hearts for what the Shepherd has prepared to deliver from our Heavenly Father and start truly worshiping our God.

For Additional Reading: Psalm 96:7-13; Luke 24:50-53
Lisa, Age 24
Schoolteacher

WEEK FIFTY

■ ■ ■ ■

JOY AND PATIENCE OUT OF WHAT?

TEXT FOR THE WEEK: JAMES 1:1-18

KEY VERSE: JAMES 1:2   "Consider it pure joy, my brothers,
                                          whenever you face trials of many
                                          kinds."

DAY ONE ■ Commentary on James 1:1-3

Christianity is more than a philosophy, a theology, a religious
institution, or a denomination. It is a life; a life that is based
on a relationship—a personal relationship with God. It is a
relationship of ultimate intimacy and total dependency. We are
no longer to live for ourselves; we are to live for Him. Without
Him, we could do nothing, but through Him we can do everything.

The Book of James is a book about practical Christianity
based on that kind of personal relationship with Jesus Christ.
Without a personal relationship with Christ, the Book of James
is an impossible book to understand or to live by. James is
concerned with the matter of faith. For him, faith is not merely
something which is believed; faith is something you do and
something that is continuously built up in our lives.

I would guess that the average person really does not enjoy
trials. In fact, most people would do almost anything to avoid
them. James is writing to people who are not different than
those who will read this book. Most of the people to whom he
was writing faced severe trials to the point of losing their homes,
families, and careers. They faced severe persecution and felt like
aliens in a foreign land. Yet in these verses we see some practical principles on how to profit and to grow through the trials we
face.

The first principle is "to consider it pure joy . . . whenever you face trials." Not only are we instructed to face trials with joy, but we are to face all trials with joy. Understanding what some of the words mean may help in our understanding of what it means to face all trials with joy. The Greek word for trial is the same word that is sometimes translated as "temptation." We see this word used in the Lord's Prayer, and also in the Book of Hebrews describing the temptations that the nation of Israel faced. When connected with 1 Corinthians 10:13, we see the reason to count trials as joy. It is with this promise that we can face the trials of life with a sense of hope, optimism, confidence, and most of all, joy.

The second principle is that the testing of our faith develops perseverance. God is not the author of evil, suffering, or trials; but He has a wonderful capacity to use them for our good. Within this context James contends that there is a very practical result of facing trials with pure joy and with deep faith in Jesus Christ. The result of such trials is patience and perseverance. The testing which God allows to take place in our lives is of greatest spiritual significance to our faith. It is by faith that we come to God; it is by faith that we follow Him, and it is by faith that we receive His wonderful promises — including eternal life.

As we face temptations, our faith grows. We trust God more fully and ourselves less fully, for it is our faith in Christ that gives us the victory to be overcomers. The testing of our faith results in a perseverance or quality of unswerving endurance — the ability to keep on going on. The suffering, the temptations, and the trials of life are never wasted when we give them and our total selves to God, and the final result of perseverance in our lives is that we will become mature, complete, and lacking in nothing. God will use the negative experiences of life to bring about a very positive result and develop in us a Christlike character.

For Additional Reading: Psalm 116:1-6; Revelation 3:10-13
Andy Morgan is the Minister with Singles at Ward Presbyterian

Church in Livonia, Michigan. Six singles from the greater Detroit area contributed the following devotionals.

DAY TWO ■ James 1:1-3

I must confess that before I went through my divorce, I had no idea at all how painful, lonely, hurtful, and miserable it was to be thrust into the "D" world. It's no picnic, that's for sure! Each day brings forth a new trial: no money, sick children, no food, a broken-down vehicle, children failing school, counselors, pastors, loneliness, having to move, runaway children, stolen checks, police, desperateness, lawyers, overeating, judges, smoking, rejection, friend of the court, social services, sleeplessness, restlessness, court again and again, custody battles, child support, alimony, visitation, referees, tears, hurts, and oh so much pain—will it ever stop?

I don't think in my case that it will ever be completely over, but because I was led into a personal relationship with Christ, I have found a fantastic support group and have been able to work through most of the hurtful events of the past. Through the Lord's help, I have healed much and have been able to go to school and am now a senior at the University of Michigan in Flint. I am preparing to be an elementary school teacher.

Because of my experience and because of seeing what others have gone through, I'm now better prepared to be an even more sensitive teacher and I can help others get through the "D" days. Until you go through it yourself, you don't realize how overwhelming the whole ordeal can be.

For Additional Reading: Isaiah 40:29-31; James 5:1-12
Judy, Age 44
Student

DAY THREE ■ James 1:1-3

I don't know about you, but when trials come into my life, the last thing I feel is happy. So, it's no wonder that when I read in James 1:1-3 that I am to consider these trials "pure joy," I struggle with it. Why can't the Christian life just be easy? That would be something to rejoice about. But that isn't what God says here. He tells me that my faith will be tested and tried.

Perhaps the reason for this is in the first verse where James calls himself "a servant of God and of the Lord Jesus Christ." What does that really mean? For me anyway, it means that God is in control of my life, not me. Yet, too many times I forget this and try to run things my way. It's as if a trial needs to come along to teach me once again to rely on the Master. My faith tends to be too immature. When I'm in a bind, I'll call on God but when things seem easy, I rely on my own strength.

In Jesus' day a real servant owned nothing for himself and was totally reliant on his master. He had to believe that his master would take care of him. I need this same "faith" in my life.

Each time that I face a trial and rely on God to overcome it, my faith matures. God becomes a greater part of my life: a loving Father. Can I rejoice in that? Yes, and with the confidence that He is sufficient to meet all my needs and more!

For Additional Reading: Psalm 88:1-9; Revelation 2:1-3
Paul, Age 41
Administrator for Single Point Ministries

DAY FOUR ■ James 1:1-3

So, not only are we to be tested, but we are to be joyful about it? I've never really enjoyed being tested, and the more important the outcome the more anxious I become. Avoiding the test sounds pretty attractive. Couldn't we just profess that we believe and be done with it?

This world is an inhospitable place for Christians. Our beliefs are contrary to those of the world, and each day our faithfulness is being tested. It would be so much easier to lead a life obedient to God if only we weren't tempted and tested so much by our jobs, by our peers, and by our culture. But until we've been tempted and proven ourselves faithful, can we know if we are living what we believe or merely doing what is convenient? Just as an exam in school often proves more to the student than to the teacher, the spiritual trials that we face prove our faith—not to God, but to ourselves. As we remain faithful, we experience more of His steadfast love for us, and our faith and assurance become even deeper.

Through our faith we know that God is with us in our troubles. As our faith in Him grows and we come to know Him better, we are able to take comfort that He is with us whatever our circumstances. All of our trials may serve to spread God's Word and to glorify Him. As we persevere in our faith, our faith becomes richer because we experience more clearly His enduring love for us. This knowledge brings us a joy that can endure any hardship that we may face.

Thought: Remaining faithful does not spare us life's trials and hardships, but strengthens us as we face them.

Prayer: Dear Lord, as we face life's troubles may we know that You are at our side. Help us to remain joyful. Amen.

For Additional Reading: Psalm 47:1-9; Matthew 28:5-10
John, Age 39
Computer Analyst

DAY FIVE ■ James 1:1-3

I don't know anyone who would choose to die from a terminal illness such as cancer. It can be a long, painful ordeal for both the patient and his loved ones. Working for Hospice, I've witnessed many people who *choose* to use their suffering and sorrow to grow and to become an inspiration to others.

Several months after his wife of 51 years died, a wonderful gentleman attended a grief support group I was leading. He had done a beautiful job caring for the woman he loved at home during her illness, learning to cook and care for her needs. This man thought that at age 77, his life was surely over. He was *not* a willing participant in the group and fought me every step of the way. Being a fairly stubborn person, he stuck it out and by the end of the series he realized that he could go on and even make new friends. He *chose* to try. Since that time, he has become a hospice volunteer, calling newly bereaved men, helping in the office, and hosting grief support groups in his home. He has found much joy in all of the new friendships he's made. He is truly an inspiration to others.

You can choose to let tragedy defeat you or use it to bring others joy and new hope. The second choice will almost surely give you a whole new outlook on your own life and you'll be amazed at how joyous you can feel again.

For Additional Reading: Psalm 102:1-12; Acts 11:19-24
Cathy, Age 40
Grief Counselor

DAY SIX ■ James 1:1-3

James tells us to face trials and challenges with joy knowing that the testing of our faith produces perseverance. As I look back over the years, I can see God's hand guiding me through each trial. I remember the fears of facing the world alone as a young mother with two small children, finding a job only to learn that it wouldn't provide enough food for our table, and feeling so alone and scared wondering where tomorrow would take us. Through it all, God remained faithful, challenging me and giving me the courage to try new things — sales, real estate, and finally producing a single's radio show aired five nights per week — and realizing that He was always there!

What are the challenges facing you today? Maybe you're being challenged to begin a new career, to move into a new neighborhood, face the breakup of a marriage, experience the challenges of raising a child alone, or a financial crunch like you have never experienced before.

Trust God no matter how difficult the situation. Ask Him to direct your path and then take charge — experience "faith in action." If we walk with Christ, there are bound to be dark days, but they are of His arrangement and only He can bring great blessings to us even out of a seemingly desert wasteland. I challenge you to put your faith into action today. God bless you!

For Additional Reading: Job 23:10-12; Revelation 7:13-17
Kathy, Age 38
Radio Show Executive Producer

DAY SEVEN ■ James 1:1-3

Joy in trials? Sounds rather ridiculous. But I believe it is the Lord's way of showing us He loves us on a regular basis.

When I encounter trouble, I thank the Lord for the problem. I ask the Lord to point out any sin in my life, then ask Him what lesson He is trying to teach me. Always, the Lord solves the problem by giving me answers through His Word, sermons, or radio programs. The lessons I learn are faith-strengthening and improve my Christian walk.

Thoughts (verses) that seem to often run through my mind are: Rest in the Lord and wait patiently for Him. Know that *all* things work together for good to them that love God. But my God shall supply all my needs according to His riches, in glory by Christ Jesus. He who does not love does not know God for God is love. Thou wilt keep Him in perfect peace whose mind is stayed on Thee because he trusteth in Thee. Finally, for God has not given us the spirit of fear, but of power, and of love, and of a sound mind.

Trials and tribulations have become joyful for me because I always draw nearer to God and God nearer to me.

For Additional Reading: Psalm 73:21-28; Acts 5:41-42
Michael, Age 38
Dry Cleaner

WEEK FIFTY-ONE
■ ■ ■ ■

CAST YOUR CARES, EXPERIENCE GOD'S CARE

TEXT FOR THE WEEK: 1 PETER 5:1-11

KEY VERSE: 1 PETER 5:7

"Cast all your anxiety on Him because He cares for you."

DAY ONE ■ Commentary on 1 Peter 5:7

I can remember one of the first times that I went fishing at my grandfather's summer cottage on the lake. Together we baited the hook (I watched, and Granddad put the worm on the hook) and then I started to fish. Fishing was simple, but rather boring. All I did was sit in the boat, throw out the baited hook with a sinker, bobber and extra feet of fishing line . . . and wait. When I was totally bored, I learned to reel in the line and throw it out again. This process is called casting. I threw out the line and brought it back in, over and over again without catching anything.

That is just how I handle my anxieties, worries, and cares. I take all of those things that are heavy on my heart and mind and begin a casting process. I will go to the Lord in a time of devotion or prayer and "cast" my cares on Him, only to reel them back to myself. And I do that over and over again, receiving nothing more than the original care plus a little more anxiety accompanied by a longer waiting list of frustrations and fears.

In 1 Peter 5:7 the word "cast" is the same word for "deposit." And that is exactly what God wants me to do with all of my cares. He desires that I deposit each and every care item into His throne room of grace and mercy during my time of need (Heb. 4:16).

When I was about nine years old, my father took me to a

bank to "deposit" my first silver dollar received as a birthday present. As I opened my first savings account, I proudly placed my dollar on the teller's counter and received a free mailbox bank and a book recording my financial investment. About a month later, I asked my dad to take me back to the bank so I could look at my dollar. Then he told me the earth-shattering news. His explanation was something like this, "Son, your silver dollar is in a huge kettle in the back room of the bank mixed-in with thousands of other silver dollars. We will never be able to find your dollar again." I was devastated, heartbroken.

But that is exactly what God means when He tells us to deposit all our anxieties on Him. He takes our cares, worries, fears, and every concern and removes them from us. He will care for them, we don't have to worry about that troublesome issue, that heavy burden anymore. He will take care of it. And He will return into our lives an investment beyond what we could ever ask or think (Eph. 3:20; Luke 6:38).

Oh, yes, we must trust Jesus completely. Just like we learn to trust the bank to take care of our finances. But the greatest reason for our trust is His love for us. We can deposit all of our concerns with Him, "because He cares for [us]." Jesus cares! He really does. He cares more than our employer, more than a best friend, more than any family member, and certainly more than the local banker.

First John 4:10 and John 3:16 tell us just how much Jesus really does care. He cares so much that He gave His life for your cares. Would you trust Him as your Saviour today? And would you deposit that one major concern and worry that has been heavy on your heart? Give your life and worry to Christ today and be assured that you need not reel it back in. He will take care because He cares.

For Additional Reading: Psalm 94:16-19; John 6:35-40
Doug Fagerstrom is the Single Adult Pastor at Calvary Church in Grand Rapids, Michigan. Six single adults from the various singles groups at Calvary Church write the following personal applications.

DAY TWO ■ 1 Peter 5:7

Anyone ever hear of an anxiety closet? This is how God dealt with one stubborn man who would not give God his closet's key. Mine was bursting, yet I still kept on stuffing it—instead of depositing my anxieties into His open arms. May you not be as resistant to God's open hand for your key.

I had just moved out *again*, into a rough area, no phone, and the single blues. About five o'clock one morning, I woke up gasping as it felt like a spike had been hammered into my forehead. I could only squint, and my balance was gone. I drove to the hospital emergency room and almost passed out stumbling into it. The pain peaked with each heartbeat, and they spent an hour trying to dull the pain before injecting a nerve block into the forehead (grade AAA). The doctors never did find anything wrong physiologically.

Bottom line—God had to break my grasp on that key by showing my inability to handle all of life's anxieties; that His love for each of us therein shows through (Prov. 3:11-12). Who has the key to your anxiety closet?

For Additional Reading: Lamentations 3:25-33; Luke 12:22-26
Philip, Age 26
Computer Programmer

DAY THREE ■ 1 Peter 5:7

Like so many Americans I have been somewhat a product of my culture. Nowhere has this been more true than in the area of turning my anxieties and needs over to Christ.

My culture brought me up to believe that a person had to make his or her own way. Therefore, turning my problems over to Christ was a sign of weakness. At that time I was unaware that behind my thinking was a spirit of pride and self-sufficiency.

Fortunately God not only showed me the error of my thinking, but also that He wanted to help me. He was able to do this by bringing into my life a number of trials which were beyond my capacity to solve. As a result I began to learn the importance of giving my worries and trials over to Christ.

Even with this progress I often had difficulty leaving these matters with Christ. We live in an age of immediate gratification and often this factor causes us to doubt whether God is working in our lives. Therefore, we put parameters on God that are not only wrong but also counterproductive to what He is trying to accomplish in our lives.

Scripture is very clear when it states that God's timing is different than that of mankind. Add to this the fact that God has promised to be faithful in His relationship with us—How can we not cast our anxieties on Christ?

For Additional Reading: Zechariah 7:7-8; 1 Corinthians 1:4-9
Mike, Age 41
Sales Manager

DAY FOUR ■ 1 Peter 5:7

Lord Jesus, here I am on this Saturday morning and I've made a list of To Do's. Help! I feel overwhelmed. There are times everybody feels overloaded, but being single seems doubly hard because we'd like someone to lean on just for a small break.

There is the everyday living with housecleaning, gardening, clothes washing, Bible study, and devotions and. . . .

Oh, yes, the body—daily workout to keep healthy and have good self-esteem. Then there is the business—reading, calls, selling, and designing. These are my personal needs—but:

- What about my three precious children? Their marriages.
- My son's physical problem.
- My sweet granddaughter Mary Rose.
- Then my friends—there are so many and I wish there was more time for their needs.

But where is the *time* to help others?

Jesus promises we can lean on Him because He cares for us.

My answer to each day is moment-by-moment living and trying not to think too far ahead.

I start my day with prayer and devotions. My faith and belief must keep growing by studying His Word. If I have complete trust in Him, then I don't have to control so much of my life or others'.

I truly know and believe that all things are possible with the Lord in my life. I can get my energy and strength by asking for the Holy Spirit to work in my life. Then I can experience calmness and peace by obeying and asking for the Lord's help.

For Additional Reading: Psalm 68:19-20; Ephesians 4:1-7
Lynn, Age 50
Floral Consultant

DAY FIVE ■ 1 Peter 5:7

While living in Anchorage, Alaska I was invited to a family's house for dinner after the morning service. To get to their house I had to go up a hill on a one-lane road and turn a sharp corner at the top. Unfortunately, we had just gotten eight inches of snow, making it difficult for my rear-wheel drive car to get around. I managed to get up the hill, but when I slowed to take the curve I lost momentum and could not go any further. I put it into reverse to back up a little and try again, but ended up on the edge of the road, with a 30-foot drop just beyond. What a predicament! My rear left wheel was on the edge. I could not steer the car back into the center of the road without swinging out over the drop-off. I could not go forward. To back up would put me over the side.

Fortunately, God knows what we are facing and what we need. Some people who lived at the bottom of the hill came up, bringing some chains with them. We laid the chains out in front of my rear tires, and this gave me the traction I needed to get back into the center of the road. I then carefully backed down the hill, parked my car, and walked up to the house where I was to have dinner.

There are often times when it seems like we are spinning our tires and not getting anywhere. Disaster may be near. It is comforting to remember that God knows our need and is able to take care of it.

For Additional Reading: Genesis 22:6-18; Luke 9:12-17
Mike, Age 33
Administrative Assistant

DAY SIX ■ 1 Peter 5:7

I am reminded of the times I have listened and grieved with hurting friends while desperately wanting to be the channel through which God administered healing and encouragement. Many times I have felt responsible for their happiness and have become so caught up in trying to meet the individual's every emotional, psychological, and spiritual need that I have lost sight of reality. Suddenly, helping someone I care about becomes a source of great anxiety.

I find that when I remember who the Creator is—Lord and Master over all the earth and over the hearts of men and women, I am liberated from the responsibility to make other people be happy. I can listen to them, empathize with them, pray for them, and help them in every way according to my provision from God, but God is in charge of their hearts. How freeing!

I need to surrender not only my own anxiety, but also the anxiety that I carry for others at the feet of Jesus who cares for all. He has already accepted the responsibility. I must do what I can, as God enables me, to help others and let God do what only He is able to do.

For Additional Reading: Daniel 3:17; Hebrews 6:10-12
Char, Age 23
Marketing Associate

DAY SEVEN ■ 1 Peter 5:7

I like to look at this verse backward: "Because He cares for you, cast all your anxiety on Him."

I may not have a spouse with whom I can share all my worries, but I have a God who can take them completely away and give me peace instead (Phil. 4:6-7). I have a God who loves me so intimately He knows the number of hairs on my head and what I'll say before I say it. Not only that, but I know out of love this same God suffered pain and torture so He could be near me. When I look at it this way, His love is irresistible!

In addition I have discovered that I'm much better at casting than at making deposits. The analogy holds true for the way I often handle anxiety. I am learning, though, that the best way to "deposit" my cares with the Lord is to give Him thanks (Phil. 4:6-7) for who He is to me amid my circumstances: my Provider and Sustainer who loves me and will never leave me. Reflecting on God's attributes in this way comforts me by helping me see that God is truly big enough and near enough to take care of my worries. And I've learned that God can be very creative in the way He meets my needs, often by using other people—like the time He sent along a marine with a broken foot to help me change a flat tire!

For Additional Reading: Psalm 55:22-23; Luke 21:34-36
Jena, Age 24
Editorial Assistant

WEEK FIFTY-TWO
■ ■ ■ ■

THE LAST WEEK — YOUR WEEK

Editor's Note: This last week is designed for you, the reader and seeker of our Lord, to share and record steps in your own spiritual journey. Much like those in the previous chapters, here are eight opportunities to open God's Word and respond with your own insight and personal application. Journaling is a marvelous discipline in the Christian life. These next eight days may begin a marvelous spiritual walk of reflection and consecration as you continue to draw near to the Saviour and God who loves you and gave Himself for you.

The next eight days are basically divided into two sections alternating every other day. The first section is basic Bible study. The second section is to encourage and enhance your prayer life.

Read the passages as indicated. Write your personal response in the spaces available. Search through the Bible for additional verses to enhance your understanding of these very special verses of Scripture.

DAY ONE BIBLE STUDY: "GOD LOVES ME!"

Read Jeremiah 31:3-4.

How long will God love you? _____

Write down one time when God demonstrated His loving-kindness to you. _____

Read Romans 8:38-39.
    What can separate you
    from the love of God?

    Write down one time
    when you didn't feel
    God's love for you.

Read John 3:16-17
    How much does God
    love you?

    Share what it means to
    believe in Jesus Christ.

DAY TWO PRAYERTIME: "PRAISE GOD"

Read Psalm 9:1-2
    How can you praise the
    Lord?

    Share a recent "praise
    time" that was meaning-
    ful to you.

Read Revelations 4:11
> Write down several things for which you can praise God.

_____

_____

_____

_____

_____

Read Psalm 34:1-3
> Write your personal prayer to God. Include praise and one or two special needs. Then pray!

_____

_____

_____

_____

_____

_____

_____

DAY THREE BIBLE STUDY: "GOD'S JOY"

Read John 15:10-11
> How can you experience God's joy?

_____

_____

> Share a verse from the Bible that has brought you great joy.

_____

_____

_____

> Share a time when obeying God really "paid off."

_____

_____

_____

_____

_____

Read John 16:22-24
> Share a time when you felt like all of your joy was gone.

_____

_____

_____

_____

What did you do?

Read Psalm 118:24
    Share your plan for know-
    ing and experiencing
    God's joy.

DAY FOUR PRAYERTIME: "THANKS TO GOD"

Read Psalm 75:1
    What reasons do we have
    to thank the Lord? Name
    some that are personal to
    you.

Read Psalm 30:12
    To what extent can you
    give thanks to the Lord?
    Share some ways that you
    can express your thanks
    to God.

Read Psalm 118:28
Write your prayer of
thanksgiving to God. _____
Share it with a friend. _____
_____
_____
_____
_____

DAY FIVE BIBLE STUDY: "GOD'S CARE"

Read Psalm 23
Share your thoughts on _____
who the Good Shepherd _____
(Jesus) is to you. _____
_____
_____
_____

Read Matthew 6:25-26
List some of the things _____
that have been of great _____
concern or worry. _____
_____
_____
_____

Read Philippians 4:19
Share a time when God _____
met a need that was out _____
of your control. _____
_____
_____
_____
_____
_____

DAY SIX PRAYERTIME: "AGREE WITH GOD"

Read Psalm 32:5
What simple thing did King David do with his sin? If agreeing with God is confession, how much of our sin should we confess?

_____
_____
_____
_____
_____
_____
_____

Read 2 Samuel 12:13
Whom do we sin against? Then to whom should we confess our sin?

_____
_____
_____
_____
_____

Read Luke 18:13
Write your prayer of confession. Agree with God on a specific sin in your life. Claim His forgiveness. Ask for strength to start clean and new.

_____
_____
_____
_____
_____
_____
_____

DAY SEVEN BIBLE STUDY: "GOD FORGIVES"

Read Ephesians 1:7
How does God forgive sin? (Be sure to thank Him!)

_____
_____
_____

Write about one time that God took a heavy weight of sin away.

Read Jeremiah 31:34
   Express your gratitude to God for what He does with your sin.

Read 1 John 1:9
   Write your thoughts on the importance of confession and claiming God's forgiveness.

   Thank the Lord for forgiveness.

THE LAST DAY "A FINAL PERSONAL RESPONSE"

Read Isaiah 25:9
   Is God personal to you? In what ways are you close to Him?

   Where do you feel distant to God?

Read John 1:12 and Ephesians 2:8-9
How can we know God personally as His children?

_____
_____
_____
_____
_____
_____

Write down your personal prayer to invite Jesus Christ into your life as Saviour and Lord. Make your prayer personal.

_____
_____
_____
_____
_____
_____
_____
_____
_____

And God bless you on your journey with the God of this universe and the Saviour of your soul.